AF560477

NATURE AND GROWTH OF CULTURAL TRADITIONS OF ISLAM

NATURE AND GROWTH OF CULTURAL TRADITIONS OF ISLAM

Taukir Ahmed

RANDOM PUBLICATIONS
NEW DELHI - 110 002 (INDIA)

Nature and Growth of Cultural Traditions of Islam

ISBN 978-93-51117-28-5

Published in 2015 in India by

RANDOM PUBLICATIONS

4376-A/4B, Gali Murari Lal, Ansari Road
New Delhi-110 002
Phone: +9111-43580356, 23289044
E-mail: randomexports@gmail.com; sales@randompublications.com;
info@randompublications.com

Reprinted 2021

Type Setting by: Friends Media, Delhi-110089
Digitally Pritnted at : Replika Press Pvt. Ltd.

Preface

Every culture, besides a number of other things, has its own distinct set of customs, traditions and etiquettes. In fact, one of the important distinguishing features between one nation and one tribe and another has generally been its distinct set of customs, traditions and etiquettes. The nation or tribe formed by the followers of the prophets and messengers of God is no exception. In the formation of this group, the prophets of God directed their followers to conform to a particular set of customs and etiquettes, which would distinguish them as a nation of the followers of God's prophets. However, because the basic objective of all prophetic teachings is to cleanse the human mind, body and soul from all that has the potential of defiling it, the customs and etiquettes for this group of people have also been fixed and promoted with the same target in perspective.

The Arab culture, originally, being one consisting of adherents of the Abrahamic traditions, had a number of these customs, traditions and etiquettes in vogue, even before the advent of the Prophet (peace be upon him). With only a few minor exceptions, the Prophet (peace be upon him) did not alter or add anything to these traditions and customs of the Abrahamic legacy. Thus, these traditions, generally, are a more primitive part of Islam, as compared to the Qur'an. After the approval of the Prophet (peace be upon him), they have been transmitted to the Muslim community through the conceptual consensus and the practical perpetuation of the companions of the Prophet (peace be upon him). Thus, the source of these customs, traditions and etiquettes is the conceptual consensus and the practical perpetuation of the companions of the Prophet (peace be upon him) and every subsequent generation of Muslims. Tradition means truths or principles of a divine origin revealed or unveiled to mankind. In the case of Islam, tradition describes furthermore the words, sayings and actions reported from Prophet Muhammad may Allah bless him and grant him peace, which have been recorded in the hadith collections together with the entire

Islamic religion, such as the Islamic schools of law, spirituality, saintity, etc. Muslims believe that the Quran is the final and complete revelation of God to all people. At the heart of the law are five fundamental obligations or duties which constitute the five pillars of Islam: 1) the confession of faith, 2) worship, 3) almsgiving, 4) fasting, and 5) the pilgrimage to Mecca. Muslims are called to prayer five times each day (dawn, noon, mid-afternoon, sunset, and evening) by the muezzin who stands atop the tower (minaret) of the mosque.

This book explores the role of the intellect in the legal, theological, philosophical, and mystical traditions of Islam, and of its continuing relevance in the efforts of the contemporary Muslim world to address the challenges of modernity.

I thank all members of my team who have helped in the preparation of the book. My special thanks go to "Random Publications" who have published the book.

— *Taukir Ahmed*

Contents

Chapter 1

Muslim Society

Eating for Living

On account of these principles Islam does not favour the idea of being a slave to the belly and the sex, and man should adopt the ideal of going all out for pleasures because life comes only once and should make living for eating as his purpose in life.

All efforts in life should not be confined to the activities of eating and enjoying. If he gets delicious and rich food, he is happy otherwise he grumbles against luck.

Those who are fully occupied with eating to their hearts' content and meeting every demand of their carnal desires, they spend their days and nights only in activities which revolve round these things. They cannot work not any high ideals, and their cowardice and lack of interest comes in the way of Jihad and sacrifice.

The Prophet has said:

> *"Those who are gluttonous eaters will be the most hungry on the Day of Judgment."* *(Al-Bazzar)*

It is well known that many diseases are caused by indiscreet eating. Man goes on eating and his desire is not satisfied, and his stomach is unable to digest. That is why in the Hadith it is mentioned:

> *"Adam's children do not fill any vessel worse than the belly."* *(Tirmidhi)*

Mere worshipping and abstinence from irrelevant things cannot save a man from the disease of gluttony. The correct method is that man should fix a great ideal and should busy himself in reaching that ideal. By this he can be saved from pleasure seeking and gluttony.

It is said that an infidel once was a guest of the Prophet. The Prophet ordered a goat to be milked, and the guest drank all the milk. The Prophet then asked to get a second goat and it was also milked, and the guest drank all the milk. Even then his hunger was not satisfied. In all, seven goats were milked and the guest singly drank all the milk. In the morning he embraced Islam. The Prophet again asked a goat to be milked. One goat's milk was drunk by the guest, but he could not finish the second goat's milk, on which the Prophet of God said:

> *"Momin drinks in one stomach while the infidel drinks in seven stomachs."* *(Muslim)*

The reason for this is that when a man comes from non-belief to Islam and when he realises this new responsibility, his deep relationship with his Lord, the reckoning which he has to undergo in the hereafter, on account of the loftiness of his courage and elevation of his senses, all these things become insignificant for him and he is satisfied with eating merely whatever is available.

The fact of the matter is that all these excesses, carnal desires and amusements are of no value, because by involving himself in them man falls down and disgraces himself, and which we can see today all around us.

The Prophet has said: "Man's food has been made an example for the world, if it is mixed with condiments and made tasty. Just see how it ends."

In another tradition it is mentioned:

> *"Whatever comes from man Allah has related it as an example for the world."* *(Ahmad)*

From these verses and traditions like these many people are likely to fall into a misunderstanding. They think that a Muslim should remain aloof from the world and the matters of the world, and the things declared *halal* and permissible by Allah should also be given up, although this is not at all the intention of Islam. To make a *halal* thing *Haram* is as big a crime as to make the *Haram* thing *halal.* Allah has a right over every Muslim that he should be an epitome of patience. He should not make his forbidden (Haram) things permissible (halal). He should adopt the attitude of gratefulness and should not make clean and permissible things forbidden.

To enjoy life and to receive benefits from it is his right:

> *"On those who believe and do the deeds of righteousness there is no blame for what they ate (in the past), when*

> *they guard themselves from evil and believe,—and do deeds of righteousness, (or) again, guard themselves from evil and believe, (or) again, guard themselves from evil and do good, for Allah loves those who do good."*
> *(Maida: 96)*

And we have seen our holy great grandfather, Hadrat Ibrahim rushing and placing a roasted calf before his guests:

> *"Then he turned quickly to his houeshold. brought out a fatted calf, and placed it before them. He said: "Will you not eat?"* *(Zariyat : 26, 27)*

The holy Prophet and his companions used to act an this command of Allah :

> *"O you who believe ! Make not unlawful the good things which Allah has made lawful for you, but commit no excess for Allah loves not those given to excess."*
> *(Maida : 90)*

There are certain requirements and demands of the body, and if they are not met, the intellectuals say that great harm will be done. The worship and the mysticism which prevent these lawful demands being met are not the concern of Islam. The attacks which it has mounted on materialism is mainly with the purpose of discouraging and preventing men from losing themselves in the forbidden carnal desires and unlawful pleasures.

Balanced Living

Islam commands that a balanced policy be adopted in the matter of clothing. It is unliked by Islam that man should either be proud and conceited in respect of his clothes. For Islam good clothing is not included in the quality of manliness or in excellent moral character, because many times a man dressed in tattered clothes proves to be much more valuable than the heaps of gold and silver.

> *Allah's Messenger has said: "How many persons in wretched condition and dressed in rags are such that if they swear by Allah for doing something, they will accomplish that thing."* *(Tirmidhi)*

It will be a first degree foolishness if a man should clothe himself in costly clothes in order to display himself and his clothes, and should look upon them with pride and strut before others in vanity.

Here you will find innumerable young men who spend hours together in their homes to dress and make themselves presentable. If they are asked to spend their valuable time in acquiring knowledge and in making efforts to awaken their religious consciousness, they will run away startled. According to them, dressing beautifully and appearing in a presentable form is the height of perfection, that is all!

Islam has stopped men from indulging in such acts very strictly, and has warned Muslims to avoid acting in this foolish manner. Allah's Messenger has said:

> *He who puts on the clothes of fame in this world will be clothed in the clothes of disgrace by Allah on the Day of Judgment, and He will put the clothes afire."*
> *(Ibn Majah)*

The fact is that the victims of this wickedness, men and women, when they find themselves wanting in etiquette and good manners and morals, they try to hide their defects in costly clothing and valuable dresses. A great pity on this kind of thinking!

> *Abu Barida narrates that he went to Hadrat Aishah and she showed a sheet of cloth having patches and a lungi made in Yemen and said swearing by God that Allah's Messenger breathed his last while wearing those two pieces of clothing.* *(Bukhari)*

> *Hadrat Jabir narrates that they attended the feast (walima) of the marriage of Hadrat Ali and Hadrat Fatima, and they did not see any better feast than that. They filled in the leaves of the palm in the bedding, and they ware presented with dates and raisins,* (munaqqa), *and they ate them. Their bedding on the wedding night was the shin of a sheep.* *(Bazzar)*

Avoiding wasteful spending and being satisfied with the necessities of life only are the signs of perfect morals and manners.

But it does not mean that Islam only likes poor and mean clothes, or wretched looks and ugly appearances are its favourites, or it desires that old, torn and patched up clothes should be worn, as some uneducated worshippers think. There is no room for such kind of thinking in the religion.

> *One fellow asked Abdullah Ibn Umar as to what kind of clothes he should wear. He replied that he should wear such clothes which should not provoke the fools to taunt him and the intellectuals to consider objectionable. He*

> *again asked as to what should be its cost. He replied : "Between five dirham and twenty dirham."* *(Tibrani)*

The prices mentioned were according to the conditions obtaining in the time of Hadrat Umar. In our times the prices will be higher.

> *A man went to the Prophet. He was dressed poorly. The Prophet asked him : "Have you any wealth ?" He said: "Yes." He asked : "Of what kind ?" The man replied : "Allah has blessed me with all kinds of wealth." The Prophet said "When Allah has given you wealth, then display the effect of Allah's benevolence and blessing."*
> *(Nisai)*

There is another Hadith:

> *"If a man is well to do, what will he lose if he would keep two pieces of clothing for Friday in addition to his working clothes."* *(Abu Daud)*

You must have realised that Islam desires that its followers should put on good clothes and they should be clean and presentable. But there is a big difference. On one side is a man who conceals the real state of affairs and displays his wealth and spends his wealth on beautifying his body and clothes. On the other side how lofty is the behaviour of another man who safeguards his reality and perfects his morals and considers these things as the main purpose of his life, and in this abundance of duties and responsibilities, he does not miss the opportunities of displaying Allah's favours, good manners and good taste.

The world is moaning under the burden of the innumerable clothes and dresses for the different months of the year. Certain clothes are worn during the summer only while other dresses are put on during the winter months. And the clothes donned during the spring have different styles and different fashions. In the Kharif season there are altogether different dresses. Nay, we can see varied clothes during the different hours of the day. The clothes to be worn for work and during the waking hours should be diverse, and for the sleeping hours something else. This unnecessary formality and imitation is common in the societies of east as well as the west. The fair sex, and the youths running after them and men like them, are all tied in the same knot of custom and convention. Islam is unconcerned with this kind of selfish desires, and exhorts people fearing God to avoid them.

> *Allah's Messenger has said : "There is ruin for the women covered with gold and coloured in the yellow colour."*
> *(Ibn Habban)*

This warning is given to those women who are mad after ornaments and who are negligent of their duties and responsibilities.

These Islamic teachings are quite known that wearing gold and silk is Haram (forbidden) for men. There is some room for other things, but it is against the dignity of men that they should use ornaments and should be always enveloped in seems. As regards women, they are allowed to use gold and silk, but they should not be entangled in beautifying and adorning themselves in such a way that it may result in waste of time and money.

Pleasure of Almighty

In the fields of learning and culture deep sincerity is extremely necessary. Knowledge is such a pure and high thing that on its basis Allah granted superiority to man over all the other creatures. Therefore it would be a very mean thing if it is utilised in furtherance of human motivations and if it is reinforced with mischief, corruption, and carnal desires. The world received a great setback at the hands of those learned men who did not possess good moral character, and were deprived of purity and loftiness.

Islam has made it compulsory for the teacher and the taught to give proof of sincerity in the matter of knowledge, and should give preference to high values and public interests over all other things. This activity of learning and teaching is however undertaken with the purpose of merely earning wealth. This limits its utility to individuals only. In this way this valuable treasure is wasted, as is seen in the case of lakhs of people. In fact, it amounts to depreciate the value of learning and to waste this great message.

Allah's Messenger has said :

> *"Any one who has obtained a learning by which Allah's pleasure could be obtained, but his purpose was merely to achieve success in the world, then on the Day of Resurrection he will not be able to smell the fragrance of Paradise."* *(Abu Daud)*

Islam severely disapproves that a man should attain learning and when he gets proficiency in that line, he should start impressing others of his learning and his greatness, and open a battle-field of debates and controversial discussion.

> *It is mentioned in the* Hadith *: "Do not attain learning in order to express pride before the Ulama, nor by its help quarrel with the foolish people, nor through it try to*

overwhelm the meetings, but he who does so, his destination is fire." *(Ibn Maja)*

These religious and worldly learning which are flying their banners over the world have reached this position when they were seekers of truth, and avoided mean purposes. But it does not mean that the Ulama and students must necessarily face trials and tribulations and have definitely to pass through hard times. No, its meaning is never this, for it is not an inevitable demand of the honest intention that the sincere people should be subjected to difficulties and be confronted with adversities. The diseases that are generated for want of sincerity are many. When these diseases grow, they destroy faith ; and when they are less in number then they bore holes in it and give a chance to Satan to enter through them.

The Almighty Allah is displeased with the slaves of wealth and position because it is determined for a Muslim that he would sacrifice all interests, relations and ambitions in the cause of Allah, and it is not for him that he should go after them and forget his Lord and His pleasure.

The magicians of Firaun (Pharaoh) established a perfect example of true belief and high sincerity, when they rejected all the threats of Firaun, and trampled below their feet the love of wealth and position, and replied to that tyrant king's challenge in these words:

"So decree whatever you desire to decree ; for you can only decree (touching) the life of this world. For, we have believed in our Lord; may He forgive us our faults, and the magic to which you did compel us ; for Allah is Best and most Abiding." *(Ta Ha : 72-73)*

What a great difference between these two groups! One group disdainfully kicks at the material world, and the other group, in order to reach up to some big personality or to achieve some small gains, makes fun of its own religion and faith and sacrifices it for achieving success in the world.

Perseverance

"Patience is a light." *(Muslim)*

In the intricate paths of life when difficulties and hardships confront a man, and the darkness of adversities and suffering becomes long, it is patience only that acts like a light for a Muslim, that keeps him safe from wandering here and there, and saves him from the muddy mire of disappointment, desperation and frustration. Patience is such a basic quality that a Muslim needs it to shape his life in this world and in the next.

On this basis only he should attend to all his work. He should make it a torchlight for guiding his way, else be will be defeated in the field of life. He should prepare his self to tolerate the hardships and difficulties, and should not holler or raise hell. He should not sit waiting for the results, however late that may take. He should not run away from responsibilities, whatever they may be. No doubts and misgivings, no hardship of trouble should prompt his intellect to indulge in violence. He should have plenty of self-confidence. He should not be frightened by the dark clouds appearing on the horizon of life, even if they may be appearing continually, nay, he should be fully sure that these clouds of adversities and hardships will disappear, and the clear and bright atmosphere of success and glory wilt appear again.

Therefore, the demand of wisdom and far-sightedness is that its coming should be awaited with patience, peace and conviction.

The Almighty God has stressed this point sufficiently that no man can escape tests and trials, so that man may be alert and ready at the time when these hardships and difficulties descend on him, and he should not be frightened by these heavenly and earthly tribulations, and need not be disappointed and disheartened.

> *"And verily We shall try you till We know those of you who strive hard (in the cause of Allah) and the steadfast, and will We test your record."* *(Muhammad: 31)*

The poet has expressed the same idea in these words.

"We had anticipated the hardships of the night before their coming. So when they descended, there was no addition to our knowledge."

Undoubtedly if accidents and debacles are faced with a clear sight and full preparations, it will prove advantageous for man and this will help in stabilising and consolidating his position.

The Two Pillars of Patience : Patience relies on two important realities.

The first reality is concerned with the nature of this worldly life. Its details are : Allah has not made this world a house of peace and satisfaction or of rewards and recompense, but He has made it a house of trials. The time that a man spends in this world is really a time for unending experiences. He comes out of one trial in order to undergo another trial which is harder and different from the one through which he has already passed, that is man is tested once by one thing and again by its opposite, as iron is first heated in the fire and then it is put in the water. Similarly man is tested by favourable as well as opposing means.

When Allah blessed Hadrat Sulaiman with a grand and magnificent empire, he knew about these natural laws of the world. He had said:

> *"This is of the bounty of my Lord, that He may try me whether I give thanks or am ungrateful. Whoever gives thanks, he only gives thanks for (the good of) his own soul; and whoever is ungrateful (is ungrateful only to his own soul's hurt). For surely, my Lord is Absolute in independence, Bountiful."* *(Nahl: 40)*

The causes of trial through sadness and hardships are vague and unfixed. However, we can understand them properly by the example of the soldiers fighting in the battle-field. In the battlefield some groups are made to fight till they have to lose their valuable lives, so that the lives of other groups may be saved.

The security of other sections is dependent on the remaining groups being made to fight in new battles. This strategy is followed in the wider interest of the country and for greater advantages, by the great leadership of the army. In this fighting the life of a man has no importance, because the problem is much wider.

Same is the position of luck or fate. A certain man is put to different kinds of trials, till he falls down defeated, as there is no other way for him, except that he should greet the hardship that has arrived with patience and submission. Since this life is a testing ground, we should strive hard for success in it.

What is the trial or examination of life ? It is not words that they can be written, or talks to which attention may be paid. The questions of the examination are these hardships and difficulties which confront a man, and which open before him the path of fright, terror, and frustration. Examination is the name of the anti-reality defects which prompt a man to be jealous and nourisher of rancour against his sincere friend ; examination is the name of the tyrannies for which a nation occupies the place of god and the other people offer their blood as sacrifice for retrieving their usurped rights.

The history of life on this earth from the first day till today is very sorrowful. The right thing is that man should himself make his own way in this life, and he should be sure that the way to his destination is full of thorns and filth.

The second reality is concerned with the nature and temperament of faith.

Faith is the name of the relationship between man and his Lord.

As in the relationship of men, the true friendship and sincerity can only be judged when it is confronted with unfavourable and bitter conditions, when they have to deal with the hardships brought about by the vagaries of time, and when they are surrounded by various kinds of problems. At such a time a man's real worth and sincerity is known. Exactly similar is the case of faith. To find out the truth and sincerity about faith it is necessary that a Muslim be tried, he should be put in the crucible of fire to see whether he comes out glowing like the gold or whether he will he burnt away with the impurities. Undoubtedly, Allah's knowledge covers all manifest and concealed matters, and from this examination there will be no addition to His knowledge, because He knows all the conditions from the beginning till the end. The Divine knowledge cannot be made a basis for man's reckoning. His reckoning will be on the basis of his own personal deeds. If some criminals deny their crimes, then on the Day of Judgment in what way proof can be brought against them except by putting them to trial in this world and man's own parts of the body may give evidence against him?

About such people Quran has to say this :

> *"And on the Day We gather them together: We shall say to (hose who ascribed partners (to Allah). Where are (now) those partners of your make believe ? Then they will have no contention except that they will say : By Allah, our Lord, we never were idolaters. See how they lie against themselves, and (how) the thing which they devised has failed them !"* *(Al-Anam : 22-24)*

How can the reckoning of such criminals be taken in the light of the Divine knowledge ? Their justifiable retribution will be proper only when all their misdeeds are placed before them. Their efforts and striving to create corruption and mischief among others and all their misdeeds will be repeated before them.

On these two bases the foundation of patience has been kept. And for this reason religion demands it, but he who shuts his eyes from realities by force of his nature is dumbfounded when he has to face hardships and his hands and feet become inactive when he has to fight difficulties. His rashness dislikes waiting and patience and he is unable to tolerate it.

Therefore, when anything untoward happens, or he has to suffer some kind of failure, or when he meets with an accident, the earth with all its great vastness becomes narrow for him, and the conditions become exasperating for him. He wants to come out of these conditions in the twinkling of an eye, but it is obvious that in this effort he will not be successful for it is against the temperament of the world and the religion. It is proper for a Muslim to earn to be patient and to wait and to wait for long.

> *"Man is made of haste. I shall show you my aim, but ask Me not to hasten."* *(Al-Ambiya. 37)*

It is written in a *Hadith:*

> *"He who will adopt the policy of patience, Allah will give him patience, and no man has been given a greater and better gift than patience."* *(Bukhari)*

Patience is the Sign of Manliness : Patience is a symbol of greatness, glory and perfection. It is a means of security against the environmental conditions and losses. That is why 'Sabur' is one of the beautiful names of Allah, because He gives respite to His sinning slaves and does not hasten to punish them. If they are quick in committing crimes, he enforces his destined decisions and verdicts in centuries. He gives respite to people for a longtime. He does not catch them immediately on their wrong action:

> *"And they will bid you hasten on the doom, and Allah fails not His promise, and surely, a day with Allah is as a thousand years of what you reckon."* *(Hajj: 47)*

Patience is included in the factors of manliness, heroism, bravery and courage, because the burden of life cannot be borne by the owners of weak and puny bodies. When a man has a heavy load, and he wants it to be carried from one place to another, he does not employ for the purpose of infants, sick persons or cowards, but he engages such persons as have strong shoulders and powerful arms. Same is the case of life. The burden of this great responsibility can be lifted and it can be shifted from one place to another place by only that person who is lion-hearted and is a mountain of patience and determination.

For this reason the leaders, rulers and the great men of the nation have to face hardships and troubles in accordance with their capabilities and qualities.

Allah's Messenger was asked: Which people have to face the hardest trial. He replied:

> *"The Prophets, and then the people of the lower rank, and then lower and still lower. People are tested in accordance with their religiousness. The man whose relationship with the religion will be strong and firm, his trial will be hard. And the man whose religiousness will be weak, his trial will also be lenient. A man's test goes on till he is successful in his tests and then he walks on the ground and there is then no sin on him."*
>
> *(Ibn Habban)*

The fall in the achievements of the people on account of tiredness, hard labour, harassment and hardship is really in proportion to their power of endurance, patience and forbearance.

The knowledge of this secret of greatness and success compelled an American leader to remark: "Do not pray to God to make your burden light, but pray to Him to make your back strong." If the burden is light, and the hands are empty and there is no fear of any danger, then infants also can do a lot of things. But the busy schedule of life, sorrow and harassment in connection with duties, bitterness of the fighting, the hardship and tiredness of striving are the conduct of the fighters and builders of life.

The man who sits in his house, how can he be affected by the dirt and dust of the road ? How can the soldier running away from the battle-field taste the difficulties of carrying heavy weapons and the pangs of fighting ? But those who are participating in the battle of life, and are bearing its hardships, they will have to face difficulties, they will receive wounds, and they will have to experience extreme fatigue and hard labour.

Because of this Islam has honoured those who have been involved in the trials and tribulations of the worldly problems, and it has comforted the tired and fatigued people, in order that they may get relief in their sorrow and their burden of adversities may be lightened.

> *"A Momin is like a soft and delicate plant, which is moved by the wind. Sometimes it bends it and sometimes it raises it up, till he completes his span of life. But the example of an infidel is like that of a hard plant, whose roots are not deep. One blow of the wind uproots it."*
>
> *(Muslim)*

A Momin who is striving in the field of life is subjected to various difficulties and hardships, but he who is helpless and weak, and who has run away from the battle-field, how can he suffer? This is the meaning of the following sayings of the Prophet:

> *"Whom Allah wants to bless with virtue, He inflicts on him wound."* (Bukhari)
>
> *"If Allah likes a nation, He puts them to trial.*
>
> *With whom He is pleased, for that (nation) His pleasure is sufficient, and with whom He is displeased, for that His displeasure becomes a cause of suffering."* (Tirmidhi)

A man who fights with the hardships of life, some times he defeats them and many times he is defeated by them. The value of such a man before Allah is much higher than the man who sees the fun from a distance, neither he has to fear any danger nor is any other thing afraid of him.

The reward that the patient and hard-working fighters in the field of life will get on the Day of Judgment, the prizes and the honours that they will receive, will be much more than what the other persons who were performing other compulsory duties (worships) will be getting.

> *"People who were in comfort and ease will wish on the Day of Judgment, when they would see the reward and honours received by those who were successful in the trials, that would it that there skins were cut by the scissors and they would also have got the same reward that day."* (Tirmidhi)

To Invite Adversities is Against the Faith : It is a strange thing that some people have, from these Islamic teachings, misunderstood that Islam honours adversities and hardships, invites difficulties and sorrows and wishes for them, because these things become the cause of giving honour and mutual brotherhood.

This is a great misunderstanding. Anas bin Malik narrates :

> *"The Prophet saw an old man walking with the support of his two daughters. He asked him 'What is the matter?' The people informed him that man has taken a pledge that he would walk on foot. The Prophet said : 'Allah is unconcerned with the act of subjecting oneself to hardships.' He ordered him to take a mount."*(Bukhari)

Ibn Abbas says that the sister of Uqba took a pledge to go for Hajj on foot, and Uqba related this to the Prophet and complained that she is not fit to walk on foot. The Prophet said:

> *"Allah is unconcerned with your sister's walking on foot, she should take a mount, and for kaffara (atonement) she should give the sacrifice of an animal." (Abu Daud)*

Allah has said:

> *"What concern has Allah for your punishment if you are thankful (for His mercies) and believe (in Him) ? Allah was ever Responsive. Aware." (An-Nisa : 147)*

Islam praises people who are in difficulties and who are subjected to trials, so that they may get encouragement, and their faith and belief may be increased.

When it talks of difficulties and diseases, it means that these are the question papers of the examination and they should be solved with strength, patience and equanimity, and one should not fall a prey to laziness, and weakness and should not complain of the fate fixed by Allah, as beautifully put by an Urdu poet:

"Why is there no storm in your waves?

Why is your self not Muslim?

Your complaint of the fate fixed by Yazdan is useless,

Why you yourself are not the fate fixed by Yazdan?"

It is mentioned in a tradition that the Prophet went to see a sick woman, and found her cursing her sickness and reproaching her fever. He dissapproved of this act of hers and spoke to her in a sympathetic way:

> *"This fever removes the faults of the sons of Adam, as the oven removes the dirt and impurities of the iron." (Muslim)*

Then, does it mean that we should rear germs of the diseases and give them as gifts to our relatives and friends ? There are some people who think like this and went to explain like this ! This is sheer madness and senselessness!

During war time man gets dirtied with dust and mud, and sometimes he is confronted with distressing troubles, but every hardship that befalls a man in the battle of life raises his rank and takes him nearer to God, if his faith is strong and not wavering.

It is extreme foolishness if one thinks that when a man is troubled by an unending series of sufferings then he is forgotten by Allah and he has been deprived of Allah's blessings. It is a pity in the time of our decline and disruption this idea has spread far and wide, although we have shown earlier that adversities and hardships come in proportion to man's determination and will to fight.

Allah's Messenger has said :

> *"Undoubtedly, that decent man whose father, grandfather and great grandfather are decent, is Yusuf bin Yaqub bin Ishaq bin Ibrahim (bpuh.)." (Bukhari)*

Yusuf is such a Prophet as was brought up in the lap of Prophets, and he belonged to a noble and decent family. By selecting him for Prophethood, Allah has put a seal of confirmation on his chastity and decency. Have a glance at this noble man, how he passed through the early stages of his life. He is brought out from one difficulty to be put in another difficulty. His mother passes away during his childhood. Then his brothers conspire against him, and throw him into a well to deprive him of the love of his father. A passing caravan takes him out from the well and makes him a slave.

Then he is sold for a paltry sum in the market of slaves. He is bought by the King of Egypt. Only after a few days since his coming to the palace, he is made a victim of trickery, deception and waywardness. He comes out chaste and innocent out of this trial. But inspite of his being innocent he is sent to jail with some unlucky persons. Not for a few days, nor for a few months, but for years he has to remain in the prison.

Any other man would have found these hardships unbearable and a sufficient cause to curse his fate, but no, the true believer remained firm like a tower of light, and carried on his task of inviting people to believe in the unity of Allah and conveying the ignorant and illiterate people His message.

> *"O my two fellow-prisoners! Are diverse lords better or Allah, the One, the Almighty ? Those whom you worship beside Him are but names which you have named, you and your fathers. Allah has revealed no sanction for them. The decision rests with Allah only, Who has commanded you to worship none save Him. This is the right religion, but most men know not." (Joseph, 39-40)*

Really great and talented people have such character. If the charms of the world are taken away from them, they do not care and their sincerity in their belief does not suffer. If any adversity befalls them or they suffer an accident, they do not feel disgraced in their own eyes. A poet who strives for greatness and honour of the world also invites the difficulties and hardships and says very proudly:

"Decent and purified selves have to become a target of the world's dust and dirt. If they keep away from sorrows, then how can they achieve nobility and glory."

From the lives of the Prophets, Siddiqueen, martyrs, and our righteous forefathers we learn that honoured people and persons of high reputation can only be those men who can bear the hardships and carry the burden.

Allah's Messenger has said:

"For the slave high position is written from Allah, but through his deeds he cannot reach there when Allah puts him to test in respect of his body, wealth and children. Then he is successful in that trial and he reaches that high position, which was written for him by the sanction of Allah." *(Ahmad)*

In other words the series of difficulties and adversities that confront a man is the proof that the paths of goodness and prosperity are being made ready for him, and his position is being raised. Sometimes the difficulties come so that a faithful man should get himself totally entangled in the material world, should not feel proud over abundance and may not be under the influence of the deception of the world for a long time. A number of disadvantageous things become advantageous and a number of stages of the trial prove to be the gates of blessings.

Law of Nature

Patience, steadfastness, waiting and consistency is the law of nature. On sowing seeds sprouts do not appear immediately, and when they come they are not immediately ripe for cutting. It requires a waiting of months.

In the mother's womb the embryo remains for months and then it takes proper shape. Allah has informed us that He created this universe in six days, although He could have accomplished this task in the twinkling of an eye. The passage of morning and evening and the rotation of day and night mark man's growth, their development and bring maturity in their consciousness. And they return to their Lord:

"As He brought you into being, so return you (to Him). He has guided a group a right, and waywardness has taken hold of another group." *(Al-Aaraj: 29-30)*

Time is the raiment of every kind of action and inaction of life. If we do not display patience and steadfastness, it can blast us in the fire of our impetuosity. We cannot also change the temperament —

inherent attributes — of things, that are moving according to the pre-determined destiny.

There is a Necessity for Every Type of Patience : There are many varieties of patience. One is that patience which manifests itself as steadfastness in obedience. Another variety is the name of keeping away from trouble, and to stand firmly in adversities and display courage in difficulties is also a kind of patience.

The basis of the first kind of patience, that is to be steadfast in obedience is the performance of the basic items of Islamic worship correctly, and for remaining constant on it requires patience and perseverance. For example, salat (prayer) is a worship and compulsory duty of life which is required to be performed repeatedly. About this Allah says:

> *"And enjoin upon your people prayers, and be constant therein."* *(Ta Ha : 132)*

In the holy Quran the mention of exhorting one another to patience is made with the mention of exhorting one another to truth. The Almighty Allah has sworn that the human welfare is equally dependent on both these:

> *"By the Time. Indeed, man is in the state of loss, except those who believe and do good deeds, and exhort one another to truth and exhort one another to patience."*
> *(Al-Asr : 1-3)*

Opposed to the sins, it is only patience and steadfastness which counter the pleasures and temptations which glamorize the crimes.

Allah's Messenger has said:

> *"Paradise has been surrounded by the unliked things, while the hell is surrounded by carnal desires."*
> *(Muslim)*

To invite undesirable and unliked things and to keep away from carnal desires is a quality which can be found in an epitome of patience only. Here patience is generated as the outcome of an unshaken belief and the desire for seeking the pleasure of Allah. And this is the soul of purity and chastity which saves a true believer from the tricks of the evil and snares of the mean things.

> *"O our Lord! Vouchsafe to steadfastness and make us die as men who have surrendered (to You)."*
> *(Al-Araf : 126)*

Here a true believer has to show patience when his life, property, family and position receive any harm, and if he is hurt, he has to be patient. It is inevitable that a man should pass through one of these stages. Pitiable is that life which does not get a taste of these waves of storm. If he is not subjected to these storms, he cannot be prepared to face dangers squarely.

But when a Muslim goes under the shelter of Allah and seeks His help, then the weapons of accidents and calamities become blunt and useless, and they do not leave any effect on his body. Many times their irrevocable faith and unshaken belief make the assault of calamities futile, as the anaesthesia at the time of surgery makes the patient unaware of the pain. A Muslim cannot be separated from the favours and blessings of Allah until his belief is shaken on account of the onslaught of the calamities, and his faith is weakened in adversity:

> *"And surely We will test you with something of fear and hunger and loss of wealth and lives and fruits ; but give glad tidings to those who persevere patiently ; who say when a misfortune strikes them 'Surely to Allah we belong and to Him: shall we return.' These are the persons on whom are the blessings and mercy from their Lord and they are the people who are rightly guided."*
>
> *(Al-Baqarah : 155-157)*

Ummul-ula narrates that she was called by the Prophet when she was sick, and said

> *"O Ummul Ula ! Be happy that a Muslim's sickness removes his faults, as fire cleans the dirt of iron and silver." (Abu Daud)*

It is written in a Hadith:

> *"When a faithful slave's dearest person in this world is snatched away from him, and he displays patience and seeks Allah's pleasure, then Allah does not agree to give him anything less than paradise in compensation.'*
>
> *(Nisai)*

We should not forget the fact that the things with which we establish our relations, and on which we claim our rights, are things which have a stronger relationship with Allah and He has prior and greater rights on them. What can be a dearer thing for a man than his son ? The son is the dearest of all his relations. He is part of his blood and flesh. He grows in his lap and is cared for by him. And when death snatches him away from the father, the world becomes dark for him and he cannot help weeping.

But in spite of all this sorrow and sadness, truth compels us to say that while the father has been separated from the son, the real king has called back his slave. The Being who had given sight to the eyes has taken away the sight.

When the father says : "My son," the real Creator says : "No, this is my slave and My right is first on him prior to that of others."

Qasim bin Muhammad says that when one of his wives died, Muhammad bin Kaab al-Qarzi came to give him condolences. He narrated an incident. There was in Bani Israil a learned and a pious man. He had a wife whom he loved very much. She suddenly died. This accident so much affected him that he closed the doors of his house and went on mourning her death inside his house. Nobody could go to him. A woman of Bani Israil came to know of this and she said that she wanted to ask him something, which is not possible without meeting him, and she stationed herself at his door. At last the learned man was informed of this and gave her permission to see him. "I have come to ask your opinion about a problem. " He inquired what was the problem. She said : "I have borrowed some ornaments from a neighbouring woman, and I have been using them for a long period. After a long period she has demanded her ornaments. Should I return them to her ?" The learned man said : "Undoubtedly, by God there is no other way than this."

> *The woman said: "But they had been with me for a very long time." The learned man said : "Even then it is more proper to return them." Then the woman stated : "May Allah have mercy on you. Are you sorry for a thing which Allah had given you as a loan, and then He has taken it away, though He had greater claim on it ?" The learned man understood the point and this wisdom of the woman benefited him.* *(Malik)*

Away from Mutual Enmity

When the quarrel intensifies and its roots go deeper, and its thorns become branches and branches increase in number, then the freshness of the fruits of faith is adversely affected. Softness, sympathy, satisfaction and peace which are encouraged by the Islamic teachings receive a setback. Performance of worship loses its righteousness, nor does the self get any benefit from it.

Many times the mutual quarrels perturb the persons who claim to be wise. In this they take a recourse to the lowly and superficial things, and sometimes indulge in such dangerous acts which only increase difficulties and bring troubles. When a man is displeased, his eyes become prejudiced and ignore the camel and object to gnat. Such eyes do not appreciate the beauty of the peacock, for they only see its ugly feet and claws.

If a slight defect is present, it turns the molehill into a mountain. And sometimes the internal rancour and jealousy affect them so badly that no hesitation is felt in inventing imaginary stories. Islam disapproves of all these manifestations of ill-feeling and advises to abstain from them. It declares their avoidance as the most virtuous form of worship.

> *The Prophet has said : "Listen, may I not tell you something more important than salat, fasting and charity?" The people requested him to do so. He said : "To keep the mutual relationship on the right footing, because the defect in the mutual relationship is a thing which shaves a thing clean, I do not mean that it shaves the hair, but that it shaves (removes) the religion." (Tirmidhi)*

Many times Satan is not able to persuade wise men to worship idols, but since he is very keen on misguiding and ruining open, he manages to succeed in driving them away from God, so much so that these wise men become more indifferent in respecting the rights of God than the idolaters themselves.

The best method adopted by the devil for this purpose is to sow the seeds of enmity in the hearts of the people. When this enmity develops into a fire and open hostilities result, he enjoys the scene. This fire burns man's present and future into ashes and totally destroys their relationship and virtues.

> *The Messenger of Allah has said : "The Satan has been disappointed that he would not be worshipped in the Island of Arabia, but he has not been disappointed from kindling the fire of fighting among the people." (Muslim)*

It means that when wickedness takes roots in the hearts, and people start hating love and brotherhood and when these are destroyed, people revert to cruelty and enmity, and break all those relations and connections for joining which Allah has given command; and thus they spread corruption on this earth.

Not Severing Relations

Islam is fully alert in respect of the destructive causes of aggression and excesses, and tries to remedy them before they may go beyond the limit. It is common knowledge that men differ from one another in their nature and temperament. If their mutual contact does not result in clashes and estrangement, then inevitably there will appear narrowness and perturbation. For this reason Islam has formulated such principles as may keep the Muslims away from disruption and mischief, and as may generate in their hearts the feelings of love and friendship. For this purpose Islam has forbidden its followers from severing relations and mutual enmity.

In human life it so happens if the slightest excess is experienced from some other persons, then it causes us pain, and immediately we sever our relations. But Allah does not like that the mutual relationship among Muslims should be subjected to such adverse consequences.

> *Allah's Messenger has said : "Do not sever relation. Do not, indulge in mutual enmity. Do not entertain rancour and jealousy against one another, and do not be jealous of others. Be brethren among yourselves and become Allah's slaves. It is not permissible for a man to have severed his relations with any of his brethren for more than three days."* *(Bukhari)*

> *In another tradition it is mentioned : "It is not permissible for a Momin to have no connection with another Momin for more than three days. After three days have elapsed and he happens to meet him, he should salute him. If he answers the salute, then both will share the rewards (Ajr), and if the other person does not answer the salute, the sin will be on him, and the Muslim will be innocent of the sin of severing relations."* *(Abu Daud)*

In this *Hadith* the period of three days is kept so that during this period the intensity of anger will be reduced and his wrath will be cooled. After this it will be the responsibility of every Muslim to restore his relationship with his brethren and to revert to his old routine, as if the severing of relation was a cloud that had gathered due to some causes, till the wind blew and drew away the cloud and cleared the atmosphere. In every dispute or quarrel, a man is necessarily in one or the other condition, he is either an oppressor or the oppressed. If he is an oppressor, he has usurped the rights of others, then he should give up this wrong policy and should reform his character. He should understand that his opponent can abandon his hostility and rancour towards him only when he takes a satisfying and pleasant step in this regard. In such a condition Islam has commanded that he should request his opponent to come to a peaceful settlement and he should please him.

> *The Prophet has said: "He who has harmed his brother's rights or has hurt his honour, then he should please him today, before the day comes when there will be neither dirham nor dinar with him. If he would have virtues, then they would be taken in proportion to the aggression that he had committed. If there would be no virtues in his record, then the evil deeds of the oppressed would be thrust into his (oppressor's) account."* *(Bukhari)*

This is Islam's advice for the oppressors, but those who are the oppressed and whose rights have been harmed-for them the advice of Islam is that when the oppressor may ask for their pardon and may seek his Lord's forgiveness, then he should pardon him and should show softness. In such circumstances, to reject the request for pardon is a great sin.

It is mentioned in the tradition:

> *"A Muslim brother apologises to another Muslim, and the latter does not accept his apology, then on him will be the same sin as is on the person who collects a tax which is not due."* *(Ibn Maja)*

> *"If a person pleads his innocence to the other, and the other one rejects it, then he will not be brought to the water-tank."* *(Tibrani)*

In this way it brings the Muslim society on the high level of a life full of love, friendship and justice. Islam considers it a meanness of the human nature and lowliness that the hatred should take roots in the hearts and may not come out, but continue to burn inside like a volcano.

Those who nurse rancour and hatred against others in their hearts are always in search of opportunities to vent their inner hatred. They feel satisfied only when they shout in anger at the top of their voices and indulge in abuses. They hurt the feelings of others and spread corruption and mischief on the earth.

> *It is narrated by Ibn Abbas : "Allah's Messenger has said : May I not show you the sign of the wicked people ?" The people said : "If you are pleased, you may tell us." He*

said : "The most wicked person among you is he who keeps himself aloof, is harsh on his slave, and does not give any gifts to others. May I not tell you of another person more wicked than this ?" The people said "Definitely, O Messenger of Allah ! If you are pleased." He said: "He who has rancour against the people and the people have rancour against him." Then he asked : "May I not tell you of a more wicked person than this?" The people said "Definitely, O Messenger of Allah ! If you are pleased." He said : "He who does not pardon the errors of others, does not accept their apologies, and does not forgive their crime." Again he asked : "May I not tell you of a more wicked person than this ?" The people said : "Definitely, O Messenger of Allah ! If you are pleased." He said: "He from whom no good may be expected, and from whose wickedness there may not be security."

(Tibrani)

The wicked tendencies covered by this Hadith are the different stages of rancour and hatred, which occur in proportion to the defect and disease. This is not a strange thing, because from the olden times the people knew about them. Even in the pre-Islam days (Jahiliyah) rancour was considered to be the lowest stage of the wicked conduct, and decent people always avoided it. A poet of that period, Antara says:

"People of high position do not have rancour in their heart,

"One who has rancour in his nature cannot reach high position."

Causes of Ills

There are many evils in the society about which Islam has warned. If we think seriously, it will not be difficult to find out their source.

Inspite of all these evils having different shapes and forms, they revolve round only one basic disease, and that is rancour and enmity.

False accusation of innocent people is a crime, the real cause of which is ill-feeling and hatred. Since it is extremely effective in mutilating the realities and to condemn the innocent persons, Islam has declared it to be the worst kind of falsehood.

Hadrat Aishah narrates that Allah's Messenger asked his companions: "Do you know what is the worst aggression?" They said:

"Allah and His Messenger know it better:" He said : "Before Allah the worst aggression is to make halal (permissible) for oneself the honour of another Muslim." Then he recited the following verse of the Quran:

> *"Those who have caused pain to the Momin men and Momin women without any fault of theirs, surely they pure earned the (consequences of) false accusation and open sin."* *(Al-Ahzab)*

Undoubtedly the tendency to unnecessarily search out defects in other people and to foist it on them is the proof of meanness and wickedness. For being guilty of falsely accusing any person, Islam has decreed punishment in this world also, and it is difficult to imagine the punishment that the perpetrator of this sin will receive in the next world.

> *Allah's Messenger has said: "He who, in order to find fault, says something about a person which was not there, Allah will throw such a man in hell till ha tastes fully what he had fabricated."* *(Tibrani)*

In another tradition it is mentioned: "If a man spreads a rumour about another person of which he was innocent in order to bring him into disrepute, then it is Allah's task to melt him in fire on the Doomsday till he gets the full taste:"

Abstain from Backbiting : The meaning of the cleanness and purity of the bosom is this that if a man does not work for the good of others, then at least he should wish well of others. But if a man who does not see any defects in others, and yet he accuses them of those defects and tries to entangle them in baseless charges, such a man is a liar, a deceiver and shameless. Allah has said:

> *"Those who want that obscenity may spread in the group of those who believe, for them there is very severe punishment in this world and in the next world. Allah knows and you do not know."* *(Noor : 19)*

This is a great favour of Allah on His slaves that He approves of covering the defects of the creatures, even if those defects are present. And it is not permissible for a Muslim that he should feel pleased by condemning another Muslim, even if his condemnation may be correct, because men of healthy mentality feel pain when they see others in pain, and they wish for their recovery and welfare. As regards having pleasure from the disgrace suffered by others, from relating others' defects, and from uncovering their evils, this cannot be the course of action of a true Muslim.

Because of this Islam has declared backbiting as *Haram* (forbidden), for in this the latent rancour gets a chance to come out and man is deprived of grace and blessing.

Abu Hurrayrah has narrated that Allah's Messenger has said : "Do you know what is backbiting ?"

> *The people said: "Allah and His Messenger know better." He said: "You remember your brother in a way that may be disliked by him." He was asked: "If my brother has the defect which I am relating, then is that also backbiting ?" He replied "If that defect is in him, then it is backbiting; and if the defect stated by you is not in him, then it is a false accusation."* (Muslim)

The etiquette and principles formulated by Islam for the security of friendships and for a safeguard against divisive tendencies includes the forbidding of telling tales. (backbiting), because it creates ill-feeling among friends, and it destroys the cleanness of the hearts.

> *The Prophet used to restrain his companions from saying things which could hurt the feelings of others. He has said : "None of you should convey to me any hurtful thing about my companions, for I want that as long as I may come to you my bosom should be clean in respect of every one of you."* (Abu Daud)

If some one hears a wrong thing about some other person, then he should not widen the hole of the torn cloth by putting his finger in it. Many evil gossips die their own death, if they are left to themselves, and many statements give rise to wars, because large numbers copy them and encourage them. They are like sparks which fly carrying destruction with them.

> *Allah's Messenger has said : "No tell-tale can enter Paradise."* (Bukhari)

In another tradition, the word "Qattat" has been used. Ulama say that `Qattat' and 'Nammam' have the same meaning. But there is also a contention that Nammam is one who hears some people talking and then goes on quoting them, and Qattat is one who eavesdrop other people talking and then goes on quoting them here and there.

> *In the* Hadith *it is stated : "Telling tales and rancour will go to hell. These two things cannot gather in the heart of a Muslim."* (Tibrani)

The essential outcome of enmity and rancour is that man should be under a wrong impression, should be in search of defects of his adversary, should grieve internally on seeing others in good position and well-placed. Islam has severely disapproved of all these things.

> *The Prophet says : "Any one who knows about the defect of his another Muslim brother and he has concealed it, then Allah will cover (his defects) on the Day of Judgment."* *(Tibrani)*
>
> *In another tradition, it is said : "He who has veiled the defect of a Momin, he has acted as if he has revived a girl placed in a grave."* *(Tibrani)*

The majority of persons who are always in search of the defects of others commit more abominable crimes than those committed by the professional criminals. The hearts of such people are miles away from their Lord. To be in search of a crime in order to give it publicity is more reprehensible than actually committing that crime.

What a mean difference is there between these two feelings and attitudes? One feeling is that there is consideration against the things forbidden by Allah and concern for safeguarding it, while on the other side there is rancour against Allah's slaves and wish and desire to disgrace them.

The first feeling may even reach the limit, but it is not so bad as the second feeling, which secures pleasure and satisfaction from the ruin of the fellow-creatures it waits for their faltering, and laughs in their adversities.

Walk Away from Rancour

The safety of a Muslim's bosom and its purity is such a good gift that does not allow to attach his life to his fate or fortune or his sensibilities to the people, because many times he fails to achieve something, when others succeed. Sometimes he remains among the 'also ran' in the race of life, and others go ahead.

But this would be a very mean and uncivilized thing if a man is overcome by the feeling of selfishness and wishes others to sustain loss and setbacks only because he himself has not been able to forge ahead and derive benefits. Then a Muslim must be broad-minded, a benefactor of humanity and a sympathiser of the people. He should look at all things from the viewpoint of public good. He should not keep his own selfish gain in view. Generally people entertain the feelings of rancour and enmity because they see that their wishes and desires are not being satisfied, while others are having more than their share of the spoils. This is the trouble which does not allow them to rest awhile.

In the ancient times, the Devil had seen that the rank and position which he himself wanted had gone to the share of Adam; therefore, he decided that he would not allow Adam to enjoy these blessings

> *"Because You have thrown me out of the way, lo! I will lie in wait for them on the straight way then will I assault them from before them and behind them, from their right and their left, nor will you find in most of them gratitude (for your mercies):"* *(Araf: 16-17)*

This Satanic tendency develops in the nature of the spiteful people and destroys their hearts. Islam has severely warned people to keep away from this forbidden tendency, and to give place to tranquillity and satisfaction in life.

Anas bin Malik narrates that we were sitting with the Prophet when he said : "Just now a man of Paradise is coming to you." Immediately a man from Ansar came there. His beard looked dishevelled from the water of ablutions (Wudu), and he was carrying in his left hand his shoes. On the second day also the Prophet repeated the same words, and the same man again appeared before them, in the same condition. On the third day also the Prophet repeated the same thing and the man of Ansar again appeared in the same condition.

When the Prophet stood up, Abdullah bin Amar went after that man, and said to him: "I have had a quarrel in my house for three days. If you give me shelter, it would be most desirable." He said : "It is all right."

Anas says that Abdullah bin Amar says that he spent three nights in the company of that man, but he did not find him praying in the night, but whenever he went to bed, he used to remember Allah till he used to get up for the prayer of the morning. But Abdullah bin Amar says that he did not hear anything from his mouth except words of goodness. Abdullah says:

> *"When three nights passed and in my eyes his conduct did not hold any importance, I told that man : 'O slave of God! I have neither quarrelled with my father, nor have I severed relation with him. The fact is that I have heard the Prophet of Allah saying that a man of Paradise is coming before us, three times, and you appeared before us. Then I desired to stay with you and to see what act of*

yours is that-so that I may follow the same, but I did not see you doing any extraordinary work. What is the reason that the Messenger of Allah has said such a nice thing about you ? He replied:

"The reality is what you have seen." When I was returning he called me and said : "The reality is the same that has been witnessed by you ; however, I do not keep any spite against any of my Muslim brethren, and if Allah has blessed someone with any good thing, I am not jealous of him. Abdullah bin Amar said: "This quality of yours must have reached the Prophet of Allah." (Ahmad)

In another narration the words of the Hadith are as follows:

"The thing that you have seen is correct. O my nephew! I do not pass a night keeping spite against a Muslim." (Bazzar)

Islam has declared jealousy as *Haram* (forbidden). Allah has commanded his Messenger to seek shelter from the mischief of jealous people, because jealousy is a spark that burns inside the bosom and hurts the jealous person as well as others.

The man who wishes that the good things of life should be destroyed, he becomes a source of trouble for the society. His conscience is not satisfied with anything. Allah's Messenger has said:

"In the stomach of a man, the dust flying in the path of Allah and the flames of hell cannot be together, nor can the faith and jealousy dwell together in the stomach of a man." (Baihaqi)

In another tradition it is mentioned: "Keep away from jealousy, for jealouy eats up virtues in the same way as fire eats up wood." (Abu Daud)

The person who hates the rewarded person or the one deserving Allah's favours and wishes that they should have been deprived of those things, for such a man there are a number of causes which repel him from the realities of life. The first cause is that he is imprisoned by the world and the lure of the wealth of the world. He fights against it, and he sheds tears for not achieving his material goat, and he entertains feeling of jealousy against those who are successful in this world. He is angry with them.

This is a great misunderstanding about omprehending both the worlds ; and the fact is that he has completely ignored the next world and has closed his eyes from the necessity of makng preparations for that world. This negligence on his part has resulted in his reaching this condition. It is necessary that every man should prepare for the next world, and should be sorry for losing opportunities to do so.

> *"O mankind! there has come to you a direction from your Lord and a healing for the (diseases) in your hearts, and for those who believe, a guidance and a mercy. Say: `In the bounty of Allah, and in His mercy, in that let them rejoice; ' that is better than the (wealth) they hoard." (Yunus : 57-58)*

The man who is jealous is weak of determination helpless, forgetful of his Lord, and unaware of his Lord's principles operative in this world. For this reason when he fails to achieve something, he conspires and schemes against the successful people. As an Arabic poet says:

> *"People became jealous of the young man because they could not reach up to his successes. So every one appears to be his enemy and opponent."*

The proper thing for him was to turn to his Lord, to seek His favours because his treasures are not limited to or reserved for any single person. After this he should again strive for his objective. It is quite likely that what he could not achieve in his first attempt culd be available in the second. Undoubtedly this is much more desirable than nursing spite and rancour in his bosom.

There is a very big difference between jealousy and high ambition, in jealousy and desire and envy, in jealousy and not desiring any deviation in straight dealing, and in charity and in expressing displeasure against contamination. It is obvious that these two things cannot be placed together.

Ambition is the name of the desire for reaching the high pinnacle and of achieving it, and this is the quality of Allah's faithful slaves. Hadrat Sulaiman prayed to his Lord thus:

> *"My Lord ! Forgive me and bestow on me sovereignty such as shall not belong to any after me. Surely, You are the Bestower." (Sad: 36)*

A quality of the slaves of the Most Gracious that has been mentioned is that they pray to their Lord thus

> *"Our Lord! Vouchsafe us comfort of our wives and of our offspring, and make us patterns (leaders) of the righteous." (Furqan: 74)*

To achieve Allah's blessings it is necessary to strive for it and primarily to have a sincere desire for it. To grieve internally over another person's achieving His blessings is an abominable tendency. There is a great difference between these two.

Envy is the name of the desire to have those gifts which Allah has bestowed on others. But since nursing such a desire and envy can also open the gateways of mischiefs, can encourage the inclination towards wong desires, and can also incite for achieving that which is apparently beneficial but in the ultimate analysis harmful. Islam has, therefore, fixed the norms for the things for which a man can have desire and for which competition is permissible.

Allah's Messenger has said : "Excepting two things, in no other thing jealousy is permissible: one—it is permissible to be jealous of the man who has been given wealth by Allah and who is spending it in the cause of truth unhesitatingly, and second, that man whom Allah has blessed with wisdom, in whose light he takes decisions and imparts education in it to others." The sense in which the word jealousy has been used in the Hadith does not include the desire for bringing to an end the blessing or the favour, but it means the efforts to achieve that blessing and having envy for that blessing has been termed as jealousy.

The idea is that the thing which a man should make his objective should be great and magnificent. It is lack of ambition or courage that a man should desire for small things, and should entertain expectations from them. There are many things which do not yield anything but distress and sorrow, and the spite against other people is generated because they think in an unhealthy manner as to why other people have achieved those things from which they are deprived.

About such things Allah says:

> *"In no wise covet those things in which Allah has bestowed His gifts more freely on some of you than on others ; to men is allotted what they earn. And to women what they earn ; but ask Allah of His bounty ; for Allah has full knowledge of all things."* *(Nissa: 32)*

As regards disliking the unstraight dealing in general conditions and matters, this is the rightful demand of justice and assertion. It has nothing to do with despicable jealousy. If we feel angry that some person has earned a lot of benefits from a little labour, or has obtained a high-ranking position, then such an anger is understandable and praise-worthy. This is a kind of public welfare which has nothing to do with jealousy. Islam has been hearing and watching individuals at intervals, so that it may clean them of the impurities of spite and enmity, and may nourish in the hearts of the general people clean and pure feelings for their good, and for itself also.

Every day, every week and every year arrangements are made for the cleaning of the individuals, so that their dirt and filth may be removed, defects may be done away with, and even the slightest trace of spite and rancour may not be found in the faithful heart. About the daily *Farz salat* (compulsory prayer) it has been clarified that its reward will not be given to a Muslim unless his heart is not found free from ill-will against others, and is not bereft of all disputes, quarrels enmity and rancour against the people.

> *Allah's Messenger has said : "There are three persons whose prayer does not rise even a fist above their heads. One is that man who leads the prayers of others who do not like it. Second is that woman who spends her night in such a way that her husband is displeased with her. And third are those two brothers who have severed their relations with each other."* *(Ibn Maja)*

The Test

Every week the acts of Muslims are evaluated. Allah sees every week what a Muslim has collected for the next world, and what feelings are hidden in his heart. If his bosom is free from spite and rancour, then he is saved from destruction, and if it is filled with the feelings of displeasure, jealousy and ill-will then he remains backward in the field of action.

> *Allah's Messenger has said : "Every Monday and Thursday men's acts are placed before Allah. On these days Allah forgives the sins of everybody, except the polytheists. However, if there is a person who has spite and rancour against his brother, He says about them : 'Leave these two alone in their condition till they come to a settlement."* *(Muslim)*

It is not correct for a Muslim that the days and nights may pass off and he should be shackled for the whole year in the chains of enmity and spite, and tied with the handcuffs of rancour and ill-will. Allah grants gifts to those who are sincere and broad-minded. In the *Hadith* it is mentioned:

> *In the night of the 15th of Shaban, Allah acquaints himself of the conditions of His slaves. So He forgives*

those who seek His pardon, bestows mercy on those seeking mercy, and leaves the spiteful people alone."

(Baihaqi)

Even after this much cleansing if a man leaves this world carrying the dirt and filth of spite, rancour and jealousy, then he deserves to be burnt in the fire of hell. The man whose cleansing has not been possible by the Shariah, the fire of hell will reach him and it will not be helpless in burning his sins and his enmity.

Spite and jealousy and the diseases which were created by them have been condemned by Islam, and they have developed and progressed because man is a prisoner of the world and the desires to achieve it, and the longing to enjoy the pleasures and luxuries of life to the utmost keep him in trouble.

But if some one is hated for Allah, if a man gets angry in the cause of truth, or if tumultous enthusiasm and liking is displayed to achieve righteousness and virtue, then this is quite a different matter.

It is no sin for a Muslim if he severs his relation till the end of his life with such persons as disobey the commands of Allah, or who cross the limits of Shariah.

If he hates such persons or declares his enmity towards them, then he cannot be blamed for that; on the contrary it is a sign of his perfect faith, selflessness and sincerity.

Allah has commanded us that we should keep away from His enemies, even if they may be our relatives:

"O you who believe ! Choose not your fathers nor your brethren nor friends if they take pleasure in disbelief rather than faith. Whosoever of you takes them for friends, such are wrongdoers." *(Taubah : 23)*

Or whose company is bad, who has the habits of meanness and of talking glibly and endlessly, to keep away from such a one is necessary. And one who has committed a wrong against Allah, to punish such a one there is nothing wrong if that one is boycotted for a fixed period, because the Prophet had severed his relation with some of his wives for a period of forty days and Abdullah bin Umar did not have any relation with one of his sons till his death, because he had rejected one command of the Messenger of Allah. His father, Abdullah bin Umar narrated a Hadith in which women were allowed to go to the mosques, but his son had rejected this *Hadith.*

High Objectives

The rightness of intention and sincerity are the two things which enliven a man's worldly action and make it a prayer that is answered. But if there is perversion in the intention and corruption in the heart, a man, inspite of offering prayers, is degraded. He commits sins and inspite of his showing interest in and taking pains for performing worship is doomed to failure and loss. But as against this many times a man builds high and lofty palaces, constructs broad and spacious buildings, lays out a beautiful garden full of fruits, and starts living in this paradise, and he is called a king. But since in his efforts and labour of building these high and lofty palaces, etc. the purpose was to benefit humanity, then for these acts he will be a recipient of an unending reward (sawab).

Allah's Messenger has said:

> *"Anybody who, without subjecting another person to cruelty or aggression, builds a magnificent building, or plants saplings without indulging into cruelty and rancour, he will be getting reward for that till the time Allah's creatures would be benefitted by them." (Ahmad)*
>
> *In another tradition it is stated : "If a Muslim lays a garden or does farming, and if a bird or a man eats something from it, then he will get a virtue (neki) in its place." (Muslim)*

Even carnal pleasures are also counted as acts of prayer, if behind them there is righteous intention and clean purpose. When a man goes to his wife so that he may be able to save his chastity, and protect his faith, he gets a recompense for this act.

Whatever he feeds his body, or whatever he does to sustain his wife and children, for that also he gets reward, provided there is goodness and righteousness in his intention.

Saad Ibn Abi Waqqas narrates that the Messenger of Allah has said : "If you spend even an ordinary thing for seeking the pleasure of Allah, you get its reward, so much so that even putting a morsel of food in the mouth of your wife is a virtuous act."

Another tradition has it:

> *"Whatever you feed your father, it is a charity from you. Whatever you feed your child it is a means of reward for you, and whatever you feed your servant, it is also a charity from you." (Ahmad)*

The fact is that as long as man keeps himself as an obedient slave of Allah and his intention is pure and sincere, then all his acts and movements, his sleep and his waking are considered to be for seeking the pleasure of Allah. And sometimes it so happens that a man wants to perform a righteous act, but on account of his poverty he is unable to do so, then Allah, who knows the secrets of hearts, gives the man desirous of reform the honour of a reformer, the man desirous of fighting in the cause of Allah the honour of a Mujahid (the fighter in the cause of Allah), because for Him high courage and righteous intention is more appreciable than the want of resources.

During the days of scarcity and poverty a battle was to be fought. Some people came to the Prophet with a view to joining his forces and offered themselves to be sacrificed in the cause of Allah. But Allah's Messenger did not allow them to take part in the Jihad because of their incapability. They returned with a heavy heart and sorrowfully. They were very much grieved for not being allowed to participate in Jihad. About them the following verses were revealed:

> *"Nor (is there blame) on those who came to you to be provided with mounts, and when you said: `I can find no mounts for you,' they turned back, their eyes steaming with tears of grief that they had no resources wherewith to provide the expenses."* *(Tauba: 92)*

Do you think that a firm and strong faith and belief would be wasted? And this burning desire for sacrifice would be just lost? No, never. For this reason the Prophet appreciated their faith, and said to, the soldiers going with him:

> *"There are some people whom we have left behind in Medina ; in whatever place or valley we may camp, they will be with us. For them their excuse is enough." (Bukhari)*

As their intentions were honest, they were the recipients of the reward (sawab) of the mujahidin (fighters), because they had stayed in Medina against the wishes of their hearts and with great unwillingness.

If this is the achievement of the honest intention that the person having it is so favoured, then the dishonest intention also earns the punishment reserved for the bad deed, although apparently the act was righteous. Such a hypocrisy has been condemned:

> *"So woe to the worshippers who are neglectful of their prayers, those who (want but to be seen (of men), but refuse (to supply) (even) neighbourly needs."* *(Al-Maun : 4-7)*

The prayer based on hypocrisy is considered a sin, because after losing the essential sincerity it has become dead, and is, therefore, useless. Similar is the case of zakat. If it is paid merely to seek Allah's pleasure then it can be acceptable to Allah, otherwise it wilt be a waste:

> *"Waste not your charity by reminders of your generosity or by injury—like him who spends his wealth to be seen by men and believes not in Allah and the Last Day. His likeness is the likeness of a rock on which there is (some) dust of earth ; on it heavy rainfalls, which leaves it a bare stone. They will be able to do nothing with anything they have earned."* *(Baqarah : 264)*

The heart which is bereft of sincerity cannot be acceptable, as the rock with some dust on it cannot grow any grain when rain falls on it. If the kernel is rotten, beautiful outer skin will not be of any use.

However, if the self is full of sincerity, then its blessing helps to make an ordinary thing as weighty as a mountain. If it is devoid or sincerity, then what reward can mounds of chaff and husks achieve from Allah ?

That is why Allah's Messenger has said:

> *"Make your faith pure ; a little (righteous) act will be sufficient to save you from hell."* *(Al-Aakim)*

In the *Hadith* the reward for virtuous acts has been mentioned to be from ten times to hundred times, depending on the performer's intention and sincerity hidden in his heart, which is known only to that Being who knows about all the manifest as well as hidden things. Accordingly the reward increases according to the sincerity and honesty of the intentions.

The external acts of man can neither achieve the pleasure of Allah nor the grandeur of the worldly life. Allah gives his attention to his faithful and sincere slaves accept only those of their acts which bring them nearer to Him. As regards the worldly show and human trappings, they have no importance and no value.

The Prophet has said:

> *"Allah does not see your bodies nor does he look at your faces, but he sees your hearts."* *(Muslim)*

It is mentioned in the Hadith :

> *"When Doomsday would occur, the deeds done in the world will be presented to Allah. From them the acts*

performed for Allah will be separated. And the other acts performed for other purposes will be thrown into the fire of hell." *(Baihaqi)*

One who would adopt these realities in one's life would experience relief and comfort in this world and would also achieve eternal bliss in the Hereafter. He will not be harmed by the loss of anything nor will he grieve for any act.

The Prophet has said:

"The man who has left his world in the condition that he had performed acts sincerely for the one and only Allah, had established prayer and had paid zakat, then Allah is pleased with him." *(Ibn Maja)*

This Hadith is in conformity with these words of Allah:

"And they have been commanded no more than this; to worship Allah, offering Him sincere devotion being true (in faith) to establish regular prayer ; and to practise regular charity; and that is the religion, right and straight." *(Baiyina :5)*

Sincerity : the Desired Thing

In the times of scarcity and adversity the rays of sincerity throw their light with full force. At such times man separates himself from his carnal desires and yearnings. He severs his relations with their defects and errors. He repents before Allah and weeps and wails and prays for His blessings. He shakes from the fear of Allah's wrath.

The holy Quran has drawn a very fine picture of such a man, who is surrounded by adversities, and is appearing to his Merciful Lord so that He may lift him out of this mire:

"Say: 'Who is it that delivers you from the dark recesses of land and sea, when you call upon Him in meekness and silent terror; if He only delivers us from these (dangers), (we vow) or shall truly show our gratitude ?' "Say : 'It is Allah that delivers you from these all (other) distresses ; and yet you run after false gods' ?" *(Al Anam : 63-64)*

This sincerity is temporary. Those conditions which befall a man and sometimes do not befall, how can they be called moral conduct? Allah wants that He should be truly and correctly known and recognised and should be respected and honoured in good or bad condition, as deserving of Him. People should give their due place to honest and sincere intention and good conduct in their lives. Their attachment to these qualities should be strong and should not break at any time, and they should not make any other thing but selflessness and Allah's pleasure as an ideal to follow in their life.

This heat of sincerity dies down gradually as passion for greed for wealth, self-love, egotism, hunger for position and office, hypocrisy and desire to be famous increases. But to Allah only that act is desirable which is free from all these undesirable impurities:

> *"Surely, pure religion is for Allah only." (Zumar : 3)*

The example of the superior nature is like that of a ripe fruit, which requires to be protected from diseases and mishaps in order to preserve its sweetness and cleanness.

For this reason Islam has considered hypocrisy in righteous acts as most abominable and has declared it as, shirk, associating some one else with Allah.

The truth is : this hypocrisy destroys all acts as white ants destroy slowly all things they come in contact with. When the habit of hypocrisy takes roots in any man's dealings, as germs of an infectious disease spread in the society, then it becomes a sort of idolatry and throws its practitioner into the fire of hell.

The Prophet has said :

> *"A little hypocrisy is also polytheism. He who is hostile to Allah's friends, he openly declares a war against Allah. Allah likes those who are righteous, who fear him and who pray secretly, those who would not be missed if they disappear and would not be recognised if they are present. Their hearts are the lamps of guidance. They remove darkness from every piece of land." (Hakim)*

Ibn Abbas narrates that one man asked the Prophet : "O Messenger of Allah ! I take up a stand with the intention of seeking Allah's pleasure, and I wish that the people of my country should see it. What do you think of it?" The following verses were revealed before the Prophet gave an answer

> *"Whoever expects to meet his Lord, let him work righteousness, and in the worship of his Lord, admit no one as partner." (Kahf : 110)*

The severe criticism and attacks which Islam has unleashed on the evils emanating from hypocrisy and want of sincerity is because it is a kind of corruption that is not discernible, and keeps the carnal desires and the wicked wishes of the self hidden. The evils which can be seen give rise to other evils and increase the rate of corruption of the society considerably. Such evils are considered very low and mean, and on account of this consciousness and feeling it is quite possible that the man who commits them may give them up sooner or later, and may turn a new leaf.

But that sinning which puts on the garb of worship has its evils hidden from the sight of the sinner himself and the society is also not able to recognise it.

It is so because such a criminal remains absorbed in the ramifications of his acts. He is under the impression that he is also working for the pleasure of Allah, then how can he realise that he has committed a sin? And how can he turn away from a thing which he considers righteous ?

As regards the general society, it is harmed more by the learned (Ulama) hypocrites than by the poor and needy people, who are the habitual criminals of this type. Want of sincerity in the talented people makes their ability a curse for the country, and such a society suffers a set back instead of making progress.

It is also true that to pollute a virtue with the impurities of the self is to downgrade its value. This is another crime which is committed for want of sincerity. The man wants to please other men and is neglecting to seek the pleasure of his Lord ; he does not understand, on account of his foolishness, as to what his sin signifies. He is turning away from the Being who is Most Powerful and who is Independent of everything, to those beggars who have neither power, nor riches. That is why Allah's Messenger has said:

> *"When on the Day of Resurrection, about the occurrence of which there is no doubt, Allah will gather all the people who came first and last, a caller will give a call : "Whoever has associated another with Allah in his acts should seek his reward from that partner because Allah is more free from partnership than all the partners."* *(Tirmidhi)*

Soldiers should Prove Sincerity : Whether it may be a common soldier or a commander, the soldiers should keep their Jihad free from all the impurities of worldly show and trappings, because they have attached their life and death with a sacred duty, compared to which ranks, medals, honours, salaries, etc., have no value..........They should give preference to whatever is with Allah, and should sacrifice their desires for pure devotion and sincere submission.

It is narrated by Abdullah bin Amar bin Aas that he said:

> *"O Messenger of Allah! show me the difference between Jihad and battle." The Prophet replied: O Abdullah bin Amar! If you fight displaying patience and for seeking the pleasure of Allah, then He will lift you in the same state ; and if you fight with pride on the largeness of your numbers and to show to the people, then Allah will lift you is the same state. O Abdullah bin Amar ! In whatever condition you fight or you are killed, Allah will lift you in that condition."* *(Abu Daud)*

Employees in the Cause of Allah : The writing work that the employees do in their offices, the accounts that they maintain, the intellectual energy that they spend, the manual work which they do with their hands, all these activities should be conducted by them is the interest of their country and for seeking the pleasure of Allah.

An animal labours for the whole day for its fodder. The efforts and labour of a common man has the value of an animal's labour, and all his work and labour are in proportion to his salary, and that is his purpose and centre of activity.

But an intelligent and wise man knows the value of his ideas and his acts and employs them in the cause of some great objective.

It is very regrettable that the general employees are suffering from this disease. They do not understand anything else but wealth, ranks and promotion. They consider their world and their religion also limited by this circle only, and they think that it is the axis of their happiness and sorrow, action and inaction, desire and ambition, and their lives revolve round that only.

Allah's Messenger has said : When the last period would come, there would be three sects in my Ummah. One sect will sincerely worship only Allah. The second sect will worship as hypocrites. The third sect will worship so that they may defraud others of their wealth. When Allah would gather them on the Day of Judgment and say to the last sect : 'By My honour and grandeur, what did you expect to get from My worship? He would answer: 'By Your honour and grandeur, I was fraudulently taking others' property by that.' Allah would say that whatever he had collected was of no use to him and would command him to be sent to hell. Then He would address the sect whose worship was governed by hypocrisy: 'By My honour and grandeur, tell Me what was your purpose? He would say : 'By Your honour and grandeur, the purpose was to show to the people.' Allah would say: 'Nothing from it has reached me. Take him away to hell.' Then the Almighty Allah would ask the sect that was sincerely worshipping Him: 'By My honour and grandeur, what did you expect to get from My worship? He would answer: 'By Your honour and Your grandeur, You are better aware of the condition of the person who sought Your words and Your pleasure.' Allah would say:

> *'My slave has spoken the truth. Take him to Paradise':"*
> *(Tibrani)*

Respect and Misbehaviour

To express greatness and pride over mankind is the attribute of their Lord, Who has created them, proportioned them, shaped their destiny, then showed them the path, Whose wrath appears as a terrible punishment and Whose favours and blessing, when manifested, stun human intellect

> *Then praise be to Allah, Lord of the heavens and Lord of the earth, Lord and Cherisher of all the worlds! To Him be Glory throughout the heavens and the earth; and He is Exalted in Power, Full of Wisdom. (Jathiya : 36-37)*

The bowing of the slaves before their Lord and adopting servility before Him is bowing before Truth and not before Falsehood, because creation, command, Unconcern, and Power are reserved and specific for Him, and the slaves' good or bad fate depends on His will. The slaves are in the best and the most purified condition when their foreheads are lowered in prostration before their Lord, and when they truly pay His dues without committing any excesses or being guilty of any shortcomings.

But the bowing of humans before humans like them is undoubtedly false and wrong and baseless . Here who claims greatness, who is proud and a wrong-doer under a baseless wishful-thinking, and the one who bows does not realise his own value. He has lifted such a heavy burden that he has no strength to carry.

That is why Islam, on the one hand, has declared pride as *Haram* (forbidden), and on the other hand treated the disgraceful behaviour and undue honouring as equally undesirable, and has enjoined on its followers to be respectable.

Allah's Prophet (S.A.W.) has said:

> *"Whoever has pride in his heart equal to a poppy seed, Allah will throw him into the hell face downward."*
> *(Ahmad)*

In another tradition it is written:

> *"In the meanwhile a man was walking in his best clothes. He was very pleased in his heart of hearts. He had combed his hair. There was pride in his gait, and Allah entrenched him in the earth. Now he will go on getting entrenched more and more till the Doomsday. (Bukhari)*

The reason for this is that pride and greatness is the attribute of Allah, and it befits Allah only. It is not proper for a man to try to usurp this right of Allah. The foundation of pride is on superficialism and meanness, which include evils like denial of Truth, ignorance of the facts, wicked-living, crossing one's limits and considering others mean. Islam has declared it Haram for a Muslim to consider himself mean, of no significance, weak and disgraceful, and on seeing some rich and powerful person, to feel sorry and inferior.

Anas bin Malik (R.A.A.) has narrated that the Prophet (S.A.W.) has said:

> *"A man who has expressed sorrow in connection with the achievement of the material world, he has expressed displeasure against his Lord, and he who creates an uproar and cries loudly on some hardship, he complains against Allah. He who adopts servility seeing somebody rich and powerful, displeases Allah, and he who, after receiving Quran, acts like the people of hell, becomes deprived of Allah's blessings."* *(Tibrani)*

In another *Hadith* it is stated:

> *"Whoever sits in the company of a rich man and adopts an attitude of servility for himself looking to his grandeur and honour in the world, his two-third religion is ruined and he will go to hell.*

This *Hadith* is a serious warning for those who grumble loudly when they are confronted with hardships, they shout and create big noise when they experience any difficulty and call men for help, and for getting their work done become servile and cringe before the wealthy and rich persons.

To feel pain as a result of lack of facilities is not an inferiority, but the conversion of lack of facilities and riches into disgrace and ignominy is despicable in the eyes of Islam.

From the ancient times the sign of manliness is that the wounded bears his pain till he is cured and starts on his journey again, and does not sit accepting defeat and waits for somebody to lift him up from the dust to which he has fallen.

In a *Hadith* it is stated: "One who accepts disgrace with willingness and pleasure, is not from among us."

Islam allows a Momin to settle in a place where there is decency and honour, and where full freedom is given to him. It is the duty of every Muslim to act on these righteous ideals, and if it is not possible then he should leave this place of disgrace and dishonour. Allah says :

> *When angels take the souls of those who die in sin against their souls, they say: "In what (plight) were you ?" They reply : 'Weak and oppressed were we on the earth.' They say: 'Was not the earth of Allah spacious enough for you to move yourselves away (from evil)?' Such men will find their abode in hell, —What an evil refuge it is !*
>
> *(Nina : 97)*

Allah has exempted those helpless persons who were unable to shift and could not find any other way of relief, in these were included women and children.

Except those who are (really) weak and oppressed-men, women and children-who have no means in their power nor (a guide post) to direct their way. For these there is hope that Allah will forgive; for Allah does blot (sins) and forgive again and again.

These verses show how undesirable and reprehensible are tolerance and bearing of disgrace and insults, and these verses create in man, the strength and will to make efforts to seek deliverance from them.

A Muslim's respecting and honouring his self, his religion and his Lord is really a sign of the greatness of his faith. And there is a very big difference between the greatness of the Faith and the greatness of Falsehood. It is really against the self-respect of a Momin that he should feel inferior before a man in power, or he should be insulted or disgraced at any place, if he should live as a supplement of another person. In it there is an avoidance of transgression and disobedience and also an aversion from disgrace and dishonour.

The greater the sense of inferiority before God, the greater is the superiority and elevation before men. This faith is far beyond all the things of the universe, all human beliefs and all false ideas about life. A Momin considers himself a servant for serving the Muslims, for establishing intimate relations with them, and for respecting their rights, he visits their houses and in the true sense of the word nurtures the feelings of greatness and impressiveness

> *If any do seek for glory and power,—to Allah belong glory and power. To him mount up (all) words of purity ; it is He who exalts each deed of righteousness. Those that lay plots of evil, for them is a penalty terrible ; and the plotting of such will be void (of result).* *(Fatir : 10)*

Hard against Disbelievers

The sense of honour, assistance, and self-confidence are those prominent qualities on which Islam has given great emphasis. It has given them a basic place in the formation of the society. For nourishing them and developing them, it has established a never-ending series of instructions. To these qualities had Hadrat Umar Ibn Khattab (R.A.A.) referred when he said: ""That person is extremely dear to me, who, when subjected to disgrace and insult, refutes them with all his might."

It is also worth considering why a muazzin repeats the call of greatness of Allah in the beginning and end of his call, five times daily. Why does he repeat these words for the prayers (salat) and why are the movements of qayam (standing) and sujud (Prostration) dependent on these words ?

In order that a Muslim should have an unshakeable faith that every claimant of greatness beside Allah is false, and every proud person beside Allah is mean and disgraceful. In other words this is a spiritual food that is being fed repeatedly to Muslims against problems of the world, attractions of the materialistic gains and the forces of darkness, so that the steps of Muslims may not falter or flounder.

In view of the importance of these attributes and to emphasize that Allah has fixed for Himself the best names, which are called 'Asma-e-Husna' (Beautiful names), so that by repeating them in bowing and prostrating during prayers, the sense of Allah's greatness and uniqueness is fully imbibed into them.

Respect is a man's birth-right, and its achievement is enjoined on every man. It is not proper for a man that he should pay his dues only when they are demanded from him.

The better thing is that when a man has been made responsible for a certain job, he should complete that work to the best of his ability, so that nobody should be able to find fault with him, and no one, either a well to-do person or a poor man should criticise him.

He should safeguard his honour and respect on that day when from every side there will be showers of curses and reproaches, and his worst enemies will be afraid of him:

> *To those who do right is a goodly (reward) yes, more (than in measure)! No darkness nor shame will cover their faces ! They are the people of Paradise; they will abide therein for ever. But those who (have earned evil will have a reward of like evil; ignominy will cover their (faces); no defender will they have from (the wrath of) Allah ; their faces will be covered, as it were, with pieces from the depth of the darkness of night; they are the people of hell-fire; they will abide therein (for ever) !*
>
> *(Yunus : 26-27)*

To disobey Allah and His Messenger is to invite disgrace and dishonour and to throw the individuals and the group into the pit of ruin. In the holy Quran Allah has clearly stated that the defeat in the Battle of Uhud was the result of the disobedience of some individuals.

> *Those of you who turned back on the day the two hosts met,—it was Satan who caused them to fail, because of some (evil) they had done. But Allah has blotted out (their fault); for Allah is Oft—Forgiving, Most Forbearing.*
>
> *(Al-i-Imran : 155)*

When Islam has advised and instructed a Muslim to be respectful and honourable, it has pointed out to him its sources too, and has made the means of achieving it easy. It showed that decency and nobility is on account of Fear of God, superiority and elevation is achieved by worshipping Allah; and honour and power are gained by obeying Allah.

A Muslim who finds this recipe, or wants to share its wealth, riches and position, its defence will be considered as a Jihad (striving) in the cause of Allah, and it will not be merely a defence of the individual rights, but the defence of the public rights and of the higher values. That is why in the Hadith it is written that the person who is killed in defending his rights should be considered a martyr. A man went to the Prophet and said: "O Messenger of Allah! If someone comes to usurp my wealth, what should be my attitude?"

The Prophet (S.A.W.) said :

> *"Do not give him your wealth." He asked "If he is prepared to fight with me?" He replied "Then you fight with him." He asked: "If he kills me?" He replied: "You will be a martyr." He asked: "If I kill him, what would be his fate ?" The Prophet replied: "He will go to hell."* *(Muslim)*

Yes, it is the demand of the honour and respect of a Muslim that he should not become an easy prey to an oppressor and a usurper. He should not become the target for a greedy and ambitious man, but that he should die fighting in the defence of his life, property and honour. There is nothing wrong if blood is shed in this connection, for it has no value where the defence of higher values are concerned.

Islam has allowed taking of revenge so that the oppressed may be comforted and honoured, and the oppressor may be disgraced and put to shame. Islam has made the rights of Muslims dear and likeable for them and has induced them that they should strive to achieve them, and should not be ready to accept anything less than their rights, except that the oppressor may request for pardon and they themselves, giving a proof of their high moral values and excellent character, forgive him. It will add to their honour.

First the Muslims were taught faith and good moral conduct, and then Allah acquainted them with the high ranks of elevation and kindness, and said:

> *And that which is with Allah is better and more lasting; (it is) for those who believe and put their trust in their Lord: those who avoid the greater crimes and shameful deeds, and, when they are angry even then forgive; those who hearken to their Lord, and establish regular prayer ; who (conduct) their affairs by mutual consultation ; who spend out of what We bestow on them for sustenance.*
> *(Shura: 36-38)*

These teachings indicate the honour and greatness of Muslims. Immediately after this, it is said:

> *And those who, when an oppressive wrong is inflicted on them, (are not cowed, but) help and defend themselves. The recompense for an injury is an injury equal thereto (in degree); but if a person forgives and makes reconciliation, his reward is due from Allah; for (Allah) loves not those who do wrong.* *(Shura : 39-40)*

The character of a Muslim be such that if he is angry with his inferior, he should forgive him ; and whoever dares to harm him in any way and he is a powerful person, then the demand of good character is that such a person should be taught manners and should be punished, until he is subdued and the balloon of his greatness is pricked.

In such a condition it is a Muslim's responsibility that he should display his strength so that the criminal and guilty should be frightened. If a Muslim who is powerful and adopts the policy of forgiveness, it is much better for him, and if he adopts such a policy even if when he is neither weak nor feeble then this is another form of punishing the criminals and the decency of the faithful.

The conduct that has been described in the former verses is different from the one described in the latter verses.

In the former verses forgiving the crimes of the criminals has been termed as good conduct, and in the latter verses the criminal has been placed before justice so that he may be punished and the sword of Qasas (revenge) should have sway over him, so that his power is broken and his undue pride is put down, and thereafter the mention of kindness, obligation and forgiveness has been made. It will ensure the due punishment of the criminals and increase the honour and greatness of the Muslims.

Strength of the Faithful

Since the elements of weakness and frailty are found in the nature of man, many times he adopts a policy of servility before the concerned persons in order to get his work done and his purpose served. In this way his self-confidence and honour is adversely affected. Therefore, Allah's Messenger has taught us that in such matters we should not be weak, but should display the character of steel, should have our chins up, and should continue to strive to achieve our objective. He has said : "Try to get your needs fulfilled with self-respect, because these matters are governed by destiny."

And he explained that if all the people of a man's family may try to snatch away from him a thing with which Allah has blessed him, it would not be possible to do so. Similarly it is also not possible to return him a thing which Allah has taken away from him, even if all the people of his family may try to do so. Therefore, it is the duty of a Muslim that he should leave the reins of his affairs in the hands of Allah and have full confidence in Him.

He should understand the importance and greatness of his religion. He should not consider it inferior. He should value himself and should not give an opportunity to an idiot to prove himself superior to him, because whatever happens in the world it is with the will and decision of Allah alone.

> *"What Allah out of His mercy does bestow on mankind there is none who can withhold; what He does withhold, there is none who can grant apart from Him; and He is the Exalted in Power, Full of Wisdom". (Fatir: 2)*

Many times we feel that in our affairs we have been defeated, but this feeling is not correct, for such a feeling negates the existence of the Almighty and All-Powerful Lord of the Universe, Whom nothing can make helpless:

> *"And Allah has full power and control over His affairs; but most among mankind know it not". (Yusuf : 21)*

Nearer to truth, more profitable and helpful in solving the problems is this attitude that a Muslim should maintain his self-respect, should always be mindful of the values, standard and balance, should not bow for getting his needs fulfilled, nor should he surrender in any adversity.

He should only pray to the Real Master, should have relationship with Him alone, should display his inferiority in His presence only, and should not cry before any other creature.

> *And if Allah touches you with hurt, there is none who can remove it but He; and if He designs some benefit for you, there is none who can keep back His favour; He causes it to reach whomsoever of His slaves He pleases. And He is the Oft forgiving, Most Merciful.(Yunus: 1-7)*

In the foregoing chapters you have seen how the Prophet (S.A.W.) has been teaching his dear companions to adopt the attitude of disregard for material wealth, unconcern for the riches, and the habit of economy, and how he had been teaching them to avoid asking for even ordinary things from others, so much so that "they were taking so much precaution that if the hunter fell from their hands they did not ask others to pick it up but themselves dismounted and picked it up."

Common men ruin this world and the next and make themselves disrespectable, owing to two causes, or at least one of these two causes : either they are afraid of their poor economic condition or their life is very dear to them.

The minds are occupied by earning wealth and property, although Allah has not kept either of these two things in the control of men.

In fact the desire to live and the fear of losing the means of livelihood are two such diseases that the superstition arising from them makes a man disgraceful, and when the fear of being disgraced rules the mind then man really is disgraced.

Similarly the fear of starvation makes a man lose everything, though Islam has taught men to revert to Allah in happiness as well as in sorrow, and it has built up the edifice of the Unity of Allah on the basis of keeping relationship with Him.

What is the use of attaching any desires, aspirations and expectations to humans who, compared to Allah, are not masters of anything, and have no control over any loss or profit:

> *Nay, who is there that can help you, (even as) an army, besides (Allah) Most Merciful ? In nothing but delusion are the unbelievers. Or who is there that can provide you with sustenance if He were to withhold His provision? Nay, they obstinately persist in insolent impiety and flight (from truth).* *(Al-Mulk : 20-21)*

Allama Ibn Qayyim (R.A.A.) in his poem pleads to Allah in this way:

> *"O God, in all my aspirations I think of You alone, And from the things which I fear, I seek Your refuge. All the men of the world cannot join the bone that You have broken, Nor can they break the bone which you have kept joined."*

This is perfect belief in the unity of Allah. It is the cure for all those weak and helpless people, who in their tattered and old clothes wander from door to door with begging bowls in their hands, without caring for the reproaches and the curses of the world.

Islam desires to throw away from the hearts the factors of pain and restlessness and to shift them from the environment of narrowness and suffering to a pleasant atmosphere. Allah's Prophet (S.A.W.) says:

> *"Livelihood itself searches the man, as death searches man."* *(Tibrani)*

The Prophet (S.A.W.) does not mean that the people should be negligent about earning their livelihood. This is the thinking of the ignorants. He has given this assurance so that people should form the habit of getting their desires in a desirable way and should avoid crying before men and placating and being crying before others. The meaning of this swearing of Allah is the same

> *And in heaven is your sustenance, as (also) that which you are promised. Then, by the Lord of heaven and earth, this is the very Truth, as much as the fact that you can speak intelligently to each other.* *(Zariyat : 22-23)*

Abdullah bin Masood (R.A.A.) narrates that the Prophet of Allah has said: "There is nothing that would take you nearer to Paradise but the commands which I have given ; and there is no act that will take you nearer to hell but the forbidden things which I have asked you to avoid. None of you should show any laxity in earning your livelihood, because Jibbrail (A.S.) has put this thing in my heart that none of you will leave this world unless he takes his full share of the livelihood destined for him.

Therefore, O People! fear Allah and earn in a desirable way. If any of you lags behind in the matter of earning his livelihood, he should not try to get it by disobeying Allah, because He does not send down His kindness in exchange for sin."

By these advises Islam has raised the honour of a Muslim, and has urged him to live in this world as 'the leader of the caravan'. He should be like the sky in the depths of this world, and lead his life like a decent gentleman. Then it has also taught that the people whom we approach for fulfilling our needs are merely means of the grace and favours of Allah.

Abdullah bin Masood (R.A.A.) narrates that the Prophet (S.A.W.) has said:

> *"Do not please anybody by displeasing Allah. Do not praise anybody for the favour granted by Allah, and for the thing which Allah has deprived you, do not reproach anybody, because Allah's provision cannot reach you by anybody's greed, nor can anybody's dislike stop it from reaching you, and Allah, in His justice and fair way, has kept happiness and satisfaction, in belief and seeking His pleasure, and has kept sadness and sorrow in displeasure."* *(Tibrani)*

But it does not mean that man should not thank a person who obliges him, and should reject every offer of obligation from others, when the Hadith says:

"One who does not thank the people cannot be a thankful slave of God." *(Tirmidhi)*

The purport of the above quoted Hadith is that man should not become a slave of a person who obliges him or shows favour to him, and that his self-respect and decency is trampled, because the first obligation is to Allah.

It is also not permissible for the giver to buy men's hearts through his gifts and obligation and use them anywhere he likes. It destroys his obligation and reward. This is the attitude of those whose ideal is not seeking nearness to Allah, therefore, decent and pious people do not accept the gifts of such men.

But those who give for Allah, and pay the dues of the slaves of Allah for seeking His pleasure only, about them Allah's Prophet (S.A.W.) has said:

"One who has been given a gift should give something in its return, if he has the means, otherwise he should praise it. He who has praised it, has thanked for it he who concealed it; he was unthankful." *(Abu Daud)*

As regards man's fear of death, and his accepting disgrace for a desire to live, this is foolish, because by cunning away, the life-span cannot be increased and by making efforts it cannot be reduced. How is it possible, when:

To every people is a term appointed; when their term is reached, not an hour can they cause delay. *(Araf : 34)*

Fiscal Matters

A great portion of Islamic teachings comprises the commands and directions concerning the special life of Muslims, so that their physical and spiritual training may be accomplished.

The foundation of this training is most excellent and purified. These are the etiquettes and regulations which are concerned with their eating, earning, wearing, residing and satisfying all their needs, for which a man makes efforts in this world.

There is in them neither a leaning towards asceticism, nor towards greedy materialism. Its foundation is on moderation and balance, and for these reasons the enforcement of the training is simple and pleasant. In its teachings Islam keeps both the body and the spirit before it, and does not allow one to have the upper hand on the other.

It arranges for their needs in such a balanced way that a man finds them very helpful in fulfilling the responsibilities of this world and the next. As against this, the wild philosophies which men have invented in the absence of the divine revelations, to shape their lives, have not been successful in meeting the needs of the body and fulfilling the demands of the two. In these philosophies balanced concessions have not been provided for the world, from which the journey starts, to the Hereafter, where every man perforce has to return.

Some ideologies are such as crush the demands of the body. Their idea is that the soul can reach perfection only when it is freed from the chains of the body, while other philosophies declare pleasures and luxuries only as their ideal, and they move all the machinery of life around these philosophies. They cannot see anything beyond the demands of the body.

But Islam is a religion which pays attention to the principles of nature and is a balanced faith and a religion of moderation. There is no room in it of that asceticism, which has no mercy for the feelings and urges of mankind, and the entire humanity feels constrained about it. Islam has also nothing to do with that animalism and pleasure-seeking, whose centre and axis is only man's belly and sex.

In this connection we should not lose sight of this reality that a Momin who confirms the belief in the life in the Hereafter and an infidel who considers this life only as be-all and end-all of everything, have a lot of difference in their ways of living.

Many people who destroy their chastity and strive their every nerve to seek as much pleasure as they can belong to the latter kind, if they do not give up their ways. About them Allah has said:

> *"Verily, Allah will cause those who believe and do good deeds to enter Paradise underneath which rivers flow, while those who disbelieve take their comfort in this life and eat even as the cattle eat, and the Fire is their habitation."* *(Muhammad:12)*

In Surah Hijr, He has said:

> *"It may be that those who disbelieve wish ardently they were Muslims. Let them eat and enjoy life, and let (false) hope beguile them. They will come to know!"(Hijr : 2, 3)*

As regards Momin, he keeps his wishes and desires spreading over both this world and the next world. He seeks virtue and welfare in the present as well as in the future. The holy Quran has informed us that the bliss and the good fortune of this world and of the next is in remembering Allah and reciting His words and praises:

> *"So when you have accomplished your Day rites, then remember Allah as you remember your fathers, or with a greater zeal.*
>
> *There are men who say: 'Our Lord! Give us in this world,' and they will have no position in the Hereafter. And there are men who say: 'Our Lord! Give us good in this world and good in the Hereafter, and save us from the torment of the Fire.' To these will be given what they have earned." (Baqarah: 200-202)*

Chapter 2

Way of Life in Islam

Real Behaviour

When a Muslim undertakes a thing, he should respect the undertaking. When he enters into any contract he should honour it till the last. This is the demand of the faith that when a man talks of any enterprise, he should have the intention of taking it to completion, like the water which does not rest till it flows down to the lower level. He should be known among the people as a man of reliable promises, and there should be no fear of any breach of promises or of any dubious dealings from him.

Fulfilment of the promise is necessary. Similarly when an oath is taken, it should be redeemed. But this fulfilment of promise or the redeeming of the oath and pledges is necessary when the dealing is legitimate and concerns truth, otherwise honouring the promise in connection with something sinful and disobedience to Allah has no value, and there is no importance of oath in sin.

> *Allah's Messenger has said : "If someone has taken an oath, but saw an aspect of goodness in another thing, he may break his oath and pay compensation (atonement), and should perform the act which is better and has goodness."* *(Muslim)*

It is not proper for a man to insist on redeeming the oath. On such occasions it is better to break the oath. In a Hadith it is stated:

> *"It is sinful for a man among you to go to his wife with his oath (unredeemed) compared to his paying the compensation (atoning) which He has fixed for breaking the oath."* *(Bukhari)*

For this mason no promise and covenant is proper and correct except in rightful matters. When a man has promised to do a certain good thing, then he should try his best to fulfil it, as long as it appears good to him. He should very well know that he should stick to manly talk, faith and belief. There is no room in this for breach of promises or doubts and hesitation. Anas bin Malik says that his uncle Anas bin Nadar could not take part in the battle of Badr, and he said to the Prophet : "O Messenger of Allah ! In the first battle that you fought with the polytheists I could not take part. If Allah kept me with the Prophet then they will definitely see my achievements in the second battle against the polytheists."

When in the battle of Uhud, there was fierce fighting and the Muslims were retreating. He prayed to Allah "O Allah ! I ask your pardon for the mistake that they have committed, and I declare myself innocent of the transgression of the polytheists". Saying this he rushed into the battle. In the way he met Saad bin Maaz whom he said : "O Saad bin Maaz! By the God of Nadir, Proceed towards Paradise. I smell its fragrance in the valley of Uhud."

Saad said: "O Messenger of Allah! The love for martyrdom which he showed cannot be expressed. Then he advanced:"

Anas says that we found more than eighty wounds on his body, which were caused by swords, the points of lances and the shower of arrows. The polytheists had disfigured his body and it was difficult to identify him. With great difficulty his sister identified him with the help of a mole on his fingers.

Anas says that he thinks that the following verses were revealed about him or about persons like him:

> *"Among the believers are men who have been true to their covenant with Allah; of them some have completed their vow to (the extreme), and some (still) wait; but they have never changed (their determination) in the least."*
> *(Ahzab: 23)*

Memory and Determination—essential : Fulfilment of promises depends on two factors. With these two things, fulfilling one's promises would be easy. Allah had taken a promise from Adam that he would not go near the forbidden tree, but Adam forgot the promise within a few days. He became a prey to weakness and broke his promise:

> *"We had already beforehand taken the covenant of Adam, bus he forgot ; and We found on his part no firm resolve."*
> *(Ta Ha : 115)*

It shows that deficiency in memory and weakness of determination are two obstructions which come in the way of performance of duty. And this is a strange thing that man, being overwhelmed by the hardships of the times, various difficulties and different pressing problems forgets the open and clear realities.

To him the clear figures appear blurred, and the realities which are as striking as the light of the sun disappear from his sight.

There the necessity of a reminder becomes very pressing to overcome the negligence and forgetfulness, and to keep this important thing before men's eyes. There are a number of verses of the Quran which were revealed for safeguarding the memory:

> *"Follow the revelation given to you from your Lord, and follow not, as friends or protectors, other than Him. Little it is you remember of admonition."* (Aaraf : 3)

> *"This is the way of your Lord, leading straight ; 'We have detailed the signs for those who receive admonition."* (Anaam : 126)

Alive and wakeful memory and remembrance is essential for fulfilling promises. A man who forgets his promises and covenants, how can he fulfil them ? That is why the following verse has been ended on a note of admonition after giving command of fulfilling them:

> *"And fulfil the Covenant of Allah; thus does He command you, that you may remember."* (Anaam : 152)

If a man has a strong memory in respect of fulfilling his promise, it is also necessary that he should have a determination to do so — a determination which should not have any laxity or slackness in this matter — a determination which should be able to overcome all the rebellious desires, and which should lighten the coming burden of difficulties. It should be a determination which should be able to cross all the difficult valleys and blocks and should be able to set an example of selfless sacrifice for others.

The measures for weighing and appraising people are different with different people. The price one has to pay for remaining faithful sometimes is very high. At times one requires to sacrifice all the wealth, property and the most desired thing in this respect.

But these difficulties, sacrifices and trials of determination prove in the end to be the steps for achieving greatness and honour, as the poet says:

"Why he, who considers his life and heart dear, should go to (seek) the beloved in her street."

The holy Quran has severely criticised those who seek to achieve heights of success and glory in the shadow of comfortable living :

"Do you think that you will enter paradise without such trials as came to those who passed away before you ? They experienced suffering and adversity and were so shaken in spirit that even the Prophet and the faithful who were with him cried: 'When will Allah's help come ?' Ah I Verily, Allah's help is near." (Baqarah : 214)

When a man develops in himself the combined forces of a conscious and wakeful mind and a heart full of determination, then he can be considered to have been qualified to enter the group of the faithful people.

Greatest Covenant

For a Muslim the most honourable and the holiest covenant is the one which he has made with his Lord, for Allah has created him with His Power. He has nourished him under the shadow of his favours and blessings, and has demanded of him that he should recognise what is the reality and admit it. No misguiding factors should cause him to deviate from the right path lest he may deny these realities or he may lose sight of them:

"Did I not enjoin on you, O you children of Adam! that you should not worship Satan ; for that he was to you an enemy avowed? And that you should worship Me, (for that) this was the straight way ?" (Yasin : 60-61)

Those who do not listen to the Prophets and do not follow their teachings, in their nature also there is a motivator which pricks them, shows them the path of their Lord, and tries to make them realize the greatness of the Creator, however corrupt and polluted the environment may be.

This is the meaning of this covenant which Allah has taken from all the humans:

"When your Lord drew forth from the children of Adam from their loins-their descendants, and made them testify concerning themselves, (saying); `Am 1 not your Lord (Who cherishes and sustains you) ?' They said: `Yes, we do testify.' (This), lest you should say on the Day of

> *Judgment: `Of this we were never mindful.' Or lest you should say: "Our fathers before us may have taken false gods but we are (their) descendants after them ; will you then destroy us because of the deeds of men who were futile ?' Thus do We explain the signs in detail in order that they may turn (to Us)."* *(Aaraf: 172-174)*

Here no regular dialogues had taken place as is clear from the apparent sense of these verses, but this is a picture of the right-natured people showing how they are mindful of Allah, how they recognise Him, how they discover His Oneness and Greatness from the proofs scattered in the universe, and shun from all the conventional customs and habits which keep men away from this Lord, and which associate some one with Allah. This style of speech and writing is common in the Arabic language.

With honouring this Covenant, a man's faithfulness is the foundation of his respect and honour in this world and of success and glory in the next world.

It is an undue misgiving and fear from Allah that we should fulfil the covenant made with Him and still be apprehensive that some disaster would befall us:

> *"Recall the favour which I bestowed on you, and fulfil your Covenant with Me; I will fulfil My Covenant with you, and fear none but Me."*

The Prophet used to give these instructions to the tribes which came to him, while conveying the Message of Islam, and used to place before them only a few aspects in the beginning according to the intellectual and physical capacities of the people instead of giving them the complete teachings. Auf bin Malik says that he was with the Prophet when there were about seven, or eight or nine persons present.

He asked us: "Will you not take a pledge on the hand of the Messenger of Allah ?" We stretched our hands and said : "We take a pledge on your hand, O Messenger of Allah!"

He said : "(Your pledge is) That you should worship Allah. Do not associate anybody with Him, and offer salat for five times and listen and obey." And he said in a low voice : "And do not ask for anything from the people."

> *Auf bin Malik says : "I saw some of these persons who had taken pledge that when their hunter fell on the ground, they did not ask anybody to pick it up and give it to them."* *(Muslim)*

How scrupulously the pledge is being observed and how severely and strictly it is being enforced ! There was no special significance of this pledge. Every group used to be instructed according to its nature and circumstances.

The ruler used to be advised not to be cruel. The trader used to be instructed not to indulge in adulteration and deceit, and the employees were admonished against accepting bribes. Otherwise every Muslim is bound to follow the entire religion, all its tenets and principles, and he will be asked on the Day of Judgment about the entire Shariah. However, in the Islamic world there have appeared a few sects which take a pledge of a special kind.

They should not be entertained. They are like quacks who pose as physicians. They administer spurious drugs and complicate the disease and endanger the life of their patient.

Islamic teachings cannot be divided and distributed. All of them must be followed, and their enforcement is necessary in every place at every time.

Ideal Pledge

Allah's Messenger took a pledge from the Ansar that they will support this Message with their lives and properties, and try their utmost in protecting the Prophethood, till the time the Message is conveyed to the Arabs and the non-Arabs.

The Covenant entered into by the Ansar is considered as the most glorious pact in the annals of belief. In sincerity, selfless devotion and total submission to Truth, no other parallel can be found. This covenant was completed in a glorious night of the season of Hajj. After this, people went their way and busied themselves in their affairs. But the people who had pledged their words busied themselves in fulfilling this historical covenant, and they accepted willingly all its demands and challenges.

In the Battle of Badr and in other battles of Islam against idolatry they shed their blood like water. The Prophet had great confidence in this covenant for the supremacy of the religion in times of difficulty and for raising the world of Allah.

Accordingly when in the first assault in the Battle of Hunain Muslims were falling back, the Prophet did not look at the armies of the newcomer Muslims, but called his old faithfuls who had taken a pledge in the valley in the night of the season of Hajj, so that they may take the control of the situation.

Anas narrates that when the Battle of Hunain was fought, the tribes of Hawazan and Ghatfan participated in the fighting with their wealth, equipment and sons. The Prophet had an army of ten thousand men, which also included the indebted men at the time of victory of Mecca, but all left him. He was all alone.

At that time he gave a second call. He turned towards his right and called : "O People of Ansar !" They said : "We are present, O Messenger of Allah ! We are with you, rest assured." The Prophet was riding a grey mule. He got down from it and said "I am a slave of Allah and His Messenger."

The polytheists were defeated and much booty was collected by the Islamic army. The Prophet distributed the booty among the newcomers who accepted Islam on the day Mecca was conquered and among the Muhajirin (refugees). He did not distribute anything among the Ansars.

The Ansar were a little perturbed. They talked among themselves : when the situation was .critical we were called and when the booty came to hand it is distributed among others. When the Prophet came to know about this he gathered them and asked:

> *"O People of Ansar! What news am l hearing from your side?" They remained silent. Then he said : "O People of Ansar! Do you not like that others should take away the worldly goods with them, and you should return with Muhammad (PBUH) to your house." They answered : "Why not O Messenger of Allah ! We are pleased." The Prophet said : "If people walk in one valley and the Ansar in another valley, then I will walk in the valley of Ansar."*
>
> *(Bukhari)*

The fact of the matter is that this great Message needed the sharpness of the swords of Ansar. They fulfilled their promise by sacrificing their lives and everything that they had. They did not have before them the ephemeral profits of this world, nor any temporary pleasures and advantages. The policy of the Prophet in distributing the booty of the battle was based on the levels of their sincerity and faith. The Bedouin who became Muslims at a later stage were in need of financial help so that they might not be disheartened by the difficulties coming in their way as a consequence of embracing Islam. Therefore, the Prophet wanted to give them reassurance and comfort, and because the Ansar were endowed with full faith and unshaking belief, the Prophet left them to their condition.

In such conditions the Prophet has said:

> *"I give some things to a man so that he may not (on account of his bad deeds) be thrown into hell by Allah, although there are other persons more dear to me."*
>
> *(Bukhari)*

Forgetting Breach of Promise **:** The praiseworthy quality of the fulfilling of promise also demands that a man should always remember his past, so that he may take a lesson from it for his present and future. If he was a poor man and Allah has made him rich, or he was a sick man and now Allah has made him healthy, then it is not proper for him to erect a strong wall between his past and present and should not think that he was never poor nor was he ever healthy, and should not build up his present on the basis of this pride. Such a behaviour is open ingratitude and immoral.

This is a breach of promise which leads man to disruption. Many times such a man gets away from the blessings of Allah, and after this he does not get the guidance and inclination to come under the shadow of this blessing.

It is said that in Medina a man, known as Saalba, went to the locality of Ansar, and keeping them as witness declared that if Allah blessed him with favour, he would pay the dues of every rightful claimant, would give money do charity and would show kindness to his relatives. Incidentally his cousin died and he inherited all his property. He however did not fulfil his promise nor did he care for 'what he had declared. Thereupon Allah revealed the following verses:

> *"Amongst them are men who made a Covenant with Allah, that if he bestowed on them of His bounty they would give (largely) in charity, and be truly-amongst those who are righteous. But when He did bestow of His botany, they became covetous, and turned back (from their covenant), averse (from its fulfilment). He has put as a consequence hypocrisy into their hearts, (to last) till the day whereon they shall meet Him ; because they broke their Covenant with Allah, and because they lied (again and again). Do they not know that Allah does know their secret (thoughts) and their secret counsels, and that Allah knows well all things unseen ?"* *(Tauba : 75-78)*

The worst example of breach of promise, ingratitude and disloyalty is that tale of Bani Israel which Hadrat Abu Hurrayrah has quoted from the sayings of the Prophet. The Prophet has said:

> *There were three persons in Bani Israel, a leper, a bald man and a blind man. Allah wanted to test them. He sent an angel to every one of them. The angel who went to the leper asked him what he coveted most. He replied : "Fair complexion, beautiful skin and a cure for my disease, for which I am hated by the people." The angel touched his body with his hand and his leprosy was removed and he became the owner of a fair complexion and a beautiful skin. The angel again asked him : "What thing you like most?" He said: "Camel." The angel gave him a pregnant she-camel and prayed: "May Allah increase this property of yours."*

Then he went to the blind man and asked him what he coveted most. He replied : "May Allah give me back my sight." The angel touched his eyes and his sight was restored. He asked for the second time as to what thing he liked most. He replied : "A goat." The angel gave him a pregnant goat.

Then he went to the bald man and asked him what thing he liked most. The bald man replied : "Beautiful hair, and my ugliness be removed as people run away from me." The angel touched him and his disease was cured and he had a tuft of beautiful hair. Then he asked him what thing he liked most. He answered "A cow." The angel gave him a pregnant cow and prayed to Allah to give him prosperity.

All the three animals gave birth to their offshoots. Their numbers increased. One had a flock of camels, the second one had a large number of cows and the third one became the owner of many goats.

Then the angel appeared before the leper in the form of a man and said : "I am a poor man. All my relatives have been separated from me in the journeys and now my only support is Allah and through Him you. I request you in the name of the Being who gave you fair complexion and a beautiful skin, to give me a camel. Will you help me in this journey of mine ?" He replied that there is an abundance of rights. The angel said: "I recognise you. Were you not suffering from leprosy and people were hating you ? Were you not needy and Allah gave you lot of property?"

He replied : "No. This property I received from my father and grandfather in inheritance." The angel said: "If you are a liar, then may Allah return you to your old condition."

In the same form he went to the bald man and talked to him in the same manner. He also gave the same reply which the first one had given. The angel then gave a curse and said that if he was a liar then may Allàh return him to his old condition.

> *Then he went to the blind man and talked to him in the same manner, and begged for a goat to be given to him. The blind man said: "I was really a blind man, but Allah restored my sight. You may take away whatever you like and leave whatever you want to leave. By God, I cannot enter into any dispute with you about a thing which I have taken by Allah's pleasure." The angel told him to keep his things with him. The purpose was merely to test them. Allah was pleased with him and his two companions became the victims of His wrath.*
>
> *(Bukhari)*

In trade, business, and other financial and economic matters an atmosphere of confidence can be created only when the fulfilment of promise is considered a duty. It is necessary that the written conditions should conform to the limits of the Shariah, otherwise there would be no sanctity in them, and a Muslim will not be bound to honour them. Islam has given extra consideration to the marriage contract.

Allah's Messenger has said: "Among the conditions which you mutually agree upon, the most deserving of fulfilment is the contract by which you make the private parts halal (permissible) for yourselves."

For this reason it is not lawful for a husband to manipulate a single dirham that rightfully belongs to his wife, or to consider the bond with which he is tied as unimportant.

> *It is mentioned in the Hadith : "If a man has married a woman for a small or a big dower (mehr) and in his heart he has the intention of not paying that dower, then he has deceived her. If he dies and he has not paid her right, they on the Day of Judgment he will be presented before Allah as a rapist. And a man who has borrowed money from another man while he did not have the intention of repaying the debt, then he has deceived him, and consequently he defrauded him. If he dies in this condition, without paying back his debt, then he will meet Allah as a thief." (Tibrani)*

There is nothing surprising about this, as there are a number of Quranic verses which insist on fulfilling the promises and warn against indulging in disloyalty and breach of promises:

And fulfil your promise. Verily, you will be answerable for your promises." *(Isra : 34)*

"And fulfil the covenant of Allah when you have entered into it, and break not your oaths after you have confirmed them; Indeed you have made Allah your surety; for Allah knows all that you do." *(Nahl: 91)*

Allah clarifies that breach of promises and disloyalty destroy confidence, create disorder and disruption, cut relationships, reduce power and make individuals weak and low:

"And be not like a woman who breaks Into untwisted strands the yarn which she has spun, after it has become strong. Nor take your oaths to practise deception between yourselves, lest one party should be more numerous than another : for Allah will test you by this; and on the Day of Judgment He will certainly make clear to you (the truth of) that wherein you disagree." *(Nahl: 91)*

Many times a man enters into a contract, but breaks it in the greed of more profit elsewhere. Or one nation makes an agreement with another nation, but the greed of better advantages and other considerations compel her to break the agreement.

The religion considers it highly objectionable that for the sake of a temporary benefit virtuousness be trampled, and deception and trickery should enter in the dealings among men. Islam makes it compulsory for an individual as well as a group to be honest, decent and sincere, so that in all the conditions of poverty and richness, and victory and defeat the covenants be safeguarded.

That is why after giving a command to honour the covenented, Quran says

"And take root your oaths to practise deception between yourselves, with the result that someone's foot may slip after it was firmly planted; and you may have to taste the evil (consequences) of having hindered (men) from the path of Allah, and a mighty wrath descend on you. Nor sell the Covenant of Allah for a miserable price ; for with Allah is (a prize) far better for you, if you only knew."
(Nahl: 94-95)

The Entire Humanity Deserves : The promise given to everybody should be fulfilled, whether the other party is a Muslim or an infidel, for morality, greatness and righteousness cannot be cut into pieces, that some people are treated with meanness and others are treated decently. The fulfilment of promise and covenant depends on truth and straight dealing. As long as it is bound on righteousness, it should be fulfilled in relation to every individual and at every time.

In connection with the covenants with non-Muslims the Prophet is reported to have said that if in the time of Islam he were invited to enter into such a contract, he would gladly accept the offer:

> *Amar bin Al-Hamaq says that he has heard the Messenger of Allah as saying: "If a man gave shelter to a man for life, and subsequently killed him, then I have no connection with the killer, even if the murdered person be an infidel."* *(Ibn Habban)*

This statement of the Prophet shows how Islam treats even those who have not accepted it as their religion. On the other hand the behaviour of the Jews is worth noting. They do not like to fulfil their promises with others.

They do not consider it a good thing to treat others justly and decently. They consider themselves 'Allah's son and His favourite'. Their belief is that Allah has reserved his blessing and shelter for the Jewish race only.

As against this, have a look at the Islamic teachings. It makes complete arrangements for safeguarding all those whose responsibility it has assumed, and with whom it has entered into a covenant. Quran addresses the Muslims and speaks about the infidels thus:

> *"O you who believe ! violate not the sanctity of the symbols of Allah, nor of the sacred month, nor of the animals brought for sacrifice, nor the garlands that mark out such animals, nor the people resorting to the sacred house, seeking of the bounty and good pleasure of their Lord. But when you are clear of the sacred precincts and of pilgrim garb, you may hunt, and let not the hatred of some people in (once) shutting you out of the sacred mosque lead you to transgression (and hostility on your part). Help one another in righteousness and piety and do not help one another in sin and rancour."(Maida : 3)*

It is remarkable now beautifully the viewpoint of the non-believers and their beliefs have been stated. Although they are idolaters, yet they have been mentioned as seekers of Allah's pleasure and blessings, and Muslims, however powerful they may become, they have been asked to cooperate with one another in the acts of righteousness and piety and not to help one another in the acts of sin and rancour.

At another place we have taken a survey of the covenants between Muslims and Non-Muslims and the revealed teachings of Allah in this connection. (Refers to a book in Arabic by the author)

Re-payment of Debt Necessary : One of the things on which Islam has insisted most and has considered it very important is the re-payment of loan. With Allah, right behaviour in this respect is more important than attending to other rights. Islam has ended all the misgivings and avarice and greed which make the debtor their victim, as a result of which he tries to find excuses to avoid re-payment or finally does not re-pay.

In this connection Islam has advised that a loan should be taken only in inevitable circumstances. To try to borrow money in a matter where it is avoidable is a very dangerous thing, and it should be avoided. In one Hadith it is mentioned that it is one of those sins for which retribution is necessary.

> *"When a borrower dies, he will be subjected to retribution on the Day of Judgment. However, in three cases it is permitted : first when a man loses his strength fighting in the cause of Allah and borrows in order to prepare to fight against his and Allah's enemies, secondly when a man near whom a Muslim has died and he borrows to meet the expenses of his funeral, and third the man who is afraid that he would remain unmarried and to safe guard his religion he borrows to meet the expenses of marriage. Allah will pardon them on the Day of Judgment."* *(Ibne Maja)*

In another tradition it is stated that Allah's Messenger has said:

"On the Day of Judgment Allah will call the borrower and he will be made to stand before Him. Then he will be asked: "O son of Adam ! For what purpose did you take the loan? And why did you waste the rights of others ?" He will reply : "O our Lord ! You know that I had borrowed, but I did not eat it, nor drank, nor wasted it, but sometimes an accident of" fire occurred, sometimes there was a theft or it was lost, or a loss was incurred." Allah will say :

> *"O My slave! I You have told the truth. I have more right to re-pay it." Allah will call for some acts of virtue and will weigh them in a balance, and his acts of virtue will*

be heavier than his evil acts, and he will enter the Paradise with the favour of his Lord." *(Ahmad)*

This shows that Allah will accept the excuses of those who were compelled to borrow being forced by the circumstances, and were unable to repay it on account of various genuine difficulties. But there are men who are the slaves of their carnal desires and pleasures, and whose own wealth is not sufficient to meet the demands of their desires; they at once rush to borrow money, regardless of the consequences. They do not care to be free of the burden of loan. Such a person according to the Hadith is a shameless thief.

Allah's Messenger has said: "He who takes others' property (as a loan) with intention of repaying it, (then is unable to re-pay) then Allah repays his loan. And he who takes a loan with the intention of not re-paying it, then Allah wilt destroy and ruin him." *(Bukhari)*

Islam wants that the loans should be given different kinds of guarantees, so that they may be considered live properties, and their re-payment should become definite and essential, and nobody should be able to escape re-paying this due, committed to writing, although performance of other acts of worship earns great rewards.

Abu Qatada says that one person asked:

"O Messenger of Allah ! If I am killed in the cause of Allah, will all my sins be pardoned ?" He replied : "Yes, if you are killed, and if you are patient, thankful and seeker of Allah's pleasure, if you remain in the front ranks and attack the enemy and do not retreat." Then the Prophet asked him what did he say. The person repeated his question and the Prophet replied : "Your sins will be pardoned, but your loan will not be pardoned. Just now Jibbrail has informed me about this." *(Muslim)*

Since the wise people knew how the debt falls as a lightning on a Muslim's honour and his earnings for the Hereafter, they used to advise people to get themselves free from all debts before putting their lives in danger.

It is narrated through Abu Darda that while proceeding for a Jihad, the Prophet used to stop at a junction of the streets and shout to the soldiers "O people ! If anybody has to re-pay a debt. and if he feels that he would die in the battle and the debt would not be re-paid, then he should return. He need not come after me, because this thing will not be enough to save him from hell."(Razin)

Today the Muslims have made borrowing and lending an amusement. To satisfy their hunger and the sexual desires they take loan, and they indulge into paying interests to the Jews and the Christians, which Allah has totally prohibited as Haram.

As a result of this they have become aliens in their own land, and they are deprived of their properties and are wandering helplessly.

Re-payment of loan is very difficult.

How many rights would have been trampled, if there were no fear of the law enforcement!

Allah likes those of His slaves who fulfil their convents, and after destroying a number of townships has stated about them:

"We did not find most of them true to their covenant' and most of them We found rebellious and disobedient. (Aaraf : 102)

Prophet's Excellent Example

Mere teachings and commands of Do's and Dont's do not form the foundation of good moral character in a society, because only these things are not sufficient for developing these good qualities in the human nature; a teacher may merely order to do such and such things and not to do such and such things, and not to do such and such things, and the society becomes a moralist society. The teachings of good conduct which is fruitful requires long training and constant watchfulness.

The training cannot be on the right lines if the example before the society is not such that commands full confidence, because a person having a bad moral character cannot leave a good impression on his surroundings.

The best training can be expected only from such a man whose personality, by the force of its Morality, would create a sense of admiration in the beholders. They would sing praises of his nobility and feel the irresistible urge to benefit from the example of his life.

The world would spontaneously feel the urge to follow his footsteps. For nourishing and developing more and more excellent good character among his followers it is necessary that the leader must possess higher and nobler character and attributes than his followers. The holy Prophet

(S.A.W.) himself was the best example of the good moral character, to emulate which he was giving a call to his followers.

Before advising them to adopt a moral life by giving sermons and counsels, he was sowing the seeds of morality among his followers by actually living that kind of life.

> *Abdullah Ibn Amar (R.A.A.) says : "The Messenger of Allah (PBUH.) was neither ill-mannered nor rude. He used to say that the better people among you are those who are best in their moral character. —(Bukhari)*
>
> *Anas (R.A.A.) says : "I served the holy Prophet (S.A.W.) for ten years. He never said 'Uf ' (expressing dissatisfaction), nor did he ever ask me why I did this or did not do that." —(Muslim)*
>
> *It is also reported by him : "My mother used to hold the Prophet's hand and used to take him wherever he wanted. If any person used to come before him and shake his hand, the Prophet (S.A.W.) never used to draw away his hand from the other person's hands till the latter drew away his hands, and he never used to turn away his face from that person till the latter himself turned away his face. And in the meetings he was never seen squatting in such a way that his knees were protruding further than his fellow-squatters." —(Tirmidhi)*
>
> *Hadrat 'Aishah (R.A.A.) says : "If there were two alternatives, the holy Prophet (S.A.W.) used to adopt the easiest alternative, provided there was no sin in it. If that work was sinful, then he used to run away farthest from it. The Prophet (S.A.W.) did not take any personal revenge from any body. Yes, if Allah's command were to be disobeyed, then his wrath was to be stirred. Allah's Messenger did not beat anybody with his own hands, neither his wife nor a servant. Yes, he used to fight in the wars in the cause of Allah." —(Muslim)*
>
> *Anus (R.A.A.) has narrated : "I was walking with the Prophet (S.A.W.). He had wrapped a thick cheddar round his body. One Arab pulled the cheddar so forcefully that a part of his shoulder could be seen by me, and I was perturbed by this forceful pulling the cheddar. The Arab then said : 'O Muhammad ! Give me some of my share*

> *from the property which Allah has given you.' The Prophet (S.A.W.) turned towards him and laughed, and gave orders for a donation being given to him."*
> *—(Bukhari)*

> *Hadrat 'Aishah (R.A.A.) has reported that Allah's Messenger (S.A.W.) has said: "Allah is soft-hearted. He likes softheartedness. And the reward which He gives for soft-heartedness does not give for hardness, nay, such a reward He does not give for any thing."* *—(Muslim)*

In another tradition it is stated: "Softness in whichever thing it may be, will make that thing beautiful. And from whichever thing softness is taken out, it will become ugly."

> *Jarir (R.A.A.) narrates that the Prophet (S.A.W.) has said : "The reward which Allah gives for soft-heartedness He does not give it for folly ; and when Allah makes any slave His favourite, He gives him softness. Those families that are devoid of softness become deprived of every virtue."* *— (Tibrani)*

> *Abdullah bin Harith (R.A.A.) has reported that he did not see anybody smiling more than the Messenger of Allah (S.A.W.)* *— (Tirmidhi)*

> *Hadrat 'Aishah (R.A.A.) was asked what did Prophet (S.A.W.) do at home ? She replied : "He used to be in the service of his home people ; and when the time of prayer came he used to perform ablutions and go out for prayer."*
> *—(Muslim)*

> *Anas (R.A.A.) has narrated : "Allah's Messenger had the best manners of all the persons. I had an adopted brother, whose name was Abu Umayr. He had a sick sparrow, who was called 'Naghee'. Allah's Messenger (S.A.W.) used to be playful with him and ask him : 'O Abu Umayr ! what has happened to your Nagheer'."* *—(Bukhari)*

Of the habits and traits of the Prophet (S.A.W.) one trait was very well known that he was extremely philanthropic. He was never miserly in anything. He was very brave and courageous. He never turned away from Truth.

He was justice-loving. In his own decision he never committed any excesses or injustice. In his whole life he was truthful and an honest trustee.

Holy Quran

Allah has commanded all the Muslims to follow the excellent habits and the best traits of the Prophet (S.A.W.) and to take guidance from the holy life of the holy Messenger.

> *"Surely there is in the person of Allah's Messenger an excellent example for you for every person who has hope in Allah and the Hereafter and remembers Allah, reciting His name many times."* — *(Ahzab : 21)*

Qadi Ayaz says that the Prophet (S.A.W.) was the most excellent-mannered, most philanthropic and the bravest of all. One night the people of Medina were terribly frightened. Some people proceeded towards the sound (which was probably the cause). They saw that the Prophet (S.A.W.) was coming from that direction. He had rushed before all others to find out what was the trouble.

He was riding the horse of Abu Talha, (R.A.A.) without a saddle, and a sword was hanging from his neck, and he was comforting the people not to be afraid saying there was nothing to worry. Hadrat Ali (R.A.A.) says that in the battles when fighting started, we used to worry much about the Prophet (S.A.W.) because nobody was nearer to the enemy in fighting than the Prophet (S.A.W.). Jabir bin Abdullah (R.A.A.) says that whenever anything was requested of him, he never said : No.

Hadrat Khadijah (R.A.A.) had told him when he was first blessed with the Divine Revelation :

> *"You carry the loads of the weak people, you earn for the poor, and help a person if any trouble comes to him in following the Truth."*

Once he received seventy thousand dirhams. They were placed before him on the mat. He distributed them standing. He did not refuse a single beggar till he finished the entire amount.

A man approached him and requested for something. He said : "At present I do not have anything, buy something in my name, and when we will get some money we will pay for it." Hadrat Umar (R.A.A.) stated : "Allah has not made it compulsory for you to do a thing on which you have no power or control." This saddened the Prophet (S.A.W.). One Ansari said : "O Messenger of Allah! Spend and be not afraid of the straitened circumstances imposed by Allah." The Prophet (S.A.W.) smiled and his face shone resplendently. He said : "I have been commanded to do this only."

The holy Prophet (S.A.W.) used to love his companions. He did not hate them. He respected every respectable man from any other nation and he used to appoint him as a responsible officer over them.

He used to be in search of his companions and gave them their shares. No companion thought that any other person was more respectable in the Prophet's eye than the companion himself.

Any person who adopted his companionship or anybody who came to him for his need, he used to advise him to be patient, till he was satisfied.

If anybody asked anything from him, he gave it to him or else talked to him so lovingly that he came back satisfied. The river of his kindness was flowing for every body. For his companions he was a guardian, and in matters of Truth all were equal in his eyes.

He was good-looking, decent, humble and softhearted. He was not a narrow-minded and a hard person. Quarrelling was not his habit. He never spoke obscene words. To condemn others or to praise someone excessively was beyond the pale of his character. He expressed indifference towards unnecessary things, but ha was never given to pessimism. Hadrat Aishah says that there was none who possessed a better moral character than the Prophet. Whenever his friends or his home people called him, he readily responded.

Jarir bin Abdullah says : "Since the time I became a Muslim, the Prophet did not prevent me from entering (the house); whenever he looked at me, he smiled."

He used to exchange repartees with his companions, mix up with them freely, and tried to be nearer to them. He played with their children and took them in his lap.

Invitation from free men, male or female slaves, or poor persons were acceptable to him. He visited the ailing and invalid persons in the far-flung areas of Medina. He accepted the excuses of the really helpless people.

Hadrat Anas says that if any person who whispered anything into his ears, he never removed his ear from his mouth unless the whisperer himself withdrew his mouth. Whenever anybody held his hand, he never tried to withdraw his hand unless the other man withdrew his. He always used to be the first to salute any one who met him or to be first to shake hands with his companions. He never stretched his legs in the midst of his companions so that they may be inconvenienced.

Whoever came to him was duly respected by him. Many times he used to spread his cloth for the visitor, and used to place the cushion which was in his use behind the visitor's back. If the visitor was reluctant to sit on the cloth, he used to insist.

He gave new family names to his companions. In their honour, he used to call them by beautiful names. He never used to interrupt anybody's talk till the speaker either stopped or stood up.

Hadrat Anas narrates that if anybody brought a present to the Prophet he used to ask him to take it to a particular house because she was a friend of Hadrat Khadijah and loved her.

Hadrat Aishah says : "I was not jealous of any woman, nor did I feel any ill will towards Khadijah, as I used to hear of her repeatedly from the Prophet. If any goat was slaughtered, he used to send it to her friends' houses as a present. Once her sister asked for permission to come in. He was very pleased to see her. A woman came to him and spoke endearingly of Khadijah and enquired about her lovingly. When she went away, he said: 'This woman used to come during Khadijah's time. Good relationship is a sign of faith."

He treated his relatives kindly, but he did not give them preference over better persons.

Abu Qatadah has reported that when a delegation of Najjashi came to the Prophet, he rose for serving them. His companions told him that they were sufficient to serve them. He replied : "They had honoured our companions, therefore I personally want to serve them."

Abu Usamah has narrated that once the Messenger of Allah went among his companions leaning on a cane and his companions stood up. The Prophet said: "Do not stand up. Do not adopt the system of these Non-Arabs who stand up to pay respect to one another."

He said : "I am a slave of Allah ; I eat as other people eat, and I sit as other people sit." When he rode a mule, he allowed some one else to ride behind him. He used to visit poor invalids. He allowed the beggars to sit in his meetings. He mixed up freely with his companions. Where the meeting was over, he used to sit there.

The Prophet once performed Hajj on a cheap Kajawa on the back of a camel on which an old, torn cheddar was spread, whose cost could be at the most four dirhams. He said: "O Allah! This is my Hajj in which there is neither hypocrisy nor show."

When Mecca was conquered and the Muslim soldiers entered the city, the Prophet was riding a camel and his head was vowed down in humility, so much so that it appeared that his head was touching a part of the *kajawa*.

He was of a quiet nature. He never talked without necessity. And if anybody talked with a wry face, he used to be indifferent to him and ignored him.

His smile was his laughter. His talk was straight and direct, in which there was no excess. His companions, in his honour and in following him, considered it sufficient to smile in his presence.

His meetings manifested a spirit of tolerance, trusteeship, honesty, virtue and righteousness. Voices were not raised there and no backbiting was allowed therein.

Whenever he opened his mouth to speak, his companions (R.A.A.) used to keep silent, as if birds were perched on their heads.

When he walked, it was with a balanced gait. There was neither fright nor haste in his gait, nor was there laziness.

Ibn Abi Hala (R.A.A.) says : "His silence was on account of tolerance, farsightedness, estimation and thinking and contemplating."

Hadrat Aishah says that he talked in such a way that if anybody wanted to count the words, he could do so.

The Messenger of Allah liked fragrance and used perfumes many times. The world was presented to him with all her allurements and amusements. Victories were won by his armies, but he was indifferent to luxuries and pleasures. He died in such a condition that his armour was pledged to a Jew.

Ethical Foundation

Faith is such a power that it keeps men away from low attributes and mean acts, and encourages him to achieve high attributes and clean morals. That is why whenever Allah called his slaves towards virtue or whenever He wanted them to hate evil, He declared it as an essential requirement of the Faith in their hearts. For example when He, in Surah Taubah, commands men to adopt righteousness and to speak truth, He addresses them as "O you who have faith" (or "O you who believe"):

> *"O you who have faith ! Fear Allah and be with the truthful people."* *(Taubah : **119**)*

Allah's Messenger has nicely explained it that when faith is firm and belief is strong, then strong and lasting moral will be developed, and if the moral character is low then faith will accordingly be weak.

A man, who is immodest and ill-mannered and who adopts bad habits without caring for others, is like the person about whom the holy Prophet (S.A.W.) has said :

> *Once the Prophet (S.A.W.) passed by an Ansari who was scolding his brother about his immodesty. The Prophet advised him to let him go as modesty was a branch of faith.*

A man who harasses his neighbour and makes him suffer any kind of damage is called cruel and stone hearted by the religion. In this connection the decision of the Prophet is:

> *"By God, he cannot be a Momin; by God, he cannot be a Momin ; by God, he cannot be a Momin. He was asked: 'who'? He answered, "He from whose misdeeds his neighbour is not safe."* —*(Bukhari)*

The holy Prophet advises his companions to keep away from the talk that is trash, the acts that are wicked, and the deeds that are senseless. He says :

> *"A person who believes in Allah and the Hereafter should speak about good things or else should keep quiet."* —*(Bukhari)*

In this way through the truth of faith and by means of its perfection noble qualities are nurtured and developed and they are guarded and kept secure till they bear fruits.

Rows Disrupted, Hearts Sad, Prayers Tasteless : However, you will also find such people, who will be calling themselves Muslims, yet they will be lazy in offering compulsory prayers, and will be posing in the public as if they were very keen on establishing these prayers.

But they will not lag behind at the same time in acting in such a way that will be contrary to the demands of the noble character and perfect faith.

Such people have been warned by the holy Prophet (S.A.W.) and the Ummah has been asked to be careful of them.

A man who commits the mistake of performing the various forms of worship without understanding their significance can only be a man who had not understood the spirit of the worship or has been unable to rise to that standard.

Many times even a child can copy the movements of salat and is able to repeat what is recited during the prayer. Sometimes an actor also offers prayer with all humility and concentration, and performs all the necessary rites.

But these kinds of movements do not benefit belief or meet the purpose. There is only one way of offering prayers in the best manner or performing other forms of worship that will never bring out wrong results, and that is : high moral character. Any person who has this attribute in him, his prayer is useful. But one who is deprived of this attribute, his worshipping is useless.

It is narrated by Imam Ahmad : One person asked the Prophet (S.A.W.), "O Messenger of Allah ! a certain woman is very famous for her prayers, fasting and many charities. but she talks rudely with her neighbours. Tell me, what will be her fate ?"

He replied that she would go to Hell." Then that person asked : "O Messenger of Allah ! Another woman does not do much by way of prayers and fasting ; gives pieces of cheese in charity and does not harm her neighbours." He replied: "She is of the Paradise."

This reply gives an idea of the high value attached to good character. It also shows that charity is a collective prayer whose benefit reaches the society. For this reason there is no room for any reduction in them. As salat and fasting are apparently individual forms of worship, a little relaxation — to a very little extent—is allowed in not making very elaborate arrangements about them.

The holy Prophet (S.A.W.) did not merely answer a casual question that explains the relationship between morality and the religion, shows its connection with the correct forms of worship, and forms the basis of reform and improvement in the world and salvation in the next world.

The problem of morality was much more important. It was necessary that he should have continually provided guidance to his followers. He should have persisted in giving good advice to them so that its importance takes root in the mind and heart and it becomes quite clear that faith, goodness and morality are all dependent on each other. They are connected with each other and none can separate them.

Who is Poor ?

One day the Prophet (S.A.W.) asked his dear companions whether they knew who was poor. They answered that poor was one who had no *dirham* or *dinar* (money). He said:

> *"In my* Ummah, *the poor is that man who would appear on the Day of Judgment who had paid zakat ; had*

observed fast ; but he would have abused somebody, he would have falsely accused some one ; he would have unauthorisedly taken some one else's property ; he would have murdered some one ; would have hit some body. All his virtues would be given to his victims. If his virtues are finished before his wicked deeds are finished, then the errors and sins of the victims would be given to him and he would be thrown into the Hell." *(Muslim)*

Such a man is really poor. His condition is like that trader who has goods worth one thousand rupees but he is a debtor for two thousand rupees. How can such a man be called rich ?

A religious man who offers certain prayers or performs certain forms of worship, but even after that performs certain evil deeds, behaves rudely with the people, treats poor and helpless people cruelly, how then such a man will be called righteous? The Prophet has explained by quoting an example. He said that the best moral character melts errors like water and bad morals spoil man's record as vinegar spoils honey.

Identification of a Hypocrite : When wickedness is nourished in the self, and the loss caused by it has become manifest and the danger has increased, then that man has come out of his religion like a nude who has come out of his garments.

At that time his claim of righteousness or faith would be false. What will be the value of religiousness without good morality? How is it possible that a man should belong to Allah and at the same time should be a victim of corruption?

This relationship between faith and morality is clearly shown in the Hadith of the holy Prophet (S.A.W.):

"The man who has these three habits is a hypocrite even if he observes fast, offers prayers, performs Umrah (pilgrimage), and calls himself a Muslim : when he talks he speaks untruth, when he makes a promise he does not keep it, and when he is given something in trust, he commits dishonesty." *—(Muslim).*

In another tradition, he (S.A.W.) has said:

"There are three signs of a hypocrite: when he talks he speaks untruth, when he makes a promise he does not keep it, and when he makes a contract he deceives, although he may be offering prayers, observing fast and calling himself a Muslim."

He has also said:

> *"There are four habits, in whosoever they are found, he will be a complete hypocrite. If any one of these habits is found in a man, he will have one habit of disruption till he gives it up, when something is given to him in trust he commits dishonesty, when he talks he tells lies, when he makes a contract he deceives, and when he quarrels he starts abusing.* —*(Bukhari).*

A Word from the Prophet

These teachings show that Islam had come to illuminate the lives of the people with the light of virtue and good manners, to create in them brightness of character, and to fill their laps with the pearls of good conduct. It made the stages that came in the process of achieving this great objective as an important part of the Prophethood.

Similarly, it declared all attempts to create disruption in these stages as an expulsion from the religion and equivalent to throwing away the yoke of faith from one's neck.

The position of morality is not like that of the means of pleasures and luxuries, from which indifference may be possible. But morality is the name of the principles of life which the religion must adopt and must care for the respect of its standard-bearers.

Islam has enumerated all these virtues and principles and has encouraged its followers to make them parts of their lives, one after another.

If we collect all the sayings of the holy Prophet about the importance of good moral character, then a voluminous book will be prepared, about which many of the great reformers will be ignorant.

Before we enumerate these virtues and state their details, it will be proper if we quote some examples of how strongly and emphatically Islam has called upon the people to adopt good moral character.

Usama bin Shareek says :

> *"We were sitting in the presence of the Messenger of Allah (S.A.W.) so quietly as if birds were perched on our heads. Nobody had the courage to open his mouth. In the meanwhile some people came and asked : "Amongst the slaves of God who is the dearest to Him."*

The Prophet (S.A.W.) replied :

> *"One who has the best moral character."*—*(Ibn Habban)*

Another tradition has it :

> *"They asked what is the best thing given to man ?" He replied : "Best moral character."* —*(Tirmidhi)*

The Prophet (S.A.W.) was asked :

> *"Which Muslim has the perfect faith ?" He answered : "He who has the best moral character."* *(Tibrani)*
>
> *Abdullah bin Amar has reported : "I have heard the Prophet as saying : 'Should I not tell you who amongst you is the most likeable person to me? And who will be the nearest to me on the Day of the Judgment ?' He repeated this question twice or thrice. The people requested him to tell them about such a person. He said: 'He who amongst you has the best moral character.'*
>
> *(Ahmad)*

In another Hadith, he (S.A.W.) has said : "On the Day of the Judgement there will be nothing weightier in the balance of a momin than the goodness of character."

> *Allah dislikes an obscene and a rude talker and the bearer of a good moral character reaches to the level of the observer of the prayer and fasting, on account of his character."* *(Imam Ahmad)*

There would be nothing surprising if such teachings were to come from a philosopher who was busy in his campaign of moral-reform. But the great surprise is that these teachings come from a man who strived for establishing a great new faith, when all other religions turn their attention first only towards the performance of worship and such other religious rites.

The last Prophet (S.A.W.) gave a call for the performance of various forms of worship and for the establishment of such a government that was involved in a long-drawn war with its large number of enemies. Inspite of the expansion of his religion and the immense increase in the various tasks of his followers, the Prophet (S.A.W.) informs them of the fact that on the Day of the Judgment there will be nothing weightier in their balance than their good moral character, then definitely this reality is not hidden from him that in Islam the value of morality is very high.

The fact is that if religion is the name of good conduct between man and man, then on the other hand in its spiritual sense it is also the name of the best relationship between man and his God, and in both these aspects there is the same reality. There are many religions which give this glad tiding that you may embrace any belief, your sins will be washed away and offering fixed prayers of any religion will cancel your mistakes. But Islam does not believe in this.

According to it, these benefits will be available only when the axis and centre of belief is a conscious step towards virtue and payment of the compulsory dues, and when the proposed worship can become the real source of washing away the sins and generating the real perfection. In other words, evil can be removed by those virtues which man makes his own and by which he is able to reach high and lofty standards. The holy Prophet (S.A.W.) has very forcefully emphasised these valuable principles so that the Ummah may understand it very clearly that the value of morality may not go down in its eyes and the importance of mere forms and shapes may not increase.

Hadrat Anas has reported :

> *"Allah's Messenger has said : "A slave achieves, by means of the goodness of his character, great position and high honour in the Hereafter, though he may be weak in matters of worship ; but on account of his wickedness of character he is thrown in the lowest recesses of the Hell."*
>
> *—(Tibrani)*

Hadrat Aishah narrates :

> *"I have heard the Prophet (S.A.W.) as saying : 'Momin, by goodness of his character, achieves the high position of the one who observes fast and offers prayers."*
>
> *—(Abu Daud)*

Ibn Umar is (R.A.A.) reported to have narrated :

> *"I have heard the Prophet (S.A.W.) as saying : "A Muslim who observes moderation in matters of worship, on account of the goodness of his character and decency achieves the position of that man who observes fast and recites Allah's verses during prayers in the night."*
>
> *—(Ahmad)*
>
> *Abu Hurrayrah has (R.A.A.) quoted the Prophet (S.A.W.) as saying "A Momin's nobility is his religiousness, his tolerance is his intelligence, and his lineage is his goodness of character."* *—(Hakim)*
>
> *Abuzar (R.A.A.) has narrated : "Successful is the man who had purified his heart for faith, kept his heart on*

the right lines, his tongue was truthful, his self was content, and his nature was on the right path."

—*(Ibn Habban)*

Benefits of Truth

Allah has created this whole universe on the basis of love, and has demanded of the people that they should build up their life on the foundation of truth, to make truth and straight dealing a practice of their life, and should give place to truth only in their talks and dealings.

When this clear sense is lost sight of by people, and false stories, superstitions and absurd beliefs rule their self, ideas and thoughts, then hardness and harshness are generated in them, they move away from the right path, and they totally give up those realities, the adoption of which was necessary. For this reason the strong and firm pillar of a Muslim's character is straight dealing. It is his duty to be attached to truth in every matter and to see every problem and affair through the glasses of truth.

To keep it before him in every decision is the clearest manifestation of his dealing and treatment. Similarly the construction of the society in Islam is made on this foundation that mere conjectures and superstitions should be opposed, baseless things and imaginary stories should be thrown out, doubts and misgivings should not be encouraged, because strong and firm realities only deserve to be manifested ; they should have their imprint on the society , and their help should be taken in strengthening various relations.

Allah's Messenger has said:

"Keep away from ill-thinking, because ill-thinking is the greatest falsehood." *(Bukhari)*

Another *Hadith* says:

"Leave alone doubtful things, follow those matters in which there is no doubt, for truth is a means of satisfaction and falsehood is the cause of doubts and misgivings." *(Tirmidhi)*

Quran has expressed condemnation of those communities who follow conjectures and superstitions that have filled their brains with absurdities and has staked their present and future, with the help of the false stories, on the gamble of corruption and disruption:

"They follow nothing but conjecture and what their own souls desire, even though there has already come to them Guidance from their Lord." *(An-Najm : 23)*

> *"But they have no knowledge therein. They follow nothing but conjecture; and conjecture avails nothing against Truth.* *(An-Najm : 28)*

Since Islam respects truth most strongly, it turns away liars very harshly. It admonishes them very severely. Hadrat Aishah narrates:

> *"Allah's Messenger did not hate anything as strongly as he hated falsehood. If he received information that a particular man has told a lie, he used to throw away that man's respect and honour from his heart till the time he was not informed that he has repented for it."*
> *(Ahmad)*

Another narration by her states:

> *"For the Messenger of Allah falsehood was the worst habit in a person. If any man told a lie in his presence, that man's thought always troubled him until the time he was informed that he has repented."* *(Ibn Habban)*

This habit of the Prophet is not at all surprising. This was the policy of our forefathers. Their relations were formed on the basis of righteousness and good moral character. They knew each other. If any one had blemishes in his character, and if he could be singled out on account of his misdeeds, then his position in that society would be like the position of a man suffering from an infectious itching disease in a healthy society, and he was not considered deserving of any respect until he was not cured of that defect.

The distinctive characteristic of the Muslim society in its first period was truth, discipline, tolerance and cautious manner of speaking. Falsehood, breaking of promises, false accusations, and baseless things are the signs of disruption or of breaking away relation from religion. Or if they are to be termed having relation with the religion, then it would be called the religious business of the false accusers, deceivers and tricksters, or the religiosity of liars and promise-breakers.

Falsehood is a Great Curse : Falsehood is such an evil that discloses the internal corruption and wickedness of the liar; and this is a name of the wrong dealing which only acts in spreading evil, so much so that even without the needs that are troublesome or the forcing inclinations it leads persons to committing sins.

Some evils are such that a man is involved in them totally. They are like diseases which require a very long-drawn treatment; they are like fright and cowardice, which always hinder the progress of a coward and a frightened man, or like greed which makes men miserly and stingy. When some people come out for Jihad to accompany the soldiers, they are shivering in their boots.

Or some other people who are terrified when they work out the amount of zakat that they have to pay. What is the comparison of these coward and miserly natures with those brave and generous natures which rush towards death laughing and which spend their wealth in the cause of Allah most willingly! Here some excuse can be found for such persons as they become a prey of their fears and doubts where called upon to offer sacrifices.

But there can be absolutely no excuse for those who make lying their habit and who for the whole of their life go on deceiving people by their falsehoods.

Allah's Messenger said:

> *"All the evils can be found in a momin, except dishonesty and falsehood."* *(Ahmad)*
>
> *The Messenger of Allah was asked whether any Muslim could be a coward. He answered : "Yes." He was asked : "Can a momin be a miser ?" He said that yes, he could be a miser. He was again asked : "Can a momin be a liar?" He replied :"No."* *(Malik)*

The replies of the Prophet show that these factors of deficiency and weakness enter some persons' nature and when they are called upon to do their duty or pay the dues of Allah and His slaves, then these factors adversely influence them. But this does not mean that miserliness is tolerated and cowardice is a lesser evil. How is it possible when nonpayment of zakat and running away from Jihad are acts which touch the borderline of infidelity (kufr)?

The extent to which a liar and a defiant person may spread falsehood — and however wide this extent may be — his sin, before Allah will be to the same extent. Journalist, who misguide the people by false news, politicians who misrepresent important public problems and slaves of selfishness who cast aspersions against eminent persons and ladies of good character — all these sections commit terrible crimes and their punishment is very severe.

> *Allah's Messenger said : "One night I saw two men. They came to me and said:" Any man whom you see talking by widening his jaws, consider him a liar. He tells a lie*

> *which is copied through his medium, till it is talked of in the whole world. He goes on doing this till the Doomsday."* *(Fathul Bari)*

Making false promises to their subjects by the rulers also comes in this category, because the falsehood spoken from the pulpit spreads to the four corners of the world.

> *It is in the Tradition that "Three persons can never enter Paradise. First the old man who commits illegal sex, second the man who tells lies and third that poor man who indulges in pride."* *(Al Bazzar)*

To invent lies against Allah's religion is the worst evil. One who has the slightest relation with Allah and His Messenger will never indulge in this kind of activity.

This is the worst kind of liar, and the consequences which he will have to face are terrible.

> *The Prophet has said : "The consequence of inventing falsehood against me is not as bad as it is for inventing falsehood against anybody. Let the man who purposely and wittingly makes a false statement about me make his destination Hell."* *(Bukhari)*

In the list of false charges and accusations are included all those inventions and absurdities which the uneducated hve fabricated against Allah's religion, which have no place in the faith. The general public has taken them to be the religion, though they have nothing to do with it. In fact they are nothing but mere pastime and plaything.

Allah's Messenger has warned his followers against the sources of these invented absurdities, has admonished them to be wary of adopting other ways than those directed by the Quran and the Sunnah. He has said:

> *"In the last period of my Ummah there will come people who will be deceitful, iars. They will tell you things which you would never have heard, nor have your forefathers heard them. Be wary of them; let them not misguide you and let them not involve you in corruptions."* *(Muslim)*

Children should be Truthful *:* Islam commands that in the hearts of the children the seeds of the greatness and importance of truth be sown, so that they may grow up and develop on truth and may become young in its lap; and they may give it its due place in their talks.

> *Abdullah Ibn Aamir says that once my mother called me when the Prophet was present in my house. My mother asked me to come and said that she would give me a certain thing. He asked what did she want to give ? She said that she wanted to give me a date (fruit). The Prophet said : " If you had not given him this date, then the committing of a falsehood would have been entered into your record of deeds."* *(Abu Daud)*

Abu Hurrayrah says that the Prophet has said:

> *"Anybody who called a child saying that he would give him a certain thing and did not give it, then it is a lie." (Ahmad)*

It is worth noting that in what a wise way the Prophet has instructed his followers to train their children in such a manner that they should consider truth and straight dealing respectable things and should avoid telling lies. Had the Prophet ignored these things and had not emphatically reminded about them, then there was a danger that the children on growing up would not have considered telling lies as sin. Adoption of straight dealing and telling the truth has been very strictly insisted upon, so much so that it has been enjoined upon to take care about this in even small household matters. Alma Bint Yazid narrates that she once asked the Messenger of Allah:

> *"If some one of us women stated that she had no desire to have a certain thing even though she had that desire, then would it be considered a lie ?" He replied : "Falsehood is written as falsehood, and a small falsehood is written as a small falsehood."* *(Muslim)*

Prohibited to tell a Lie even in a Joke : The Establisher of the Shariah (PBUH.) has warned of all the occasions where falsehood can be used and the adverse consequences of the same, so much so that it is not possible for even an ordinary enforcer to misguide the people about the reality or to lessen its importance.

A man tends to make false statements in cutting jokes, thinking that on the occasions of entertaining people there is nothing wrong if baseless information is given or false and imaginary events are related. But Islam, which considers providing relief to hearts as permissible, has fixed only those methods proper and permissible which are within the limits of truth, because halal is much broader than Haram and that truth is independent of falsehood.

Allah's Messenger has said:

> *"Death for the man who indulges in story-telling in order to make some people laugh and for that he relies on falsehood. There is death for him, there is destruction for him."* *(Tirmidhi)*

In another *Hadith* it is stated:

> *"I give guarantee of a house in the middle of Paradise for the man who has given up falsehood, though he was required to indulge in humour."* *(Baihaqi)*

The Prophet has said:

> *"A Momin cannot have complete faith unless he gives up falsehood in his jokes and debates though in all other matters he speaks the truth."* *(Ahmad)*

This is our daily observation that people give full rein to their tongues in the matter of humorous talks to make others laugh, and do not hesitate to spread the tales and stories invented by friends or foes only for the purpose of getting some pleasure or for pulling some ones's leg, when the world has absolutely prohibited such a wrong policy, and this is a fact that this kind of entertainment and amusements and false acts create enmities and rivalries.

Avoid Exaggeration in Praise : Some people, when they praise somebody, go to the extent of exaggerating and making false statements. For a Muslim it is necessary that when he praises somebody he should do it to the extent to which he knows about that man. He should avoid exaggeration and falsehood in showering praises of the praised one, although he may be deserving of the praises, for exaggeration is a kind of falsehood which has been forbidden.

> *To a person who was praising the Prophet, he said : "Do not indulge in exaggeration while praising me, as the Christians did in the case of Ibn Maryam (Christ). I am only a slave. So only say that he is a slave of Allah and His Messenger."* *(Razin)*

A group of such people is always found who lick the boots of the leaders and rulers of the country and praise them to heaven. The main purpose of their lives is to compose very lengthy panegyrical poems or to write long-drawn essays in praise of their benefactors. Thus they try to make a mountain of the molehill and place an unknown person in the palace of fame. Sometimes they do not even hesitate to call the tyrant rulers as standard bearers of justice and coward and chicken hearted soldiers as brave and lion-hearted fighters. Their only purpose in this is to earn wealth. This is the worst kind of falsehood.

Allah's Messenger has counselled us to totally reject them and expose them till they give up their wrong practices.

> *Abu Hurrayrah says that the Prophet has commanded us that we should throw dust in the face of those who indulge in exaggeration in their praises.* *(Tirmidhi)*

The commentators have pointed out that the persons mentioned here are those who make exaggeration as their habit and through this try to earn gifts and presents from the praised ones, but those persons who praise the performers of good acts with a view to encouraging them and to inciting others to follow their example are not meant.

The limits where a Muslim stops and which keep him distinct from the bootlickers and the exaggerators are that he praises his benefactor or a good person, but he does not let him indulge in vanity and pride. These limits have been clarified by the Prophet.

> *Hadrat Abu Badr narrates that a man praised some one in the presence of Allah's Messenger and the Prophet told him : "Fie on you, you have separated the head of your companion." He repeated these words and then said: "If some one wants to praise his brother, then if he is aware of the facts then he should say that I think he is such and such and Allah is the real Knower, and he is the bearer of these qualities."* *(Bukhari)*

Keep away from Falsehood and Deception in Trade : Traders make false statements while showing their wares and stating their prices. The basis of trade in our midst is unlimited greed. The shopkeeper desires that there should be dearness, while the buyer wants to get the commodities free of charge.

It is wealth which controls activities of buying and selling in the markets and in different fields. Islam hates this kind of deceptive affair and the senseless debate and disputation latent in it.

The Prophet has said : "The buyers and sellers are free till they do not separate and if they have acted with honesty, and have explained the defects of commodities, then Allah will bless them with prosperity. And if both of them tried to deal dishonestly and tried to hide the defects- then it is likely that they may get some profit, but the prosperity will vanish from their trade."

In another tradition it is stated:

> *"The prosperity of the dealing of both the persons is terminated. The untrue and false oath will help get the commodity sold, but it reduces the earning.* (Ahmad)

The buyers who go to the shopkeepers are mostly ignorant of the real situation, and whatever the shopkeeper says they believe it. The honest thing is not to take undue advantage of the simplicity of men for the purpose of obtaining double price or for concealing the defects.

The Messenger of Allah has said:

> *"What would be a greater dishonesty than this that when you are talking with your brother, he may be thinking that you are telling the truth whereas you are deceiving him by telling lies."* (Bukhari)

He has also said:

> *"It is not lawful for a Muslim to sell such a commodity that has a defect, except that the defect is shown to the buyer."* (Bukhari)

Ibn Abi Adnan arrates that a man opened a shop in the market and swore that he would sell such a commodity as no one else would be selling, so that he may deceive some Muslims ; so the following verses were revealed:

> *"Verily, those who sell the covenant with Allah and their oaths for a small price, there is no compensation for them in the Hereafter. On the Day of Judgment Allah will not speak to them, nor will He look at them, and nor will He purify them; but for them is very severe punishment."* (Baqarah)

Disregard of truth in giving evidence is the worst type of falsehood. When a Muslim should stand up for giving evidence, he should state the truth unhesitatingly, regardless of the fact whether it is against his close friend or a favourite person. No relationship or prejudice should deviate him from the right path, nor any greed or bribe should be able to make him waver in his stand.

> *"O You who believe ! Stand out firmly for justice, as witnesses to Allah, even as against yourselves, or your parents, or your kin, and whether it be (against) rich or poor; for Allah can best protect both. Follow not the lusts (of your heart), lest you swerve, and if you distort (justice)*

or decline to do justice, verily Allah is well-acquainted with all that you do." *(Nissa : 135)*

Hadrat Abu Bakr narrates that the Messenger of Allah has stated:

"May I not tell you the major sins ?" Three times he repeated the same thing. We requested "Why not O Messenger of Allah?" He replied "To associate some one else with Allah, to disobey the parents and to murder some one unjustly." He was leaning. Then he got up and said : "And to tell lies and to give false evidence." He went on repeating it till we said to ourselves it would be better if he were silent then."

(Bukhari)

Trickery and deception is a falsehood which has layers and layers of darknesses. It does not only involve the concealment of truth but it also tries to prove that the falsehood is truth. In some special matters it harms only a few individuals but in public matters it becomes a severe and deadly danger against the whole nation.

For this reason the Prophet has very bluntly and emphatically counselled to keep away from it and has warned against it.

Do not Break your Promises : The traders and the industrialists particularly should take special care to see that they keep their promises, that they are true to their words and that they do not change their stand. It is a very sad state of affairs that among the Muslims the tendency of breaking promises and crossing the limits has become very common, when their religion has termed the false promises symbols of disruption.

The Messenger of Allah considered the words coming out from the mouth as holy and the words that fell on his ears as respectable. Before attaining Prophethood, these qualities of decency and manliness were found in his character.

Abdullah bin Abi Hama says that he entered into a contract for the sale of a commodity with the Prophet before he was blessed with Prophethood, and some commodities had remained to be sold. He promised to the Prophet that he would hand over a certain thing to him at a certain place. Then he forget all about this. After three days he remembered his Promise and went to the appointed place. He saw that the Prophet was present at the spot. He only said this:

"O young man ! You worried me. I am waiting here for you for the last three days." *(Abu Daud)*

It is narrated that the Prophet had promised Jabir bin Avauuan that he would give him some gifts from the stock of articles coming from Bahrain, but before fulfilling this promise he died. When the stock from Bahrain arrived at the place of the First Caliph, he caused an announcement to be made in the public that any one whom the Prophet might have promised to give something from this stock or any one who had lent something to the Prophet should come to him and take away his due." *(Bukhari)*

It is worth noting how the words are appraised and they are enforced, so that they may not become worthless if left uncared for. False promises do untold harm to the interests of the society. They cause inconvenience to the people and waste time. Redeeming your pledges is a commendable quality. Allah considers fulfilling of promises as one of the attributes of Prophethood

"Also mention in the Book (the story of) Ismail; he was true to what he promised, and he was a Messenger, Prophet. He used to enjoin on his people prayer and charity and he was most acceptable in sight of the Lord."
(Maryam : 54-55)

In these verses the order of the good qualities show what position the quality of fulfilling of promises enjoys ; and Ismail showed that he was true to his word when his father told him that he saw a dream in which he was slaughtering his son, Ismail, and asked him what he thought about it. The son, who was true to his word, replied: "God willing, you will find me patient and steadfast."

Sometimes man relies on falsehood when he commits a mistake, and he wants to save himself from the bad consequences of that mistake. This is very unwise and brings a bad name. It amounts to going from one evil to another, which is worse than the first evil. It is necessary that man should own his mistakes. It is likely that his truthfulness and his sense of sorrow over his mistake may save him from the bad consequences and he may be pardoned.

When a Muslim senses some danger or is afraid to speak the truth, it is proper that he should show courage and try to avoid getting ensnared in the net of falsehood.

Allah's Messenger has said:

"Adopt truth, even if you see your destruction in it, for the (final) salvation is in it." *(Ibn Abi-duniya)*

In another *Hadith* it is mentioned:

> *"When a person tells a lie, the bad odour that emanates from it keeps the angels one mile away."* *(Tirmidhi)*

If a man is truthful and straight in his speech and dealings, then inevitably there will be truthfulness and sincerity in his actions and goodness and reform in his conditions. By adopting truthful and straight methods in dealing with others, this light of truth also illuminates man's heart and mind and their darkness also vanish:

> *"O you who believe Fear Allah and (always) say a word Allah created me right ; that He may matte your conduct whole and sound and forgive you your sins; He that obeys Allah and His Messenger has already attained the highest achievement."* *(Ahzab : 70-71)*

Right action is the desired action, about which there is no misgiving, because it is the creation of certainty. There is no idea of defect in that, because it is the companion of sincerity. There is no curve in it, because its source is truth. The success of the communities and nations in the matter of conveying their message depends on the fact that the bearers of the message must be performers of right action. If they have an abundant record of right and truthful action, then they can reach the zenith of success and glory, otherwise they swerve from their destination in the way, for mere idleness, senseless activities, slogan shouting and self-praise would not be of any use.

> *Allah's Messenger has said : "Adopt truth, for truth shows the path of righteousness, and righteousness shows the path to Paradise. A man speaks the truth regularly and adopts truthful ways till he is recorded as a truthful person before Allah ; and keep away from falsehood, for falsehood leads to wickedness, and wickedness throws in the Hell. A person tells lies regularly and attaches himself to falsehood till he is recorded as a liar before Allah."* *(Fathul Bari)*

Evil and wickedness towards which the habit of telling lies leads is the last stage of the destruction of self and the lowness of faith.

Imam Malik has reported about the Hadith narrated by Ibn Masood : "A person regularly tells lies and adopts falsehood (as his policy), till a black point is imprinted on his heart, and slowly and slowly the whole heart becomes black. At that time his name is entered in the list of liars before Allah."

Allah has stated in Quran:

> *"It is those who believe not in the Signs of Allah that forge falsehood; it is they who lie."* *(Nahl : 105)*

Righteousness whose path is shown by truth is the highest peak of goodness to which only men of high determination can reach. In this connection the following verses of the holy Quran would suffice:

> *"It is no virtue that you turn your face to the East and the West, but virtue is that one should believe in Allah, and the Last Day and the angels and the Prophets ; and spend out of love for Him his wealth on relatives and orphans and the needy and the wayfarer and on those who ask and for ransom of the slaves and establish salat and pay zakat. And those who fulfil the pledges they make and steadfast in adversity and affliction and in times of struggle, such are the people as are truthful and God-fearing:"* *(Baqarah : 177)*

The Surety

Islam exhorts its followers that they will be masters of live heads and wakeful conscience, which would ensure the protection of the rights of God and humanity and which would also protect their actions from the commitment of excesses.

Therefore it is necessary that every Muslim should be Ameen, trustworthy. In the eyes of the Shariah, Trust has a very broad sense. This word contains an ocean of meaning, but underneath it all is the sense of responsibility, the sense of having to appear before Allah and to account for one's actions, the details of which are given in the *Hadith:*

> *"Every one of you is a guardian and every one will be asked about his subjects. Imam is a guardian. He will be asked about his subjects. A man is the guardian of the persons in his household. He is answerable about them. A woman is the guardian of her husband's house. She will be asked about her responsibility. The servant is the guardian of the articles of his master. He is answerable about this responsibility of his."* *(Bukhari)*

The narrator of the Hadith Ibn Umar says that he heard these things from the Prophet and he thinks that the Prophet also said:' "A man is a guardian of the stock of his father and is answerable about that."

The people take trust in a very limited sense and consider it to mean the protection of others' deposits, although in Allah's religion this has a very broad and unlimited sense.

This is a duty for safeguarding which a Muslim advises another Muslim and in this connection seeks the help of Allah. When a Muslim prepares to go on a journey, his brother prays for him in this way:

> *"I pray to Allah for your religion, your trust and for the happy ending of your work."* *(Tirmidhi)*

Hadrat Anas narrates that whenever Allah's Messenger addressed a sermon to us, he invariably repeated this sentence: "The man has no faith who cannot keep trust and the man who does not respect his promises has no religion."

Since the zenith of achievement and the highest limit of success is to be protected against the hardships of this world and the bad consequences in the Hereafter, the Prophet prays for safety from both the conditions. He has said:

> *"O Allah ! I seek your shelter from the pangs of hunger, because it is a very bad companion, and I seek your shelter from dishonesty because it is the worst friend."*
> *(Abu Daud)*

> *Hunger is the name of deprivation in the world and dishonesty is the name of destruction of religion, therefore the Prophet had prayed for being spared from both. Before attaining Prohethood he was known among the people as Ameen* *(Trustworthy).*

Similarly the trustworthiness of Moosa (Moses) was, observed when he fetched water for the flock of the two daughters of the good old man, had helped them, had respected their womanhood, and had treated them in a decent and gentlemanly way.

"So he watered (their flocks) for them ; then he turned back to the shade, and said : "O my Lord! truly am I in (desperate) need of any good that you do send me!" Afterwards one of the (damsels) came (back) to him, walking bashfully. 'She said: "My father invites you that he may reward you for having watered (our flocks) for us." So when he came to him and narrated the story, he said : "Do not fear ; (well) have you escaped from unjust people." Said one of the (damsels):

> *"O my (dear) father ! engage him on wages; truly the best of men for you to employ is the (man) who is strong and trusty."* *(Qasas : 24-26)*

This event took place when Moosa had not been made Prophet, and was not sent to Pharaoh's darbar.

And this is not at all surprising because Allah chose only those individuals for being appointed as His Messengers who were the most decent, most honest and righteous, among the people..

The self which continues to be attached to the high moral character even after undergoing the extremes or the hardship of poverty and helplessness must be belonging to a very powerful and trustworthy man; and the protection of the rights of God and His slaves demand such character only as does not change in good or bad conditions, and this is the spirit of trustworthiness.

Appointment, a Trust : There is also another sense of trust, and that is everything should be placed at its proper and deserving place. An office or a post should be offered only to the deserving person ; and responsibility should be given only to that person who is able to shoulder it and who has the capability to do justice to the trust placed in him. Governorship, responsibilities of the party, nation or country, which are granted placing confidence in the persons concerned, are trusts, about which they are answerable. A number of proofs can be advanced in support of this statement.

Hadrat Abuzar reports that he asked the Prophet whether he would not make him a governor somewhere. Hearing this the Prophet tapped his shoulder and said:

> *"O Abuzar ! you are weak, and this responsibility is a trust. On the Day of Judgment it will be a cause of loss of honour and ignominy. However, those people will be spared who will have accepted it with all its responsibilities and would have fulfilled whatever responsibilities they had in this connection" (Muslim)*

It is a fact that mere excellence of education or experience does not make a person most suitable for some office. It is also possible that a man may have good moral character and a righteous person, but he may not have the capabilities to fulfill the responsibilities of a certain office.

Hadrat Yusuf (Joseph) was a Prophet. He was the living example of righteousness and virtuousness, but he had not offered his services to shoulder the responsibilities of the country on the basis of his righteousness and Prophethood. He had taken the reins of office in his hand on account of his learning and memory.

"(Yusuf) Said: `Entrust to me the treasures of the country. Verily, 1 am protector and learned." *(Yusuf : 55)*

Trust demands that we should entrust such responsibilities and posts to such individuals as would be able to run them properly. If through bribery, nepotism and for some other reason we deviate from this principle and we select an unfit person for some office, then since we have ignored a fit person and have appointed an unfit and undeserving person, we have committed open misappropriation.

Allah's Messenger has said that whoever has appointed an administrator through nepotism although there was among the people an individual who was more desirable before Allah than that person, then he has committed misappropriation against Allah, His Messenger and all the Muslims." *(Hakim)*

Yazid bin Abi Sufyan reports that when Hadrat Abu Bakr sent him to Syria, he advised him thus : "O Yazid ! You have many relationships. It is likely that you may be influenced by them in making important appointments. I am very much afraid about you since the time the Prophet has said : "Any one who has been made responsible for some affair of the Muslims and he has entrusted some responsible job to some one, influenced by his relatives, then Allah's curse on him. No virtue or justice from him will be accepted before Allah, so much so that he will be thrown in the Hell." *(Hakim)*

The community from which the quality of keeping trust is vanished, can be recognised thus : the distribution of posts and offices in that community become a game and play of favours. The value of able men goes down and in their place unfit and undeserving men are appointed.

The tradition has it that this forms part of those manifestations of corruption which will appear in the last period.

A man came to the Prophet and asked when the Doomsday would occur. The Prophet answered: "When deposits in trust would start being lost, then wait for the Doomsday." He was again asked:

"What is the meaning of loss of trusts ?" He replied : "When responsibilities are entrusted to unfit persons, then wait for the Doomsday." *(Bukhari)*

Performance of Duty also a Trust : This sense is also included in the meaning of trust that the man to whom the responsibility has been entrusted should have the sincere inclination of satisfactorily fulfilling those responsibilities and that he should devote all his energies for doing justice to fulfil it.

Undoubtedly it is a trust. Islam considers it worthy of honour that a man should be sincere in his work, should be keen on doing his job in a better way, and should be able to safeguard the right of the people that are in his charge, for however ordinary that responsibility may be, a slight negligence is likely to cause undue harm to the whole community and society ; and the germs of corruption and mischief enter the entire body politic.

Dishonesty in performing official duties causes various moral diseases in the society. It causes great harm to the religion, to the Muslim public and to the country. This sin, its punishment and its evil appear in different forms.

The Messenger of Allah has said:

> *"On the Day of Judgment when Allah will gather all the people, past and present, a flag will be fixed for every deceiver, by which he will be recognised. So it will be said that this is the group of such and such deceivers."*
> *(Bukhari)*

In another tradition it is stated:

> *"There will be a flag near the head of every deceiver which he will raise in proportion to his deceit. Listen, there is none worse deceiver than the Amir who deceives the public."* *(Muslim)*

In other words there will be none more deceitful and deserving of bad consequences than the person who is made responsible for the affairs of men and he sleeps peacefully while the public is undergoing hardships and facing destruction.

Misuse of Office Betrayal of Trust : Trust demands that if a man is appointed to a certain high office he should not use it for self-aggrandisement or for the benefit of his relatives, for the use of public funds for personal purposes is a crime. It is a common thing that the governments and the firms give fixed salaries to their employees. Then to find out extra sources of income is disrespectful, ignominious and mean. Allah's Messenger has said:

> *"Whomsoever we wilt entrust with service, the provision of his needs is also our responsibility. If he takes more than this, then he is committing misappropriation."*
> *(Abu Daud)*

It is misappropriation because he has used that property of the organisation for himself which was to be given to the weak and the needy, and it was to be spent for a greater cause and purpose.

> *"If any person is so false, he shall on the Day of Judgment, restore what he misappropriated; then shall every soul receive its due, — whatever it earned — and none shall be dealt with unjustly."* *(Ale Imran : 161)*

But a man who takes care of the commands of Allah in fulfilling his responsibility and he is averse to indulge in dishonest practices in performing his duties, then he is considered by Allah one among the fighters for the supremacy of the religion. The Prophet has said:

> *"When the Administrator is given a job, he should receive his due and should pay the dues of others, then he is like a fighter in the cause of Allah till he returns home."*
> *(Tibrani)*

Islam has forbidden the exploitation of one's office and taking undue advantage from it. It has been very severe in closing all the avenues of earning illegal wealth.

Adi bin 'Umaira narrates that he has heard the Prophet as saying: "Whomsoever we have given some post and he has concealed a needle or a thing smaller than that, then it will be a misappropriated thing with which he will have to appear on the Day of Judgment." Thereupon a dark-skinned Ansari got up and said : "O Messenger of Allah! take away my governorship." The Prophet inquired what was the matter. He replied "I have heard all your talk just now." The Prophet said :

> *"I still say that whomsoever we may make a governor, he should place everything before us. He should take whatever is given to him, and should keep away from whatever he is asked to desist."* *(Muslim)*

It is said that a man from the tribe of Uzd, called Ibn Labtih, was sent as an administrator by the Prophet to collect charity and donations. When he returned with the collection he said : "These are your things and these have been gifted to me." The narrator of the *Hadith* says that hearing this the Prophet stood up and after the praise of God said:

> *"... I appoint, from amongst you, an administrator for these affairs for which Allah has made me responsible. When that man comes back, he says this is for us and this has been gifted to him. If he tells the truth, then why*

> *does he not sit in his parents' house. Let us then see from where the gifts come to him ? By God, if any one of you receives even an ordinary thing without it being due, he will have to appear before Allah carrying that thing. I do not want to see any one of you meeting Allah in this condition that he is carrying a camel on his head or a cow which is bellowing or a goat that is bleating." Then he raised his two hands till the whiteness of the armpits was visible and said : "O Allah ! I have conveyed your message."* *(Muslim)*

Wealth and Ability given by Allah also a Trust : Trust also means that you should take a survey of your powers of perception with which God has blessed you. You should have a look at those special abilities which God has given you. If you look at your property and your children, who are very dear to you, you will feel that all these are God's trust which has been deposited with you.

Therefore it is necessary that they should be sacrificed in His cause, and they should be utilised for seeking His pleasure.

If you suffer a loss in them, you should not start crying and wailing and you should not consider that it was your personal property that has been taken away from you, because compared to you Allah is the more rightful owner and He has the right to use it in any way He likes. If you are tested by an increase in them, then you should not hesitate to undertake Jihad when called upon to do so, and you should not turn away from obedience to Allah on account of them. Or you should not feel conceited on their strength.

> *"O you who believe I betray not the trust of Allah and the Messenger, nor misappropriate knowingly things entrusted to you. And know that your possessions and your progeny are but a trial; and that it is Allah with whom lies your highest reward."* *(Anfal: 27-28)*

Others' Secrets a Trust : Trust also means that you should protect the rights of the gatherings which you attend. You should not disclose their information and their secrets to others.

A number of relationships are severed, rifts are created in friendships and interests are endangered when the information about or the secrets of the gatherings are disclosed by someone by correctly or incorrectly quoting the source, thus jeopardising all the plans.

Allah's Messenger has said : "When a man says something to someone and then turns to you, then it is a trust."

The confidential talk of the meetings should be guarded, provided it conform to the moral laws and the principles of religion, otherwise its sanctity vanishes. If a Muslim is present to such a meeting where criminals, are conspiring among themselves, so that they may inflict some loss on others, then it is his responsibility that he should try to prevent this evil to the best of his ability.

> *Allah's Messenger has said : "The secrets of the gatherings are a trust, but three kinds of gatherings are exceptions : one in which Haram (illegal) blood is being shed, one in which Haram (illegal) sex is being indulged into, or in which property is being illegally usurped. "*
>
> *(Abu Daud)*

The conjugal relations are sacred in the eyes of Islam. The domestic relationship between a husband and wife and their mutual affairs should be fully protected. The closest man should also not be informed about them.

But foolish people relate their private matters and domestic affairs here and there to outsiders. This is a very bad habit and Allah has declared it Haram.

Asma bint Yazid reports that she was with the Prophet and a husband and a wife were sitting there. The Prophet said:

> *"Is there a man who narrates the acts performed with the wife? And is there a wife who relates her relation with her husband to others ?" People did not say anything from fear. I said : "O Messenger of Allah ! By God, husbands also do this and wives also do likewise." He said : "Do not say like this. Its example is like a devil-man meeting a devil-woman, and he covers her and performs the sexual act and people are watching."*
>
> *(Ahmad)*
>
> *The Prophet said: "On the Day of Judgment before Allah the greatest act of misappropriation will be that a man may love his wife and the wife may also be inclined towards her husband and then he may disclose his wife's secrets to others." (Muslim)*

The deposits which are given to us in trust are for keeping protected for a fixed period, and then to be turned on demand. We are answerable for these acts.

While migrating to Medina, the Prophet left behind his cousin so that he may return to the polytheists the deposits kept with him in trust, although these polytheists were the members of the same community which was driving him out of his native place.

He was being compelled to leave his home in the cause of his belief, but how can a decent man behave indecently even with indecent and infamous people?

Maimoon bin Mehran says that three kinds of treatment be always meted out to good and bad man alike keeping trust, fulfilling promise and kindness.

To consider trust as personal property is a wicked act, theft.

Abdullah Ibn Masood says that fighting in the cause of Allah vanishes all the sins except the misappropriation in trust. He says that on the Day of Judgment a person will be brought who had fought in the cause of Allah, but he would be asked to pay up amounts in trust. He would reply: "O Our Lord! how is it possible when the world has ended."

Then it would be said : "Take him to Hell." And in his presence the amounts of trust will be presented in the same form in which they were handed over to him in the world. He would see them and recognise them. He would go after them and seize them and carry them on his shoulders, till he would be under the impression that he has come out, when the trusts would slip from his shoulders.

He would again run after them. This act would continue with him for ever. Then he said that Salat (prayer) is a trust, Wudu (ablutions) is a trust, to weigh a thing is a trust, to measure a thing is a trust, and he listed many things and said the greatest trust is that wealth or articles which are deposited or handed over.

The narrator of the *Hadith* says that he went to Bara bin Aazib and asked him what he thought about what Ibn Masood said. Bara bin Aazib replied : "He spoke the truth. Did you not hear this command of Allah:

> *"Allah commands you to render back your trusts to those to whom they are due; and when you judge between man and man that you judge with justice."* *(An-Nissa : 58)*

Keeping trust protects the rights of Allah and those of His slaves. It keeps away men from lowliness and meanness.

It reaches the desired heights only when this quality is absorbed by men in their natures and consciousness, when it reaches the depths of their hearts and when it is guarded against the influences of close and distant relationships.

This is the meaning of the Hadith narrated by Hudhaifa bin Yaman:

> *"Keeping trust has been naturally ingrained in the depths of men's hearts. Then Quran came and people learned it from Quran and Sunnah." (Muslim)*

The knowledge of Shariah cannot be indifferent to the righteous conduct, and keeping trust signifies the correct knowledge of Quran and Sunnah as well as a wakeful conscience. If the conscience dies, then the quality of keeping trust is taken away. At such a time the recitation of the Quranic verses and the study of Hadith cannot be profitable, but the claimants of Islam think about others and also about themselves that they are the bearers of this quality, but one may ask how can the heart that rejects the truth be expected to keep trust?

For this reason Hadrat Hudhaifa has stated that the heart that has no belief loses the quality of keeping trusts. Accordingly he reports : "Then we started talking about vanishing the quality of keeping trust, and the Prophet said : 'When a man goes to one kind of sleep, the trust is squeezed from his heart till its effect remains equal to a point.

Then he goes to another kind of sleep, then the trust shrinks from his heart in such a way as if it were merely a scar: Then the Prophet said: "Then people indulge in buying and selling, but no one can give a thing in trust, so much so that it is said that in a certain family there is a trustworthy man, and about him it is said how tolerant, well-behaved and wise he is although there is not an iota of faith in his heart."

This *Hadith* draws a horrible picture of vanishing the quality of keeping trust from the hearts of dishonest people. It is like finding sparks of goodness in the nature of some mischievous people sometimes, although they have no influence on their lives. And sometimes the good acts overshadow their evil deeds, but it is clear that these acts cannot revive the dead heart. This conscienceless person appraises men on the basis of his desires and preferences. He does not distinguish between faith and infidelity in them.

Keeping trust is a very important quality. Men with weak faith cannot bear it. Allah has given an example of how its burden bears down man's whole existence. Therefore, it should not be considered an ordinary thing and no laxity should be shown in fulfilling its demands:

> *"We did indeed offer the Trust to the Heavens and the Earth and the mountains ; but they refused to undertake it, being afraid thereof ; but man undertook it ; he was indeed unjust and foolish."* *(Ahzab : 72)*

Injustice and ignorance are two evils which beset man's nature, and man has to face the problem of fighting a Jihad against them. His faith cannot be complete without cleaning and purifying it from injustice.

> *"It is those who believe and confuse not their beliefs with wrong-that are (truly) in security, for they are on (right) guidance."* *(Anaam : 82)*

> *"Verily, from among the slaves of Allah those who are learned fear Allah."* *(Fatir : 28)*

This is the reason why after mentioning man's bearing trust in the foregoing verses of Surah Ahzab, it is said that those who are unjust and ignorant indulge in misappropriation, they are hypocrites and are the deserving recipients of Allah's punishment; and security is granted to men of faith and keepers of trust:

> *"(With the result) that Allah has to punish the hypocrites, men and women, and the unbelievers, men and women, and Allah turns in mercy to believers, men and women, for Allah is Oft-Forgiving, Most merciful."* *(Ahzab:73)*

Main Traits

In regard to the classical theories, Hedonism, Cynicism and Stoicism all the moral philosophies are clearly the products of their times. They are called the philosophies of consolation as the collapse of the Greek city states had left no hope of social reconstruction, consequently they consist of advice to individual men for attaining personal salvation. Since men who suffer great catastrophes grasp at pleasure as providing some comfort Hedonism declared that 'pleasure is the sole good', while Cynicism and Stoicism thought it better to announce; 'learn to be indifferent to external influences'!

This was to avoid frustration, heart break and despair in a crumbling world of their times. Cynics were more depressed than stoics. They felt that they were powerless to prevent the collapse of the world in which they lived and hence renounced it. Thus, moral philosophies are the products of their times, while the moral philosophy of Islam is for all time.

It is interesting to note that according to Will Durant 'there are but three systems of ethics, three conceptions of the ideal character and the moral life. One is that of Buddha and Jesus, which stresses the feminine virtues, considers all men to be equally precious, resists evil only by returning good, identifies virtue with love, and inclines in politics to unlimited democracy. Another is the ethic of Machiavelli and Nietzsche, which stresses the masculine virtues, accepts the inequality of men, relishes the risks of combat and conquest and rule, identifies virtue with power, and exalts an hereditary aristocracy.

A third, the ethic of Socrates, Plato, and Aristotle, denies the universal applicability of either the feminine or the masculine virtues; considers that only the informed and mature mind can judge, according to diverse circumstances, when love should rule, and when power; identifies virtue, therefore, with intelligence; and advocates a varying mixture of aristocracy and democracy in government.

'It is the distinction of Spinoza that his ethic unconsciously reconciles these apparently hostile philosophies, weaves them into a harmonious unity which is the supreme achievement of modern thought.' (Will Durant, *Outlines of Philosophy*, pp. 165, 166).

Before we proceed to discuss the moral philosophy of Spinoza who is considered as one of the towering figures in the history of ethics, we deem it necessary to point out that every great religion starts with certain conceptions with regard to the nature of man and the universe. The psychological implication of Buddhism, for instance, is the central fact of pain as a dominating element in the constitution of the universe. Man, as an individual, is helpless against the forces of pain, hence salvation lies in inaction; self-abnegation and unworldliness are the principal virtues.

Similarly Christianity as a religious system is based on the fact of sin. The world is regarded evil and taint of sin is considered as hereditary to man, and man as a force against sin is insufficient, hence stands in need of some supernatural personality to intercede for him with God—a Redeemer is required to get rid of sin. Islam admits that pain and sin certainly exist but the universe is not essentially evil, it can be reformed and the seemingly destructive forces of nature may be brought under control through an appropriate study of them. Now we turn to Spinoza.

He begins by making happiness the goal of conduct and defines happiness in terms of pleasure. He is a relativist, for he holds that nothing is good or bad in itself but is only so in relation to someone. He does not believe in altruism and is a rigid determinist. This is, in a nutshell, his moral philosophy.

In holding happiness as pleasure he seems to have ignored the fact that there is a vast difference between happiness and pleasure. According to Dewey 'there is no such thing strictly speaking as a pleasure; pleasure is pleasantness, an abstract noun designating objects that are pleasant, agreeable. And any state of affairs is pleasant or agreeable which is congenial to the existing state of a person whatever that may be.' As already stated, he remarks:

> *'What is agreeable at one time disagrees at another; what pleases in health is distasteful in fatigue or illness; what annoys or disgusts in a state of repletion is gratifying when one is hungry and eager. And on a higher scale, that which is pleasant to a man of generous disposition arouses aversion in a mean and stingy person. What is pleasant to child may born an adult; the objects that gratify a scholar are repulsive to a poor. Pleasantness and unpleasantness are accordingly signs and symptoms of the things which at a particular time are congenial to a particular make-up of the organism and character. And there is nothing in a symptom of the quality of an existing character which fits it to be a desirable end'*
>
> *(Dewey,* Ethics, *p. 213)*

'Happiness, on the contrary, is a stable condition, because it is dependent not upon what transiently happens to us but upon the standing disposition of the self. One may find happiness in the midst of annoyances; be contented and cheerful inspite of a succession of disagreeable experiences, if one has braveness and equanimity of soul.' Agreeableness or pleasure, he says, depends upon the way a particular event touches us; it tends to focus attention on the self, so that a love of pleasures as such tends to render one selfish or greedy, while happiness is a matter of the disposition we actively bring with us to meet situations, the qualities of mind and heart with which we greet and interpret situations.

'Briefly, happiness as distinct from pleasure is a condition of the self. There is a difference between a tranquil pleasure of the self and tranquillity of mind; there is contentment with external circumstances because they cater to our immediate enjoyment, and there is contentment of character and spirit which is maintained in adverse circumstances' (Dewey, *Ethics*, p. 214).

Happiness is thus much higher and nobler than pleasure. As George Eliot remarked in her novel *Romola* 'it is only a poor sort of happiness that could ever come by caring very much about our own narrow pleasures. We can only have the very highest happinesss, such as goes along with being a great man, by having wide thought and much feeling for the rest of the world as well as ourselves' (Dewey,

Ethics; p. 214). Islam hates the idea of sensualistic evaluation of good as pleasure which is but Hedonistic.

Spinoza is relativist in that he admits that good or bad is only in relation to someone. From this point of view even a bad thing becomes good as a crafty, unscrupulous man considers frauds to be good. Platonism may argue in favour of Spinoza that knowledge is necessary, no wicked act can be committed if the doer knows its nature. But there are men who despite their knowledge of wickedness persist in it. Platonism has no answer to it. Kantian theory may come to defend Spinoza but its categorical imperative which means 'Do unto others as you would have them do unto you' will be of no avail and becomes inoperative in case there is a clash between one's own benefit and benefit of others.

There are occasions when self-love is uncontrollable and men have strong tendency to treat their own satisfaction as of higher value. Without the backing of moral character neither Platonism nor Kantian theory can be successful, let alone Spinoza who is a relativist to the core. Islam, therefore, lays great emphasis on moral character and builds it in its own way as specified above. Spinoza does not believe in altruism—regard for others as a principle of action. He is more inclined towards egoism—a theory which regards self-interest as the foundation of morality. The problem is that of the relation of egoism and altruism, of regard for self and regard for others, of self-love and benevolence. The issue concerns the motivation of moral act.

It is generally held that men are moved only by self-love or regard for their own self, i.e., selfishness. But 'acts are not selfish because they evince consideration for the future well-being of the self. No one would say that deliberate care for one's own health, efficiency and progress in learning is bad because it is one's own. It is moral duty upon occasion to look out for oneself in these respects. Such acts acquire the quality of moral selfishness only when they are indulged in so as to manifest obtuseness to the claims of others. An act is not wrong because it advances the well-being of the self, but because it is unfair, inconsiderate, in respect to the rights and just claims of others. Self-sustaining and self-protective acts are, moreover, conditions of all acts which are of service to others.

Any moral theory which fails to recognize the necessity of acting sometimes with special care and conscious regard for oneself is suicidal; to fail to care for one's health or even one's material well-being may result in incapacitating one for doing anything for others (Dewey, *Ethics*, p. 326).

Here it becomes clear that regard for self, if it is conscious, is regard for others. It is only the blind regard for self which is injurious to others as it often results in a war of all against all. The point becomes more clear if we study the Quranic verse (3 : 92) in its proper perspective. The verse is: 'By no means shall ye attain righteousness unless ye give of that which ye love.' The test of charity is: Do you give something which you love or value greatly?

The problem is of altruism and self-sacrifice which has been admirably solved by the Prophet. As related by Anas, Abu Talha, having heard of this fresh revelation, came to the Prophet and offered his highly valued garden to be given in charity. The Prophet appreciated the spirit but advised him to distribute it among his own relatives. Further, when Umar approached the Prophet and asked his opinion as to giving away, in charity, his best garden in Khyber, the Prophet advised him to keep the garden for himself and give away only the produce in charity. This proves that Regard for others is not disregard for self. The self is to be cared for and developed so that it may be of greater service to others. But this does not mean thoughtless development of self nor does it mean self-destruction but it means a careful development having in mind one's duties to others. This is the meaning of altruism in Islam, but spinoza is unaware of it.

A rich man is not supposed to live like an ascetic, for God, as said the Prophet, likes to see the traces of His bounty in his creature. 'Say: who hath forbidden the beautiful (gifts) of God which He hath produced for his servants, and the things clean and pure (which He hath provided) for sustenance?' is the Quranic verse. The gifts of God are to be utilized properly and not to be spent extravagantly: 'O ye who believe! Squander not your wealth in varieties (4 : 29). What is essentially required of man is the harmonious development of body and soul together. 'Thy soul has a right on you, thy body has a right on you' are the words of the Prophet which point to the importance of life in equilibrium and moderation.

General Well-being

The conception of common good, of general well-being, demands the full development of individuals. Only when individuals are well developed that they are better able to make sacrifice and serve the interests of others. Perhaps, it is on this account that the saying is: 'Regard for self is regard for others.' But, in Islam, this refers not to blind regard but to thoughtful regard for self which reminds it of its duties to others. Here it may be said that the Quran praises those 'who prefer others above themselves though poverty become their lot' (59 : 9). But this relates to grave situations which demand wholesale sacrifice or self-surrender. The Helpers at Medina, for instance, offered full help to those who, leaving all their property of Mecca, had migrated to Medina for the clause of God. Abu Bakr, for example, offered whole of has property to defend Islam on the occasion of expedition to Tabuk. On such occasions we have to surrender all that we have and even our own self. Spinoza is a rigid determinist.

To him, all things come and pass according to the eternal order and fixed laws of Nature and man can liberate himself from the pain and anxieties of this world if he understands that the course of Nature is predestined. In this, respect he is similar to the Stoics who find salvation in the 'Philosophy of Indifference' which is, in fact, the life of inertness.

Islam is dynamic and has no liking for inertia: 'And neglect not thy portion of this world; but be bounteous to others even as God hath been to thee and seek not to work mischief in the land. Verily, God loveth not the mischief-makers' is the Quranic verse (28 : 77), which enjoins man not to be inert and sluggish but to work hard and earn as much as possible by fair means so that he may satisfy his own needs and be of help to his brethren-in-want. The real happiness in life is that which comes to man in being bounteous to others as God has been to him. Charity has its own reward.

Spinoza, like Stoics, is obsessed with the idea of predestination but Islam solves it in its own way.

Good Behaviour

As described by Aristotle 'moral act is that the doer of the moral deed must have a certain state of mind' in doing it. First, he must know what he is doing; secondly, he must choose it, and choose it itself, and thirdly, the act must be the expression of a formed and stable character. In other words the act must be voluntary; that is, it must manifest a choice, and for full morality at least, the choice must be an expression of the general tenor and set of personality. It must involve awareness of what one is about; a fact which in the concrete signifies that there must be a purpose, an aim, an end in view, something for the sake of which the particular act is done' (Dewey, *Ethics*, p. 176).

A moral act, according to the above description, must be the expression of a formed and stable character. But a character of this nature is rarely to be found. No human being can claim to have an absolutely formed character unless he is especially trained so as to find pleasure in right objects and pain in wrong ends. This requires not only moral education of an excellent type but also an ideal to be followed. Nowhere can these prerequisites be found except in Islam which provides such education in the form of the Quran and an ideal in the life of the Prophet. The best course therefore is to think of moral act in the light of Divine revelation, for human thought, unaided by such knowledge, cannot discern the true values and standards of conduct. So, an act is good or bad exclusively because God has attributed this quality to it.

'To the Muslims', says Anderson, 'there is an ethical quality in every human action, characterized by *qubh* (ugliness, unsuitability) on the one hand or *husn* (beauty, suitability) on the other. But this ethical quality is not such as can be perceived by human reason; instead, man is completely dependent in this matter on Divine revelation. Thus all human actions are subsumed, according to a widely accepted classification, under five categories: as commanded, recommended, left legally indifferent, reprehended, or else prohibited by Almighty God. And it is only in regard to the middle category (i.e. those things which are left legally indifferent) that there is in theory any scope for human legislation'. (Anderson, *Islamic Law in the Modern World*, p. 3).

A survey of moral theories discloses the fact that the philosophers and thinkers have differed greatly in their opinions as to the morality of an act. There are some like Bentham who judge the goodness of an act by its consequences, others like kant by its motive, for consequences are often out of control, still others who hold an act to be good or bad by its approbation and disapprobation, praise and blame. But viewed critically, consequences do not seem to be enough to justify goodness or badness of an act, for sometimes a bad act ends in good consequences, for example, a man throws his dagger to kill his enemy but it hits his malignant tumour and instead of being killed, he is relieved of his pain.

Similarly, approbation and disapprobation cannot be the standards of moral judgement as even the most immoral customs may be praised. Female infanticide for instance, was considered to be good in pre-Islamic Arabia. Approbation and disapprobation only represent the scheme of moral values which is embodied in the social habits of a particular group. Thus a-militant community admires and praises acts of bravery; an industrialized community sets its value on amassing wealth. Hence acts are not esteemed because they are virtuous; rather they are virtuous because they are supported by social approval. The only thing that morally counts may be the motive that inspires the act and from which the act is done. Consequences, as already stated, are often out of control. According to the Prophet 'a person who has no-knowledge of medicine, yet pretends to be a doctor, is responsible for the consequences of his act'. He cannot be excused. The act itself being fraudulent, motive counts for nothing Acts are good or bad according to the classification as specified above, the importance of motive, in Islam, is due to the fact that it helps in determining the reward or punishment applicable to the act. The act, as it were a thing to be judged by the motive from which it is done, hence the Prophet's saying: Acts are determined by their motives'. For further illustration we cite the example of a person who spends his wealth in charity.

The act is, no doubt, 'good and recommended yet he may not be rewarded or if rewarded, the reward may be less than what it ought to be. This is according to his motive. If his deed of charity proceeds from ostentation and show there may be no reward or the reward may be less than what it ought to be. Acts are thus determined by their motives. Migration, for instance, is a good act and recommended for the believers to save themselves and their religion but according to the Prophet there is difference between a believer who migrates for the sake of a woman and he how migrates for the cause of God. Their acts will be determined by their motives. They will receive reward or punishment according to their motives. This is the peculiarity of Islamic morality. It searches out what is in most in the heart.

Behaving Ideally

The Quran is the code of moral conduct. Conduct and character are considered to have the same meaning. The word character expresses continuity of action. According to Aristotle 'we are what we repeatedly do'. For Schopenhauer, character is continuity of purpose and attitude. It lies in the will, not in the intellect. A good will', says he, is profounder and more reliable than a clear mind. Brilliant qualities of mind win admiration, but never affection; and 'all religions promise a reward for excellencies of the will or heart but none for excellencies of head or understanding.'

To Dewey, self-hood is expressive of character, the self, as it were, reveals its nature in what it chooses'. In consequence, a judgement upon an act is also judgement upon the character. Only that man is good who does good deeds. 'The goodness of goodman', as Aristotle said, 'shines through his deeds.'

In Islam, character lies in *taqwa*. The word *taqwa* is noteworthy for its importance as it forms the standard of judging the greatness of man: 'The most honoured among you is *atqakum* or the most God-fearing of you' (49 : 13). Says the Prophet: "The Arab is not superior to non-Arab, nor a non-Arab is superior to an Arab; neither the White to the Black nor the Black to the White except on the basis of *taqwa* or fear of God."

To start with, we refer to the Caliph Umar who once asked Ubay b. Kaab (a companion of the Prophet and distinguished for his knowledge of the Quran) as to the meaning of taqwa, who, in answer, asked Umar whether he had ever passed through prickly shrubs and, if so, how he managed to save himself from the pricks. To this Umar replied that he drew together his robe and held it firm. This, very act, said Ubay, is taqwa. Literally the word 'taqwa' means abstinence from what is harmful but it is generally used to express a life of piety. Ghazzali defines it as the 'eschewing of each and every thing that may be detrimental to faith'. In the Quran it is used in various senses, i.e. 'to fear God' in the verse: 'Enter houses through the proper door and fear God *ittaqu* (2 : 189); 'to act aright' in the verse: 'God likes those who act aright', '*muttaqin*' (9 : 4); 'to guard against evil' in the verse: 'And had they believed, and guarded themselves from evil', *attaqu*, better would have been the reward from their Lord' (2 : 103); 'right conduct', in the verse: 'And take a provision (with you) for the journey but the best of the provisions is right conduct, taqwa (2 : 197); 'piety and righteousness' in the verse: 'By the soul and Him Who balanced it, and endowed it with the talent to distinguish wickedness from piety', *taqwa* (91: 7,8). *Taqwa* is also used as opposed to transgression in the verse: 'Help ye one another in righteousness and piety', *taqwa*, and do not help in sin and transgression (5 : 2). And the Prophet has used it in the sense of 'guarding oneself against doubtful things'. He says: 'What is lawful and unlawful is evident, yet there are some doubtful cases not known to many of the people. He who guarded himself or *taqa* against doubtful things saved his faith and himself from what is unlawful' (Bukhari). On another occasion he has used this word in the sense of righteousness: 'The believer will not be righteous or *muttaqi* unless he refrains from what is unlawful in favour of what is lawful' (Tirmidhi). All this is to stress the point that one should live in strict conformity with the law of God.

Heart, as said the Prophet, is the seat of taqwa and this makes it clear that 'taqwa', in its real sense, is the fear of God which springs from the heart and expresses itself in righteous deeds. The fear of God is not the fear of a coward or of a child but of a man who wishes to avoid harm to himself and to others. And, indeed, it is the fear out of love and reverence for such a One Who has been Most Gracious and Most Merciful. The lover, in this case refrains from all such acts as would displease the object of his love. The fear of God is, therefore, out of love for God, and this is the height of morality and good sense that accords the lover a distinct place as a man of character. Character is, in fact, the mark or peculiarity which distinguishes one from the other. And, in Islam, this is in point of taqwa, so character lies in 'taqwa'.

Islam, therefore, lays great stress upon character building. Here we refer to the pillars of Islam : *I man* Salat, Sawn, *Zakat* and *Hajj*. These play a significant part in building the character. *I man* or Belief in the Unity of God aims at the Unity of Man; Salat or Prayer, five times a day, regularly reminds the believer of his duties to God and to his creatures and in its continuity and consistency is a series of acts to form a stable character on piety and righteousness; *Sawn* or Tasting, which extends over the whole month of Ramadan in each lunar year, is to teach self-restraint and to make the believer aware of the hardships that the poor and the needy are confronted with and, thus, to awaken in him the feelings of sympathy for them; *Zakat* or Poor-due is a tax collected by the Government for the help of economically depressed classes and for such as are mentioned in the Quranic verse (9 : 60), it is self-sacrifice on the part of the believer and serves to ensure social security; Hajj or Pilgrimage is to be performed at least once in the lifetime, by those who can afford the journey to Mecca (the sacred sanctuary of Muslims), its social aspect cannot be exaggerated as it affords the opportunity for the believers to meet together and confer with regard to social welfare of the community. While *Zakat* is to teach self-sacrifice,*Hajj* teaches the etiquette of social life and social behaviour.

These are the pillars of Islam devised in such a manner that they serve to purify the soul of man, and keep in check his desires. Desire is an emotion that is directed to the possession of some object from which pleasure is expected. Desire is often so personal that its satisfaction leads men to deviate from the right path. To control such desires has seemed more fundamental than their satisfaction and it is well said that it is better, by far, to be a human being dissatisfied than a pig satisfied.

Here the question arises of, human nature as to what it is like. While most of the philosophers hold it to be evil, Islam sas that it is pure and good, as man is created in the goodliest form (95 : 4). Yet it cannot be denied that man is liable to fall a prey to the temptations, for our senses and appetites are solely concerned with external things such as commit us to situations we cannot control. The solution lies in control, but the question is: 'Can we control ourselves?'

The superiority of Islam lies in this that it has its ways and means to capture and block up the very source of evil. For this purpose it adopts two methods:

1. Moral education, and
2. Purification of soul—a sort of pincers movement.

Moral education, according to Aristotle, is character training which a person receives in a good city, but this is a vague definition and bears no comparison to moral education of Islam which aims at the development of character which avoids evils and takes pleasure in righteous deeds, and which according to Iqbal, awakens in man the higher consciousness of his manifold relations with God and the Universe. The character training received by the believer, under the instructions contained in the Quran, is exemplary as was the character of the Prophet of whom the Quran speaks highly: 'A noble pattern have yet in the Messenger of God' (33 : 21).

The character of the Prophet was that of the Quran itself, as said Aishah, his wife. He actually practised what was revealed to him. His message is for all mankind. He exemplified in his deeds the moral and spiritual law and proclaimed that 'he was sent in order to complete the virtues of character' (Waliuddin, al-Tabrize, *Mishkat*, vol. 2, p. 632). To him 'an accomplished Muslim is he who is best in character'.

While the Quran and the life of the Prophet supply the believer with the best moral education, the Pillars of Islam purify his soul to such an extent that he is transformed into a God-fearing and God-conscious being. He feels the presence of God at every turn and movement in his life and his actions are the result of careful deliberation so that he may not incur the wrath of God. This attitude towards life is a key to self-control and to the success and prosperity of man : 'He succeeds who purifies it (soul), and he fails who corrupts it' (91 :9, 10). Such is the procedure adopted by Islam to build a character, stable and virtuous in form, for no moral theory can be successful without the virtues of character.

Referring to the moral theory of Kant we have to say that he seems to have drawn upon Islamic teaching and particularly the saying of the Prophet :

> *"Wish for your brother (i.e. others), what you wish for yourself; he has no faith who wishes not for his brother what he wishes for himself (Bukhari). This corresponds*

> *to Kant's categorical imperative: , 'So act as to treat humanity, whether in thine own person, or in that of any other, in every case as an end withal, never as a means only. It is in other words, 'Do unto others as you would have them do unto you'. But the Prophet's saying as above, not only precedes the formula of Kant but is much higher in point of morality as the full text of his saying as given by Bukhari in his Al-Adab al-*Mufrad *is : 'He has no faith who wishes not for his brother (i.e. others) what he wishes for himself 'of the good'. The words 'of the good' are remarkable in that they mean that none should wish for the other except What is good, not so in Kantian theory.*

From the above it is evident that Kant affirms what Islam established centuries ago but he failed to observe that man's character is the basis of morality. His theory is defunct without the backing of character. Islam, therefore, emphasizes the importance of character and also builds it in the manner specified above, hence the morality preached by Islam is deep rooted and most effective. No moral theory, except that of Islam, is complete and comprehensive.

Chapter 3

Religious Doctrines and Faith

Relation of Man with Allah

In the Islamic scheme of cultural reconstruction, the basis of social system is the family. The family is the unit of social system and a miniature society. Just as affection, rights and duties are organizing principles of the family, in the same way they are organizing principles of the society as a whole, which is conceived as a larger family or the family of God. The members of this larger family are brothers and sisters to one another. Thus, the Holy Prophet said:

> *"All creatures make the family of God. God loves him more who treats His family folks well". Another Tradition says: 'All human beings are brothers (and sisters) to one another'.* (Muslim, Abu Daud).

In order to understand a social system, knowledge of three things is needed. They are: the nature of the family, the nature of human life, and the duties of man in life.

Family Attributes

A. *God has created all human beings from a single pair of common parents:*

O mankind! We created

You from a single (pair)

Of a male and a female, *(XLIX - 13)*

The Holy Prophet aid:

> *'All human beings are the children of Adam, and Adam was created out of clay'.* (Tabri)

B. *All men are sinless and holy by birth. The Quran speaks of "God's handiwork according to the pattern on which He has made mankind" (XXX - 30).*

The Holy Prophet says that 'every child is born according to the original pattern of nature'. According to this original pattern, every man is sinless and Holy.

C. *Human beings are superior to other creatures:*

We have honoured the sons

Of Adam (XVII - 70)

We have indeed created man

In the best of moulds, (XCV - 4)

There is a Hadith-i-Qudsi which says:

The creature (man) whom I have created with my own Hands and breathed of my Spirit unto him — I shall never put him on a par with those creatures for whom I merely said: 'Be' and they came into being.

(Mishkat, *Bab Badil Khalq)*

D. All human beings have been addressed by the Word of God (revelation)

... and to every people

A guide (XIII - 7)

And there never was

A people, without a warner

Having lived among them

(in the past) (XXXV 24)

E. *God has provided equal opportunities for all.*

'God has created all that is there on the earth for the benefit of all of you', says the Quran. The Holy Prophet says:

'Except three things man does not have a right on anything else: (1) A house to live in; (2) Garments to cover the body and (3) Water and pieces of bread.'

Life of Man

(A) *The Lord of life is, not man, but God*

God hath purchased all the Believers

Their persons and Their goods (IX-111)

(B) *Life is not a futile activity; it is trust*

Did ye think
That We had created you
In jest, and that ye
Would not be brought back
To Us (for account)? (XXIII - 115)

(C) *Life is not absolutely independent or free; there are certain laws governing it.*

Does Man think
That he will be left
Uncontrolled, (without purpose)? *(LXXV-36)*

Man has two kinds of duties in life:

(1) duties related to the universe and
(2) duties related to man.

Duties Related to the Universe

(A) It means making use of human faculties to deploy the things of the universe for man's use:

It is We Who have
Blessed you with authority
On earth, and provided
You therein with means
For the fulfilment of your life *(VII - 10)*
Say: work (righteousness):
Soon will God observe your work,
And His Apostle, and the Believers. *(IX - 105)*

(B) *The means of subsistence should be developed so much that nobody may remain deprived of his living:*

And We have provided therein
Means of subsistence, — for you
And for those for whose subsistence
Ye are not responsible *(XV - 20)*
It is He Who has
Spread out the earth
For (His creatures). *(LV—10)*

(C) *Through labour and striving man should develop the things of nature:*

That man can have nothing
But what he strives for *(LIII - 39)*

... to them
We shall pay (the prize
Of) their deed therein *(XI - 15)*

The means of human power keep changing according to circumstances. For example, in modern times we have weapons like the rifles, the missiles, the machine gun, the tank etc. and then we have technology, industry, modern trade and commerce, journalism, literature and modern arts and science. All these things go to make up modern civilized life.

The Centrality of God in Matters of Duties : In matters of duties towards the universe and in all affairs of human activity, God should have a central place, and subordination to him should be recognised. Otherwise dreadful consequences may follow and such dreadful consequences can be seen in the materialistic civilization of our times. This is why in those verses of the Quran where attention is drawn towards the order of the Universe and man is encouraged to subject the universe to himself God has been mentioned or suggested in some way.

This indicates that for man's activity in the Universe God has a central place and man must subject himself to him. Only then, his reason and experience can guide him properly and further instruction may not be necessary.

Men's Responsibilities

It must be recognised that all human beings are involved with one another, so that if one human being is unjustly killed, it is as if the whole people were killed, and if one human being has been saved from destruction, it is as if the whole human race were saved from destruction. The Quran says that if anyone slew a person:

It would be as if
He slew the whole people:
And if anyone saved a life,
It would be as if he saved
The life of the whole people. *(V - 35)*

Every individual must be deemed responsible for taking care of the other. This care-taking may be material as well as moral and spiritual. The individual will specialise in that sphere of responsibility with which he is more conversant.

Matter in Life

Regarding material responsibility the Quran says:

Serve God and join not
Any partners with Him,
And do good—
To parents, kinsfolk,
Orphans, those in need,
Neighbours who are near,
Neighbours who are strangers,
Companions by your side,
The wayfarer (ye meet),
And what your right hands possess *(IV.36)*
And render to the kindred
Their due rights, as (also)
To those in want,
And to the wayfarer:
But squander not (your wealth)
In the manner of a spendthrift. *(XVII.26)*

As regards subordinates and juniors the Holy Prophet says:

They are your brothers. Allah has made them subordinate or junior to you. He to whom makes his brother subordinate must give him to eat what he himself eats, give him to wear what he himself wears, and must not have assign him any work which he himself cannot do, or if he assigns him such a work he must himself help him, as a co-worker. (Bukhari, *Kitabul Iman).*

Special commandment is given regarding treatment towards women:

On the contrary live with them
On a footing of kindness and equality.

If ye take a dislike to them
It may be that ye dislike
A thing, and God brings about
Through it a great deal of good. *(IV. 19)*
Let the man or means
spend according
To his means:
And the man
Whose resources are restricted,
Let him spend according
To what God has given him. *(LXV - 7)*

In his sermon on the occasion of his last Hajj, the Holy Prophet said:

In your dealings with women fear God. You have made a convenant with them that God has a witness.
(Muslim; Mishkat, *Bab Hajjatul Wida)*

Regarding treatment with human beings, in general, the Holy Prophet said: 'He who is engaged to fulfil the need of his brother, his need, Allah is engaged to fulfil.' At another place he said: 'The human creature does not become a complete Believer until he chooses for his brother what he chooses for himself.'

Regarding moral and spiritual duties the Quran says:

O ye who believe!
Save yourselves and your
Families from a Fire
Whose fuel is men
And Stone. *(LXVI-6)*
Help ye one another
In righteousness and piety. *(V-3)*

The Holy Prophet said: 'Listen everyone of you is a care-taker or a shephered; and everyone of you will be asked about his care-taking of those who are put under his care'.
(Bukliari, *Kitabun Nikah)*

Giving Priority to the Needs of Others Over One's Own Needs : One must always give priority to the needs of others over one's own needs. The Quran says:

By no means shall ye
Attain righteousness unless
Ye give (freely) of that
Which ye love. *(III-92)*

What has been recognised as the greatest virtue of the Helpers (Ansars) is the spirit of sacrifice. Attention is drawn to it in the following Verse of the Quran.

It is said that the helpers:

Give them (refugees) preference
Over themselves, even though
Povery was their (own lot). *(LIX-9)*

Commandment to Overlook the Defects of Others : One must meet out good treatment of others in spite of their defects, shortcomings and wrongs.

The Quran says

Let not those among you
Who are endued with grace
And amplitude of means
Resolve by oath against helping
Their kinsmen, those in want,
And those who have left
Their homes in God's cause,
Let them forgive and overlook;
Do you not wish
That God should forgive you?
For God is Oft-Forgiving,
Most merciful. *(XXIV-22)*

The historical context of the revelation of this Verse is as follows.

Some people made a false accusation against Aisha. Among them were some relations of Abu Bakr, whom Abu Bakr supported financially. After the innocence of Aisha had been established Abu Bakr felt bad about the relations whom he supported. He took an oath not to support them. Seeing him do it other companions also did the same regarding their relations.

In the context of this situation, the above Verse was revealed. It says that the bad deeds of others are for them. You must not change your good behaviour towards them. The reward is with God; always have hope of getting it from Him and pleasing Him.

Thigs Necessary for the Maintenance of Social System : The following things are Necessary for the maintenance of the social system:

(1) The standard of honour should be such as to encompass all the people and to be equaly applicable to all of them.

(2) The idols of the distinction of race, family colour and nationality should be broken down.

(3) There should be equality and amity regarding human relations on the level of practical life.

These factors have been given great attention in the Islamic scheme of cultural reconstruction. Some details in this regad would bring them home.

Respect as Prescribed

Instead of the family, wealth, race etc., the standard of honour is character and moral behaviour. This standard can be acquired voluntarily and it is also acceptable to all human beings. The Quran says:

verily ...verily

The most honoured of you

In the sight of God

Is (He who is) the most

Righteous of you. *(XLIX-13)*

The Holy Prophet said: 'One person earns excellence over the other only on the basis of righteousness and piety'. (Mishkat, *fi Shoabil Iman)*

It is very difficult to demolish the idols of race, family etc. Various efforts to do so were made in every age, but without leading to much success.

But the Prophet of Islam (peace be upon him) adopted such devices in domestic and social life that people, both of inferior and superior status, began to feel that these man-made distinction of "high" and "low" had no validity.

Islam first campaigned for the reform and purification of the minds and then it declared that the distinctions mentioned above were invalid and insignificant.

And made you into
Nations and tribes, that
Ye may know each other
(not that ye may despise each other). *(XLIX-13)*

The Holy prophet said:

No Arab excels over a non-Arab, nor does a non-Arab excel over an Arab.

(Mishkat, *Khutba Hajjatul Wida')*

About colour and language the Quran says: 'And among the signs of God are the creation of the heavens and the earth and the differences of language and colour.

The above distinctions emerge more prominently in matters of marriage, and involve many complexities and subtleties. For this reason, the Holy Prophet and his Companions began the charity at home and broke the idols of these distinctions.

The Holy Prophet got his cousin Zainab married to a freed slave, Zaid b. Harisa. Omar got married his son Asim to a milk-seller's widowed daughter. Both these evidences are famous in Islamic history. After reforming his own home Omar gave verdict in favour of marriage without the consent of the guardians, which is called 'marriage without sufficient conditions' *(Ghair Kafu).*

The following incident bears it out. A rich man Mawali, who was one of the freed slaves, sent a proposal for marrying the sister of a Quraish. The Quraish refused saying: 'We are people of a high family. The man does not suffice for my daughter. When Omar came to know of it he sent for the Quraish and said that the man was well to do as well as righteous.

If his sister was willing he should wed her to him. The Quraish asked his sister and she expressed her willingness, and the wedding was performed. *(Siyasat—i—Farooq-i-Azam,* Izalatul Khifa, Maqsad II)

Jurists have discussed at length *Kafu* or sufficient conditions for marriage, but in modern times it need not be a subject of discussion. The discussion of the jurists is guided by considerations of compromise with the circumstances.

It is not a verdict of the Shariah. The subject came up for discussion after the time of the Holy Prophet and his Companions and stirred up great controversy among the jurists. Among the conditions considered sufficient for marriage are bravery, good family, vocation, financial status, age and religion (moral character). But except religion all the other requisites are subject to controversy. The fact that all the jurists agree on the point of religion and disagree on all other points itself goes to prove that only religion is the condition laid down by the Shariah.

The other requisites or conditions are there only for making matrimonial life comfortable.

In modern time the other requisite 'sufficiency' obstruction to marriage and become a blot which is an Islamic culture. Hence in our scheme of cultural reconstruction we would consider religion *plus* social status as sufficient conditions for marriage, which were considered so in the era of Prophethood, too.

In our scheme education and the ability of earning livelihood should become more important since these are the demands of our time. These factors certainly go to make matrimonial life comfortable.

Marriage and Society

Marriage forms the basis of the institution of the family and acts as a safeguard against promiscuity and the sowing of wild oats. The Quran says:

It is He Who has
Created man from water:
Then has He established
Relationship of lineage
And marriage: *(XXV - 54)*
Your wives are
As a tilth unto you
So approach your tilth
When or how you will;
But do some good act
For your souls beforehand; *(II - 223)*

The point of the comparison of the wife to a tilth is that sexual relation is meant, not merely for the purpose of satisfying sexual desire, but for the purpose of ensuring the survival of the human race.

As the cultivator has the responsibility of not merely sowing the seed but also of providing what the land needs and of protecting it, so has the husband similar responsibilities towards his wife.

Role of Man in Family

It is natural for man to be the head of the family. Owing to the natural differences between the two sexes, man is more disposed to being active and tough while woman is more disposed to be passive and soft. Besides, man shoulders the responsibility of earning livelihood for the family.

The Quran says:

Men are the protectors
And maintainers of women,
Beacuse God has given
The one more (strength)
Than the other, and because
They support them
From their means. (IV - 34)

The Holy Prophet said:

Man is the care-taker of his wife and children. In this matter he is answerable to God. (Bukhari, Kitabun Nikah).

Benefits to Women

The recognition of the superiority of man makes no difference to the rights of woman, nor does it make man entitled to greater rewards for good deeds and virtuous behaviour. "Women have rights on men just as men have rights on women', says the Quran. At another place it is said: 'Men will earn their rewards according to their deeds, and women will earn their rewards according to theirs'. *(IV - 32)*

Purity of Mind and Heart : Islam has confined sexual relations to matrimonial life, and has commanded us to have hearts and minds purified of lustful desires as far as possible. For this purpose, it has emphasized the notion of answerability to God, which is an effective means of maintaining chastity. Thus, the Quran says:

Whether
Ye show what is in your minds
Or conceal it, God
Calleth you to account for it. *(II - 284)*

Say: 'Whether ye hide
What is in your hearts
Or reveal it,
God knows it all. (III - 29)

Seeing the Right

Men are forbidden to stare at women brazenly, for such stares stimulate erotic feelings:

Say to the believing men
That they should lower
Their gaze and guard
Their modesty: that will make
Far greater purity for them:
And God is well-acquainted
With all that they do.
And say to the believing women
That they should lower
Their gaze and guard
Their modesty; (XXIV - 30)

Women have been commanded to exercise control over their speech and voice, for these things too may stimulate erotic feelings.

If ye do fear (God),
Be not too complaisant
Of speech, lest one
In whose heart is
A disease should be moved
With desire: but speak ye
A speech (that is) just. (XXXIII - 32)

Scandal-Mongering and Immodest Talk Prohibited : Indulging in scandals and immodest talk has been prohibited:

Those who love (to see)
Scandal published broadcast
Among the Believers, will have
A grievous Penalty in this life
And in the Hereafter (XXIV - 19)

Exhibition of Beauty and Immodest Dress Prohibited : Exhibition of beauty has been prohibited because it stimulates erotic feelings — 'make not a dazzling display, like that of the former Times of Ignorance (XXXIII - 33). Tight and thin or transparent dress has also been forbidden, for it also involves exhibition of the body. Women 'should draw their veils over their bosoms' (XXIV - 31). The Holy Prophet said:

> *'The women who exhibit their bodies even after dressing up and thus try to attract others to themselves or to be attracted towards others; and the women who walk mincingly with their neck bent like that of a camel — such women will not enter paradise, nor will they catch even its fragrance'.*
>
> (Muslim, *Babul Nisa Al Kasiyatul' Aariyat).*

Coming out wearing some perfume is also prohibited. The Holy Prophet said:

> *'The woman who passes by people wearing perfumes so that they may be pleased is in fact a woman who is inviting immorality.* (Nisai, Abu Daud)

Prohibition Against Meeting of Man and Woman in Privacy: The meeting of man and woman in privacy has been prohibited because it would give an opportunity for Satan to do his work. Do not seek to meet those women in privacy who are not your close relations, for Satan circulates in man like blood *(Muslim,* Kitabul Libas wal Zinah)

Concept of Punishment

Punishment is divided into three classes:

Hadd, Tazir, and Qisas.

1. Hadd is that punishment which is said to have been ordained of God in the Quran and the Hadith, and which must be inflicted. The following belong to this class:- Adultery, for which the adulterer is stoned. Fornication, for which one hundred stripes are inflicted. Drunkenness, for which there are eighty stripes. The slander of a married person, that is, bringing a false charge of adultery against a married person, for which the offender must receive eighty lashes.

   This punishment is said to have been instituted by God, when 'Aishah, the favourite wife of "the Prophet," was falsely charged with adultery! Apostacy, for which the Murtad, or Apostate, is killed, unless he repent of his error within three days. When an

Apostate from Islam has been killed according to the law, or has left the country, his property goes to those of his heirs who still remain Musulmans (vide the "Al Siraji").

2. Tazir is that punishment which is said to have been ordained of God, but of which there are not special injunctions, the exact punishment being left to the discretion of the Qadi, or Judge.
3. Qisas (lit. "retaliation") is that punishment which can be remitted by the person offended against, upon the payment of a fine or compensation. The punishment for murder is of this class. The next akin to the murdered person can either take the life of his kinsman's murderer, or accept a money compensation (Diat). There is also retaliation in case of wounds. Qisas is the lex talionis of Moses, "eye for eye, tooth for tooth, hand for hand, foot for foot, burning for burning, wound for wound, stripe for stripe" (vide Exodus xxi. 24). But in allowing a money compensation for murder, Muhammad departed from the Jewish code.

No animal is lawful food unless it be slaughtered according to the Muhammadan law, namely, by drawing the knife across the throat and cutting the windpipe, the carotid arteries, and the gullet, repeating at the same time the words "Bismillah Allaho Akbar, i.e. "In the name of the great God." A clean animal, so slaughtered, becomes lawful food.

In the "Sharah Waqia it is said that the following creatures are lawful (halal):-

1. Those animals that are cloven-footed and chew the cud, and are not beasts of prey.
2. Birds that do not seize their prey with their claws, or wound them with their bills, but pick up food with their bills.
3. Fish; but no other animals which move in the water.
4. Locusts.

Some commentators say that the horse is lawful; but it is generally held to be "makruh". Fish found dead in the water is unlawful; but if it be taken out and die afterwards it is lawful.

Alligators, turtles, crabs, snakes, frogs, etc., are unlawful. Wine is expressly forbidden in the Quran; and, in the judgement of the learned, this prohibition extends to whatever has a tendency to intoxicate, such as opium, bhang, charas,' and tobacco.

The Akhund of Swat his issued several "fatwahs," prohibiting the use of tobacco; but the chilam (or pipe), having become a national institution, no notice has been taken of the inhibition. The Wahabis do not permit territory, the huqqa, or chilam, is never allowed in a mosque.

A Kind of Obligatory Action

Farz-i-Kifaya are those commands which are imperative (farz); but which, if one person in eight or ten perform, it is equivalent to all having performed it.

1. To return a salutation.
2. To visit the sick, and inquire after their welfare.
3. To follow a bier on foot to the grave.
4. To accept an invitation.
5. To reply to a sneeze, e.g. if a person sneeze, and say immediately afterwards, "God be praised" (Alhamdo lillah), it is incumbent upon at least one of the party to exclaim, "God have mercy on you" (Yarhamuk Allah).

There is an interesting chapter on the custom of saluting after sneezing in Ishaq Israeli's "Curiosities of Literature," from, which it appears that it is almost universal amongst nations.

Fitrat (lit. "nature") is said to be certain ancient practices of the prophets before the time of Muhammad, which have not been forbidden by him.

In the Hadith "Muslim," the customs of fitrat are said to be ten in number.

1. The clipping of the mustach, so that they do not enter the mouth.
2. Not cutting or shaving the beard.
3. Cleaning the teeth (i.e., miswak).
4. Cleansing the nostrils with water at the usual ablutions.
5. Cutting the nails.
6. Cleaning the finger-joints.
7. Pulling out the hairs under the arms.
8. Cleansing the mouth with water at thc time of ablution.

Greetings

The usual Islamic salutation is "as salamu alikum," i.e. "The peace of God be with you."

When a person makes a "salam," and any of the assembly rise and return it, it is considered sufficient-for the whole company.

The lesser number should always be the first to salute the greater; he who rides should salute him who walks; he who walks, him who stands; the stander, the sitter, etc. A man should not salute a woman on the road; and it is considered very disrespectful to salute with the left hand, that hand being used for legal ablutions.

The ordinary salute is made by raising the right hand either to the breast or to the forehead.

In Central Asia the salutation is generally given without any motion of the hand or body.

Pupils salute their masters by kissing, the hand or sleeve, which is the usual salutation made to men of eminent piety.

Homage is paid by kissing the feet of the ruler, or by kissing the ground or carpet.

In Afghanistan, conquered people pay homage by casting their turbans at the feel of the conqueror; and the heads of tribes often lessen the size of their turbans before appearing in the presence of their rulers. Shariat is the code of law for the Islamic way of life. The word Shariat means a clear straight path or example. It is the best system of law from Allah for humanity to follow. Shariat, or Islamic law, is the code of conduct for Muslims and is based on two main sources: the Quran and the Sunnah of the Prophet. It aims at the success and welfare of mankind both in this life and the life-after-death. Shariat prescribes a complete set of laws for the guidance of mankind so that Good (Maraf) is established and Evil (Munkar) is removed from society. It provides a clear and straight path which leads to progress and fulfilment in life and the attainment of Allah's pleasure.

The Quran is the main basis of Shariat. It states the principles while the Sunnah of the Prophet provides the blueprint of how to apply them. For example, the Quran says: establish Salat, observe Sawm, pay Zakat, take decisions by consultation, do not earn or spend in wrong ways — but it does not describe how to do these things. It is the Sunnah of the Prophet which shows us how to act on Allah's commands.

The Quran is the main book of guidance and the Prophet taught us how to follow it. The Prophet not only told us how to follow the guidance, he also practised it himself. Prophet Muhammad's life was the living Quran.

Shariat has rules for every aspect of life. It is complete and perfect, and its application guarantees success, welfare and peace here on this earth and in the Akhirat.

Man-made laws differ from Shariat in a number of significant ways.

Man-made Law	***Shariat or Allah's Law***
1. Men make laws when they feel the need; these laws start from a few and then grow in number over the years.	Islamic Law is complete and perfect, and covers all aspects of human life. Men of learning explain and clarify Shariat for the benefit of ordinary people.
2. Laws made by men are not permanent; they are changed to suit people's wishes and desires. For example, in a particular country at a particular time, drinking alcohol may be banned; but this can when change pressure grows.	Shariat is permanent for all people all the time. It does not change with time and conditions. For example, drinking wine and gambling are not allowed under Islamic law. No one can change this; it is law that is valid for all time and for public all places. The American Government once banned all alcoholic drinks, but removed the ban after a time because it could not be enforced.
3. Man does not have knowledge of the future. Hence, man-made laws cannot stand the test of time.	Allah is All-knowing and All-powerful; He is the most Wise; His laws are the best and are complete.
4. Man is a created being. His laws are the creation of the created.	Allah is the Creator and His laws are for Man, His creation.
5. Man-made laws may be suitable for a particular nation or country. They cannot be universal.	Allah's laws are for all nations, all countries and for all time. They are universal.
6. Men make laws to suit their own needs. If members of parliament want to decrease the rate of tax on the rich, they can do so even if the majority of the people suffered and there was high unemployment in the country.	Allah is above all needs. He is not dependent on anything, so His laws are for the good of all people and not for a few, selfish people.

Shariah has two other sources: Ijma' (consensus) and Qiyas (analogy or reasoning on the basis of similar circumstances). These sources must still be based on the Quran and the Sunnah.

Ijma', or consensus, applies to a situation where no clear conclusion can be made from the Quran and the Sunnah. In this situation the representatives of the people who are knowledgeable and well-versed in the Quran and the Sunnah will sit together and work out an agreed formula to solve the particular problem. Ijma' developed during the period of al-Khilafatur Rashidin.

Qiyas means a reference or analogy of a comparison of one thing with a similar one. It is applied in circumstances where guidance from the Quran and the Sunnah is not directly available. A solution to a problem is reached by a process of deduction from a comparison with a similar situation in the past.

Sunnah : The word Sunnah means a system, a path or an example. In Islam it refers to the practice of the Prophet, his life example. It is embodied in the Ahadith (plural of Hadith) which are the Prophet's sayings, actions and the actions done with his approval. Ahadith have been very carefully collected and compiled since the death of the Prophet. Six collections of Hadith are regarded as the most authentic. They are:

1. Sahih al-Bukhari
   (Collected and compiled by Muhammad bin Ismail known as Imam Bukhari, born 194 AH, died 256 AH/870 CE).
2. Sahih Muslim
   (Muslim bin al-Hajjaj, known as Imam Muslim, born 202 AH, died 261 AH/875 CE).
3. Sunan Abu Daud
   (Sulaiman bin Ash 'ath, known as Abu Daud, born202 AH, died 275 AH/888/CE).
4. Sunan Ibn Majah
   (Abu 'Abdullah Muhammad bin Yazid al-Qazwint, known as Ibn Majah, born 209 AH, died 273 AH 886 CE).
5. Jami' al-Tirmidhi
   (Abu Isa Muhammad bin Isa al-Tirmidhi, date of birth not recorded, died 279 AH/892 CE).
6. Sunan an-Nasai
   (Abu 'Abdur Rahman Ahmad bin Shoaib an-Nasa'i, born 215 AH, died 303 AH/915 CE).

In addition to this, the Muwatta' of Imam Malik (born 93 AH, died 179 AH), Musnad of Ahmad bin Hanbal (born 164 AH, died 241 AH/855 CE) and Mishkat al-Masabih of Abu Muhammad al-Hussain bin Masud (died 516 AH) are also well known. There are many more collections and commentaries.

Treasure of Wisdom

Man has the ability of prying into secret realities and into the causes of things. With this ability he is able to analyse situations, to have knowledge of individual and social life, and to put everything in its proper place and proper context. This is a reflection of God's Attribute: the Possessor of Knowledge and Wisdom. Thus the Quran speaks again and again of God as the Knower and the Wise and the Knower of the Secrets of the Hearts:

He granteth wisdom
To whom He pleaseth;
And he to whom wisdom
Is granted receiveth
Indeed a benefit overflowing; *(II - 269)*

Comprehensiveness

This virtue enlarges the horizons of the mind. It helps man to understand things and to extend his grasp and reach. It is a reflection of God's Attribute of being All-Encompassing in Knowledge. The Quran says:

Nor shall they compass
Aught of His Knowledge
Except as He willeth. *(II - 255)*

The Matchless

Owing to this virtue, the individual develops his unique individuality, which makes him like nobody else. This is a reflection of God's Absolute Uniqueness, and Attribute about which the Quran says:

there is nothing
Whatever like unto Him, *(XLII - 11)*

The above argument indicates the measure of human character in the Islamic scheme of cultural reconstruction; it indicates the kind of human character which should be regarded as the essential and the ideal one.

Concept of Family

Disintegration of the Family in the West : Individual life is constructed in the context of social life, and social life begins in the family which is its unit. In western culture, the institution of the family has been disintegrated, resulting in the freezing of feelings of affections, love and sympathy. There, every person feels that nobody is his or hers, and that he is alone in an alien world.

Insistence on Affection Through Family in Cultural Reconstruction : In the scheme of cultural reconstruction, the institution of the family is the basis of the life of the community. For maintaining this institution mutual love, affection and sympathy have been insisted on. The Quran speaks of these things in various ways:

Reverence God, through Whom
Ye demend your mutual (rights),
And (reverence) the wombs
(that bore you) *(IV - 1)*

AlArham (wombs) is the plural of the Arabic word *Rahm* womb which literally means the womb of a woman.

But figuratively it means family relationship and bounds of kindship—the English word 'kindness', in its original and wider meaning is the closest synonyms for the Arabic terms. *Tajul 'uroos* says:

> Rahm *means the womb of a woman. Since the various members of family come from the same womb, the term has been used in the sense of kinship. The figurative meaning of* rahm *is kinship. When an Arab says that such and such persons have* rahm *between them he means they are very closely-related.*

Rahm includes close relations which may be both intimate and non-intimate: "*Rahm* is the term used for all relations, without distinction whether they are intimate or non-intimate" (Qurtubi). The above Quranic verse (IV -I) insists on rewarding kinsfolk and condemns the rejection of kinship bonds, Abu Bakr Jassas says: '

> *The Verse insists on the right of familial relationships and prohibits their severence'. (Jassas Razi,* Ahkamul Quran) *Ibn-e-Hayyan says: Juxtaposing God with the 'womb' indicates that violation of the bonds of kinship is a great sin (*Al Bahrul Muheet).

Importance of Bonds of Kinship in Other Quranic Verses: The implications of Sympathy for, and doing good to one another because of familial bonds of kinship are not confined to this life. They extend beyond this life too. The distribution of inheritance is based on such an idea:

But kindered by blood
Have prior rights
Against each other
In the Book of God. *(VII-75)*

The bond of kinship is so strong that even differences of religion do not break it; and the claim for affection and love remains inspite of them. Thus, the Holy Prophet said to his kinsfolk:

Say: 'No reward do I
Ask of you for this
Except the love
Of others near to kin. *(XLII-23)*

Those who violate the bond of kinship have been regarded by the Quran as transgressors:

But He causes not to stray,
Except those who forsake (the path),
Those who break God's Covenant
After it is ratified,
And who sunder what God
Has ordered to be joined,
And do mischief on earth: *(II-26-27)*

Prophet's Teachings

The Holy Prophet has interpreted the reverence to kinship or wombs in various ways. He always spoke of the excellence of this virtue and insisted on the importance of maintaining it.

For example, he says:

> *God said: 'I am Allah, I am the One. I created mercy and derived it from my own name. He who joins the bond of mercy, I shall join him* (with blessings).
>
> *He who breaks this bond, I shall break him (into damnation).*
>
> (Abu Daud, Mishkat, *Babul Birre Was-Sila)*

Mercy is a twig entwined with the Merciful One. Allah said: 'He who joins it, I shall join him. He who severes it, I shall severe him. *(Bukhari, Muslim,* Kitabul Birre Wal-Sila)

Allah created all the creatures. After He has finished this work Mercy stood up and got hold of the Merciful One by the waist. The Merciful One said: 'Stop!

> *Mercy said: "This is the place of him who seeks refuge with thee. The Merciful One said: Art thou not satisfied with the decree that I burnt him who burnt thee and I severed him who severes thee? At this Mercy replied: 'I am satisfied'.* (Mishkat, *Babul Birra Wal-Sala)*

Rahm or Mercy is related to the throne of God. Mercy says: He who joins me, Allah shall join him; and He who severs me, Allah shall severe him *(Op cit).*

In the West Children and Parents are not Responsible for Mutual Care: In Western culture, parents and children have become burdens on one another. The relation between them has been broken down and so have the bonds and rights of kinship.

The children are brought up in nurseries and the old parents are taken care of by houses for the old, which are separately and specially built for them. Eventually in such a position the natural feelings which are related to blood kinship are suppressed and vitiated. Feelings of affection and love should not be looked for or expected in such a situation.

Natural Feelings and Rights in the Scheme of Islamic Cultural Reconstruction : In the Islamic scheme of cultural reconstruction due consideration is given to natural family feelings. The bond of kinship between persons has been emphasised very much and the rights and duties associated with it have been spelled out and insisted on.

Various Verses of the Quran insisted on doing good to parents. Often this command comes after the command regarding faith in one God and His worship, which, perhaps, implies that the efficient cause of man's birth (God) and the material cause (parents) both must be considered and one must give what is due to both of them.

The difference is only with regard to what is primary and what is secondary. Here are some Verses of the Quran:

The Lord hath decreed
That ye worship none but Him,
And that ye be kind
To parents. Whether one
Or both of them attain
Old age in thy life,
Say not to them a word
Of contempt, nor repel them,
But address them
In terms of honour.
And, out of kindness, lower to them the wing

Of humility, and say:
'My Lord! bestow on them
The Mercy even as they
Cherished me in childhood'. (XVII - 23.24)
Serve God, and join not
Any partners with Him:
'Do good — to parents, kinsfold *(IV- 36)*
Say: 'Come, I will rechearse
What God hath (really)
Prohibited you from'; join not
Anything as equal with Him;
Be good to your parents; *(VI - 151)*

Since in bringing up children the mother has to suffer more of trouble, priority is given to her in the matter of doing good to parents. The Quran says:

Any We have enjoined on man
(To be good) to his parents:
In travail upon travail
Did his mother bare him,
And in years twain
Was his weaning: (hear
The command), 'show gratitude
to Me and to thy parents:
To me is (thy final) Goal. *(XXXI - 14)*
We have enjoined on man
Kindness to his parents:
In pain did his mother
Bare him, and in pain
Did she give him birth. *(XLVI - 15)*

Regarding doing good to parents there are certain Traditions. Once a man asked the Holy Prophet: 'What duty is enjoined on children towards their parents.' The Holy Prophet said: 'Both of them are thy paradise or hell'.

Another Tradition says: "The pleasure of God depends on the pleasure of the parents, and the displeasure of God is the displeasure of the parents. Still another Tradition says: 'May his nose be laid in the dust! May his nose be laid in the dust! May his nose be laid in the dust! (May he suffer abjection and humiliation). The audience asked: 'Whose nose, O Prophet of Allah?'

The Holy Prophet replied:

> *'He who finds his parents or one of his parents and does not enter paradise'. The traditions, like the Quran, also command the giving of priority to the mother. Once a man asked the Holy Prophet who was most worthy of his good treatment. The Holy Prophet said: 'Thy mother'. He asked: 'Who next?' The reply was: 'Thy mother'. He once again asked: 'Who next?' The reply was 'Thy Mother'. At this he asked for the fourth time: 'Who next?' This time the reply was: 'Thy father'. Another person asked the Holy Prophet about the treatment to the memory of the parents after their death. The Holy Prophet said: 'Pray for their salvation; fulfil their vows and pacts; do good to your kinsfolk, keeping the parents in mind; and respect the words of your parents'. Doing good to parents is commanded even if their religion is different. When Abu Bakr's daughter Asma asked the Holy Prophet regarding her infidel mother, the Holy Prophet advised doing good to her out of human kindness.*
>
> (Bukhari, Muslim, *Kitabul Birre Wal Silah).*

Cherishing is the Foremost Duty of Parents towards Children : In the scheme of cultural reconstruction, just as there are the duties of children towards parents in the same way there are the duties of parents towards children. Among them the foremost duty is that of cherishing and bringing up the children. The Quran speaks of the desire and the prayers of parents before the birth of the child as follows:

> *And if Thou givest us*
>
> *A goodly child,*
>
> *We vow we shall*
>
> *(ever) be grateful'* *(VII - 189)*

By the word 'goodly' are meant particular traits of character. But the word keeps changing its meaning according to the context. In this context 'goodly' has been explained by exegetes as follows:

A healthy child, one whose body should be alright; healthy in the sense that his limbs should be intact; perfectly healthy in the sense of having the capability to do good deeds for the benefit of humanity.

Children should be brought up According to Their Needs : The bringing up of children should be done in such way as to ensure their proper development and to provide them with the things they need according to their age. Thus, the Quran speaks of breast-feeding the child as follows:

The mother shall give suck

To their offspring

For two whole years,

If the father desires

To complete the term. *(II- 233)*

The relation established by giving suck to a child is reverenced so much that if another woman gives suck to the child instead of the mother, the child and that woman have the same relation between them as would obtain in the case of the real mother. This relation is Holy and not to be violated. Hence the Quran prohibits marriage with:

foster-mothers

(Who gave you suck), foster sisters: *(IV- 23)*

The father is entrusted with supporting the woman who gave suck to the children, be she a real mother or a foster mother:

But he shall bear the cost

Of their fooding and clothing

On equitable terms. *(II-233)*

Several Traditions speak of the affection of the Holy Prophet for children. Once a rustic Arab said to the Holy Prophet: 'Do you kiss your Child? I have never done it myself. At this the Holy Prophet said: 'If Allah has taken off all mercy from your heart, what can I do'. In another Tradition the name of this rustic arab is mentioned as Iqrab Habis. He saw the Holy Prophet kissing the child Hasan and said: 'I have ten children. I never kiss them'. At this the Holy Prophet said: 'He who does not show mercy is not shown mercy'. Still another Tradition observes: 'He who does not show affection to our juniors and respect to our ancestors is not one of us.

In showing affection, it is necessary to act on the principles of equality, that is no distinction should be made between superior and inferior in this regard—it is not proper to give some gift to one person and to deprive the other person from it on the basis of any distinction. There is the story of No man.

Once his father gave him some gift. The Holy Prophet asked the father: 'Have you given such a gift to all your sons?' He said: 'No'. The Holy Prophet said: 'Withdraw the gift you have given'. Another Tradition reports this incident as follows: 'Do you like that all your children should receive equal treatment from you? He said 'Yes'.

The Holy Prophet said: 'Then do not do such a thing (do not observe partiality)." Still another Tradition gives the following advice: 'Fear Allah, and mete out equal treatment among your children'.

Special Attention to Bringing up of Daughters : Among Arabs, the daughters had no importance. For this reason, the Holy Prophet has drawn special attention to their character. He said: 'He who gets a daughter and lets her live, does not dishonour her and does not prefer her to the son—Allah will send him to paradise'. *(Abu Daud, Mishkat,* Babul Shafqa Wal Rahma alal Khalq). Another tradition says: 'He who has daughters and who metes out good treatment to them, his daughters will become a block against the fire of hell in his case. *(Bukhari, Muslim, Mishkat)* Still another Tradition says:

> *He who brings up two daughters till they come of age, he and I shall be together like two fingers of the hand on the Day of Judgment.* (Muslim, Mishkat)

Family Planning for the Sake of Proper Bringing up of Children : If poverty comes in the way of the proper bringing up of children, child births should be properly spaced through various methods. Even birth control is permitted if it becomes necessary.

The various methods of birth control that are used in modern times were not there in the days of the revelation of the Quran. So it is not fair to look for some command in the Quran and the Sunnah regarding birth control and to reject birth control on not finding the command there.

The basic consideration in this regard is that the fundamental principles of Islam are not violated. If they are violated birth control should be rejected. But if they are not violated then it is not fair to insist on opposing it. The possibility of both supporting and rejecting it should be kept open, subject to the demands of the circumstances.

Just as there may be circumstances which demand the increase of population, in the same way there may be circumstances which demand birth control. Perhaps it is for this reason that the Quran and the Sunnah have not given any definite command regarding this matter.

Birth Control in Islam According to Circumstances : Here, we give some evidences which suggest that Islam is not inimical to the policy of family planning and birth control. The Quran says:

If any of you have not
The means wherewith
To wed free believing women,
They may wed believing
Girls from among those
Whom your right hands possess *(IV - 24)*
Let those who find not
The wherewithal for marriage
Keep themselves chaste, until
God give them means
Out of His grace. *(XXIV - 33)*

In the above Verses, poverty is recognised as undesirable for marriage. It is therefore amenable to reason that if circumstances demand it the size of the family should be restricted through birth control. At the time when the Quran was revealed a birth control method, the *coitus obstructus* (not allowing the semen to go inside the women), was in vogue among Arabs. But it is significant that the Quran did not forbid it. Jabir has taken the silence of the Quran for permission: 'We practised *coitus obstructus* when the Quran was being revealed. Sufian says: 'If *coitus obstructus* was something to be prohibited, the Quran would have prohibited it'. Regarding women the Quran says:

Your wives are
As tilth unto you,
So approach your tilth
When and how ye will; (II - 23)

In connection with interpretation of this Verse, Ibn-i-Abbas, Ibn-i-Umar and Abu Haneefa provide the following comment: 'How ye will mean practising *coitus obstructus* or without it'. Another Verse of the Quran says that only one wife or slave-girl will be more suitable,

To prevent you
From doing injustice *(IV - 3)*

With regard to the interpretation of this Verse, Zaid b. Aslam, Jabir b. Zaid (Successors of the Companions) and Imam Shafai offer the following comment: 'Being contented with one wife or slave-girl implies that you should not have many children'. Sufian b. Ainia has offered the following interpretation: 'To prevent you from doing injustice' (IV - 3) comes close to the suggestions that you should not become insolvent and needy'.

Argument From the Sayings of Saints and Scholars : There are various Traditions regarding the number of children. Some of them encourage big family, others encourage small family. In the same way, there are many Traditions regarding *coitus obstructus*. Some of them imply permission, others imply prohibition of the practice.

A study of all these Traditions indicate that in this matter the Holy Prophet had a liberal outlook and was moulding his outlook according to the demands of the circumstances. Otherwise he would have no difficulty in giving a commandment for or against birth control. In the days of Caliph Omar the Conqueror and the ruler of Egypt Amroob. Al-as gave the following lecture to the people.

This lecture was moulded according to the Demands of the circumstances and it can be called a declaration of the government policy of that time: O my people! avoid four bad habits, for they cause distress after comfort, misery after prosperity and degradation after honour: (1) Avoid having a great number of children (2) Avoid low standard of life, (3) Avoid wasting your goods through profligacy, and (4) Avoid wasting time in unnecessary and pointless discussion.

> *This lecture has been quoted by Ibn-i-Hakeem in his history of Egypt*
>
> (Futuh-i-Misr wa Akhbaruha, *Vol. I, p. 139)*
>
> *Imam Ghazali and Shah Abdul Aziz have also permitted* coitus obstructus *as a method of birth control in view of poverty and destitution.*

After seeking religious sanction for birth control it does not remain important whether the man uses some device or the woman. But the sanction that has been suggested is conditional and applies only to critical cases. If a general sanction for birth control were given its consequence would be dangerous, as western and westernised cultures testify.

Education Regarding Both Man and the Universe Necessary : In addition to bringing up children, education is also the responsibility of the parents. Undoubtedly the West has made great progress in matters of knowledge regarding the Universe, but as regards knowledge about man it is still very much backward.

It is successful in understanding the mysteries of the universe but unsuccessful in understanding the mystery of man. David C. Marsh admits that our knowledge of the physical universe has become very wide. We have been able to control and harness the powers of nature to a great extent; but we are ignorant regarding innumerable aspects of man and his affairs to an unfortunately great extent.

A.W. Haslet says that a scientist is not more helpless in other matters of knowledge than he is in the matter of knowledge about man. He can split the atom; can analyse the composition of the farthest star; can harness the power of electricity—but the same scientist is confronted with difficulties when he wants to understand the nature of life and even his own or man's nature. For neither life nor man can yield to any experiment under controlled conditions.

Both Kinds of Education Recommended By the Quran : In the Islamic scheme of cultural reconstruction so much knowledge about man is available that there is no problem in solving human problems. As regards Universe, it has been insisted not only that man should acquire all kinds of useful knowledge but should also maintain progress or evolution of human knowledge, otherwise the survival of the human species will be endangered.

Hence, the very beginning of the revelation of the Quran is by the commandment: 'Read' *(Iqra)* the very first Verse of the Quran points to the fact that man is originally a clot of blood.

He does not deserve any exaltation on the basis of this origin, but it is only through knowledge that he is exalted to higher and higher stages:

Proclaim! (or Read!)
In the name
Of the Lord and Cherisher,
Who created—
Created man, out of
The (mere) clot
Of congealed blood:
Proclaim! and thy Lord

Is Most Bountiful,—
He Who taught
(The use of) the Pen,—
Taught man that
Which he knew not. (XCVI—1-5)

Similary immediately after the creation of man (Adam) this truth was revealed, through a competitive test with the angles, that supremacy is determined by knowledge. The angels themselves have to acknowledge it—

Glory to thee: of knowledge
We have none, save what Thou
Has taught us: in truth it is Thou
Who art perfect in knowledge and wisdom (II-32)

The episode of Talut also brings out the truth that supremacy is determined not by wealth, family, or racial or tribal religion, but by knowledge and physical prowess. The Quran relates the episode as follows:

Their Prophet said to them:
'God hath appointed
Talut as king over you.
They said: 'How can he
Exercise authority over us
When we are better fitted
Than he to exercise authority,
And he is not even gifted
With wealth in abundance?'
He said: 'God hath
Chosen him above you,
And hath gifted him
Abundantly with knowledge
And bodily prowess (II-247)

Conformity to Contemporary Standards of Prowess and Knowledge : It is not enough to have knowledge and physical prowess. Knowledge and physical prowess should be acquired in conformity with the standards of a particular age. For example, the modern age is an age of science and technology, so in this age the measure of supremacy should be according to modern standards of knowledge and prowess.

The words 'power' (Quwwat) and 'iron' (AlHadid) have been used in the Quran in a manner that indicates that the equipment of power and technological potentialities of man shall go on increasing day by day. Without keeping pace with this progress no community can survive:

Against them make ready
your strength to the utmost
Of your power, *(VIII-60)*
And We send down Iron,
In which is (material for)
Mighty war, as well as
Many benefits for mankind, *(LVII-25)*

Both Kinds of Education Recommended By the Traditions : The Holy Prophet has drawn attention to knowledge in various ways. For example, he says: 'I have been sent as a teacher'. Regarding the Pen (which is a means of knowledge) he says: 'Allah created the Pen first'. The effects of knowledge have been recognised by the Holy Prophet. They are progress and exaltation; undoubtedly 'wisdom' adds to the nobility of the noble person and exalts the low persons to make them sit in the company of the King.

Knowledge has been described by the Holy Prophet as the cause of the leadership of the nations and also of their influence over other people. Knowledge is a weapon against enemy and an embellishment for the sake of friends. Allah raises nations through knowledge and exalts them to the position of leaders. They are followed by other nations and their opinions become decisive for other nations.

God has made knowledge capable of infinite development. He has not confined it to any one (religious or worldly) sphere- 'wisdom or knowledge is the lost property of the knower; he has a right to it wherever he finds it.'

The Holy Prophet has recommended long journeys for the sake of all useful knowledge:

The Holy Prophet has recommended that we should undertake journeys to very remote places for the sake of all kinds of useful knowledge—and without any prejudice too. A Tradition says 'Aquire knowledge even if you have to go to China'. This Tradition has been regarded as 'weak' in terms of the degree of authenticity. But its import is very much in line with the spirit of Islam, and it does not say anything fantastic either. China and Arabia are to antipodes. But the ports of Arabia were visited by the merchant ships of China in those days, and Chinese goods were sold in some Arabian towns. Masudi writes that 'Chinese ships visited the ports of Amman, Seraf, Fars and Bahrain'.

About the port of Daba in Amman Ibn-i-Habib writes: "There was a port called Daba. On the last day of the month of Rajab, a big market or fair was set up there. In this fair came merchants from Sindh, Hindustan, China and from various places of the east and the west".

The Holy Prophet Used the Most Important Modern Weapons of His Time : The most important weapons of the days of the Holy Prophet were as follows:

Dabbaba: It was a special kind of armoured car, made for protection against arrows by coating it with layers of thick skin. It was used for the purpose of battering fortresses.

Zabr: It was made in the shape of an umbrella from skin mounted on wood, and was used for protecting the back against arrows'.

Minjaniq: It was a weapon of offence, and was a kind of sling by which heavy stones were thrown at the enemy. (*Lissanul Arab)*

Hasak: It was a kind of thorny shrub which was spread around the fortress and around the enemy army so as to make the way dangerous for the enemy. *(AlQamusul Muhit)*

The Holy Prophet was the First to Use Minjaniq and Hasak : The Holy Prophet imported *Minjaniq* and *Hasak* for deployment in the Battle of Taif. In fact, he himself was the first to use *Minjaniq* and *Hasak*. Ibn-i-Hisham says:

A trustworthy person reported to me that in Islam the Holy Prophet himself was the first to use Minjaniq *against the army of Taif.*

(Al Siyarul Nabuwiyah, Zikr *Ghazwatul Taif)*

Miqraizi says:

The Holy Prophet installed the Minjaniq on the fortress of Taif.

Another report says:

> *The Holy Prophet spread Hasak around the fortress of Taif.*

There are various accounts regarding the *Minjaniq* that the Holy Prophet used. Some reporters say it was imported, while others say it was made by Salman Farsi. After the conquest of Taif, in the year 9 H., Urwabin Masud Thaqafi and Ghailan bin Salma Thaqafi adopted Islam and went to Jarsh and acquired skill in the use of the above-mentioned weapons:

> *Urwa bin Masud Thaqafi and Ghailan bin Salma Thaqafi were not present in the siege of Hunain and Taif. They had gone away to Jarsh to learn the art of using* Dabbaba, Manjaniq *and* Zabr.*(Ibn-i-Hisham,* Al Siyarul Nabuwiya, *Vol. III, Ghazwatul Taif:* A Rauzul' Unuf, *Zikr Talim Ihlil Taif)*

Manufacturing Arms

Jarsh was a town in the suburbs of Damascus. It was under the power of Rome, which was second in greatness in those days. This town had big arms factory. It was conquered by Sharjil bin Husna in the days of Omar's Caliphate. The town was under the suzerainty of Rome, Sharjit conquered it in the days of Omar bin Khattab. *(Imtaul Asma',* Nazala Rasulullah bil' Araj, Hashiya 366)

The Holy Prophet's Command to Develop the Science of Weaponry : When, after the conquest of Jarsh, the arms factory fell to the hands of Muslims, they developed it further. The Holy Prophet incited his people in various ways to learn the arts of warfare. For example he said: 'He who gives up archery after learning it is not one of us'. On another occasion he said: 'By the virtue of one arrow Allah sends three persons to paradise: the maker of it who wants to earn a reward (from God), the archer who shoots it, and the helper who picks the arrow and gives it (to the archer)'. The above argument should make it clear that the Islamic system of education encompasses all spheres of life.

Special Attention to Character-Building : Alongwith the acquiring of knowledge skill special attention is drawn to character-building in the commandments of Islam. The commandments in this regard are addressed to parents and teachers first. In western culture there is a little standard of character. In the Islamic scheme of cultural reconstruction, the standard is there: It is the Attributes of God Himself. These Attributes are related not only to Beauty but also to Glory (and Power) and Perfection.

The qualities of character that emanate from these Attributes have been discussed above. All the qualities are needed, in due proportion, for the development of a balanced character. By innate dispositions, certain qualities may be increased or decreased; but such a thing should not be allowed to happen by human design.

Both the East and the West have Failed Here : Here, in the matter of character-building both the East and the West have failed. About the West, it can be said that it aimed at worldly gain only, and therefore it gave importance only to those qualities of character which are related to the acquisition of worldly gains.

But how about the East? The East has not been able to achieve any success in character-building beyond a few moral reforms, and this in spite of its spiritual trumpeting.

The Pattern of Balanced Personality is the Holy Prophet : In the scheme of cultural reconstruction, the pattern of balanced personality is the Holy Prophet. As the Quran puts it:

We have indeed
In the Apostle of God
A beautiful pattern (to conduct) *(XXXIII. 21)*
That the Apostle may be
A witness for you, and ye
Be his witness for mankind! *(XXII. 78)*
Thus have We made of you
An Ummat justly balanced,
That ye might be witnesses
Over the nations,
And the Apostle a witness
Over yourselves *(II-143)*

Those who are perceptive know how perfect and comprehensive the life of the Holy Prophet was.

The Life of the Companions as a Pattern of Character-Building : After the life of the Holy Prophet the life of his companions is a pattern of character-building. These companions performed in every sphere of life such feats as have no equal in human history. If their activities had been confined to any one particular sphere, Islamic civilization would not have come into existence. Nor would it have survived.

Adjacent to Masjid-e-Nabwi, there was an institution called Saffa. This institution trained the companions in character-building. Its activities encompassed all spheres of life in those days.

The products of Saffa exemplified a particular way of life. They undertook responsibilities of earning livelihood, education and other responsibilities of citizenship, and along with these the responsibilities of participating in battles voluntarily. Some eminent products of the Saffa institutions were: Abdullah b. Masood, Saad b. Abi Waqqas, Huzaifa b. Yamaan, Abdullah b. Omar, Salman Farsi, Abu Darda, Abu Huraira, Salim, Abu Zar Ghifari, Hanzala, Bilal Habshi and Suheb Roomi. *(Tabaqati Ibni-i-Sad,* Vol. I, II; *Musnad: Ibn-i-Hambal, Vol. I).* Their deeds testify to the education for character-building that the Holy Prophet initiated.

Fundamental Principles of Character-Building : From the Quran the following fundamental principles of character-building can be derived. They are : (1) Gnosis, (2) Utility, (3) Trustworthiness, (4) Responsibility of Caretaking, (5) Justice and (6) Application. We shall discuss them below:

(1) *Gnosis:* It means the realization of the self and the realization of God. On the one hand, it would inculcate virtues like self responsibility, liberal outlook, boldness, contentment and freedom from wants, and on the other, virtues like humility, hope, piety, resignation, discipline and fortitude:

As also in your own
Selves: will ye not
Then see *(LI-21)*

Because God will never change
The Grace which He hath bestowed
On a People until they change
What is in their (own) souls: *(VIII-53)*

Without the realization of the self the realization of God is not possible :

And be ye not like
Those who forget God:

And He made them forget
Their souls *(LIX-19)*

(2) *Utility:* It means that every individual should become useful according to his natural abilities. The individual should be equipped with all kinds of accomplishments, material, moral, spiritual, physical etc.

The Quran says:

He sends down water
From the skies, and the channels
Flow, each according to its measure:
But the torrent bears away
The foam that mounts up
To the surface. Even so,
From that (Ore) which they heat
In the fire, to make ornaments
Or utensils therewith,
There is a scum likewise.
Thus doth God (by parables)
Show forth Truth and Vanity.
For the scum disappears
Like froth cast out;
While that which is for the good
Of mankind remains on the earth. *(XIII-17)*

In the above parable, the useful things like silver and gold remain, and the useless things which are the scum disappear like froth. The obvious implication is that in this world only the useful things survive and the useless things gradually perish.

In our Muslim society, the concept of utility has been confined to moral betterment, and thus material power was left to the worldly people. This has resulted in degradation and lowness. Even if moral betterment is accomplished, progress can not be made without physical power. This fallacy has two reasons behind it:

(1) The wrong concept of religion led people to think that only by performing certain religious rituals they would achieve all that the worldly people do by tireless effort and striving. This is against God's law of justice.

(2) The wrong concept of miracles led to the notion that things, and even the advancement of a nation, can happen without any physical causality. This is against the law of nature. The property of the fire is to burn. He who puts his hand into it, will necessarily get burnt. If the fire was turned into a garden in the case of Abraham, it was a miracle which has no relation to the common laws of nature. But the world is run by the common laws of nature and not by miracles.

(3) *Trustworthiness* : The notion that trustworthiness is the basis of the good life should be promoted. In this world man is like a trustee *(Ameen)*. God has endowed him with a Trust and he is to answer for his deeds before God.

The Quran syas :

God doth command you

To render back your Trusts

To those whom they are due; *(IV.58)*

In the above verse, the word 'trusts' has a general meaning; it includes all kinds of responsibilities, be they related to one's duty towards God or to one's duty towards fellow human beings. The Holy Prophet has regarded trustworthiness as the basis of faith. He says: 'He who is not capable of trustworthiness, does not have faith'. Another Tradition says: 'The first thing that you will loose from your religion is trustworthiness, and the last thing that you will loose is prayers *(namaz)*. Some people will go on saying prayers but religion will not be with them.

(4) *Responsibility of Care-Taking:* Every individual should feel his own responsibility and also the responsibility of others. He should extend whatever kind of help is needed by others, be it moral or material. He should extent this help as a matter of his duty. The Quran says:

O ye who believe!

Save yourself and your

Families from Fire. *(LXVI-6)*

At another place the fulfilment of the needs of God's creature has been described as the giving of a beautiful loan to God Himself :

Who is he

that will loan to God

A beautiful loan, which God

Will double unto his credit

And multiply many times? *(II - 245)*

The Holy Prophet once said: 'Listen! everyone of you is the caretaker of others, and everyone will be asked about his responsibility towards those who are under his care. (Bukhari, *Kitabul Istiqraz) The word* Raai *means: 'Guarding the other person according to his Good'* (Baizawi) *hence Raai is: 'anyone who is the guardian of somebody else'* (AlMunjid). *At another place, it has been said: 'The creatures are the children of Allah. The person who does good to Allah's children is dearer to Allah!* (Mishkat, *Bab fil Shafqa' alal Khalq)*

The care-taking mentioned above should be carried out in a particular spirit. The Holy Prophet has elucidated it through a parable:

Think, there is a ship having many people on board. The provisions for their needs (water etc.) are kept in the upper storey of the ship. Those who are in the lower storey keep coming to the upper storey for, say, water. If the people of the upper storey allow them to have water out of a spirit of camaraderie, everything works well, and no untoward incident happens. But if the people in the upper storey deny water to the people of the lower storey just because it causes a little trouble to them, the people of the lower storey will be forced to adopt some other means for getting water. Suppose they decide to make a hole in the bottom of the ship for getting water, and start making this hole. Now if the people of the upper storey neither prevent them from making the hole nor allow them to have water, it is evident that the ship will sink. Then, neither the hole-makers will survive, nor those who ignored their responsibility towards them. (Bukhari, Mishkat*: Bab Amr bil Ma'ruf)*

In the above Tradition, life is compared to the situation of being on board a ship and the needs of life to water. The spirit of co-operation, which should not be violated in spite of some trouble, is emphasized in a beautiful way. The violation of this spirit in the ship leads to the sinking of the ship and the destruction of all its inmates, be they of the upper storey or of the lower storey.

All these elements of the parable have a significant bearing on the understanding of the human situation and the truths of social psychology.

5. *Justice*: Justice implies balance in all spheres of life, so that everything may have its course without transgression limits and along the way of temperance. We have already discussed Justice. Here we shall reinforce the argument by some quotations from the Quran and the Traditions.

The Quran has prohibited intemperance and excess, and has recommended balance and temperance in every sphere of life :

O People of the Book!

Commit no excesses

In your religion: nor say

Of God aught but the truth *(IV-171)*

Say: 'O People of the Book!

Exceed not in your religion

The bounds (of what is proper),

Tresspassing beyond the truth,

Nor follow the vain desires

Of people who went wrong

In times gone by, —

Who misled

Many, and strayed (themselves)

From the even way *(V- 8)*

The Holy Prophet drew attention to temperance, balance and justice. He said:

Do not be harsh on yourselves, otherwise Allah will be harsh on you. For when the people before you were harsh on themselves Allah was harsh on them. Their remnants are now the priests of the worshipping places of the Christians and the Jews.

Once upon a time, three companions visited the house of the Holy Prophet in order to find out the truth about his private worship and prayers. When they were told about it they thought that the worship and prayers were not very much. But they also thought that the Holy Prophet was already among the saved and they themselves were sinners, so perhaps no comparison could be drawn between them. On that occasion, one of the companions took a vow to keep awake all night in prayer. The other said that he would always keep fast. The third one said that he would not marry. When the Holy Prophet came out of his house and when he was told about their vows, he impressed it upon them that they should not be so harsh to themselves in matters of religion and that they should adopt a moderate or middle course:

"Remember I have more of piety than you, but I sometimes fast and sometimes eat, sometimes say prayer and sometimes I sleep and cohabit with women. He who deviates from my Way or Sunnah is not one of mine." (Bukhari, Mishkat, Muslim, Abu Daud, *Kitabul Itisam bil Kitab wal Sunna, Fast I)*

6. *Application :* Application means that one's belief and ideals should be translated into one's actions. It means that one's life should be a continuous enactment of these beliefs and ideals. This virtue takes an individual out of the world of self-delusion and brings him into the world of practical life. It puts this Practical life at the very center of his being. The Quran says:

And say: 'work (righteousness):

Soon will God observe your work,

And his Apostle, and the believers: *(IX-105)*

That man can have nothing

But what he strives for: *(LIII-39)*

...to them

We shall pay (the price of)

their deeds therein *(XI. 15)*

The following Tradition brings out the significance of application and the life of action:

'Suppose there are three workers. One of them works from morning till noon; the other from noon till sometime in the afternoon; and the third from sometime in the afternoon till dusk. The first two get one carat each as wages, and the third gets two carats each. Then the Holy Prophet said that the first two are the Jews and the Christians and the third one is my 'Ummat'; this third

category worker has such a great efficiency that in comparatively less time he does the same work to earn double wages.

(Mishkat, *Bab Thawabi Hazihil Ummah)*

Punishment for Evil Deeds Postponed In the Case of the Practical : Efficiency is so important that God postpones the punishment of those who are practical. In their case, immediate punishment for evil deeds would cause disturbance in the system of the Universe and in the dialectical process of its functioning. Shah Waliullah says:

Indeed, Divine justice does not let any sinner remain unpunished in this world, except that it may be done on consideration of causing disturbance in the functioning of the world.*(Hujjatullahil Baligha,* Al Jazai alal Amali fil Dunya).

He goes on to add:

Many times it happens that the commandment in consideration of the system of the universe becomes more urgent than the commandment in consideration of individual's deeds. It is for this reason that the evil doer is given a long rope and the righteous person has to face hardships. The hardships serve the purpose of breaking down his selfish desires. *(Ibid).*

We See Only One Aspect of Reality : In advanced countires, people are not getting punishment for their evil deeds. It is so because their deeds imply dynamism and practical abilities, which make for the dynamic movement of the universe. It is not that evils are not regarded as evils now, in the modern age, or that they have been transformed into virtues. In fact, we human beings have a limited view, and we see only one aspect of reality, whereas Divine Providence sees the total reality. If we were to see all the aspects of reality, we would not raise doubts regarding the functioning of Divine Providence.

In Western Culture Woman is Licentiously Free : In western culture, the supremacy of man has ended, which has resulted in the disintegration of the unity of the family and given licentious freedom to woman. Behind this kind of freedom, the motive is not so much self-reform as of revenge against man. So in every sphere of life woman is pitted against man, so much so that even in the case of immorality of sexual licentiousness, woman claims equal rights with man. In the personal affairs of a woman the husband or somebody else is not entitled to interfere.

Even marriage is regarded as a restraint because it is supposed to restrict personal freedom and frustrate one's enjoyment. Western civilization does make woman 'equal' to man, and even his rival, but it has failed to fill up the "vacuum that woman has left behind her in that particular sphere which was specifically her own. Thus, a vacuum has been created in family life and is increasing day by day and causing all kinds of trouble.

What happened was this that the wrong concept of religion and morality kept woman deprived of her natural right for a long time, and now the licentious freedom and feminine revolt that we see is actually a reaction of the age-old suppression of woman's natural right. Thus, in the present situation both man and woman are uneasy. But things have gone so far that people are helpless to put any check. If somebody dares to do so he is called conservative, which implies the greatest stigma of our time.

Superiority of Man in the Scheme of Cultural Reconstruction: In the scheme of cultural reconstruction, the superiority of man is maintained. Woman has been given her due position and the sphere of her activity has been determined and defined. She can contribute to civilization only by remaining within this natural spheres of hers. In this regard, the following considerations are involved:

- The nature of sexual relations;
- The safeguarding of sexual relations;
- The limits of the activities of woman.

The Nature of Sexual Relations : The relation between man and woman is one of pairing and of mutual assimilation. The Quran has pointed this out but has not ascribed it specifically to human beings; it is the general pattern in all living things.

And of everything
We have created pairs;
That ye may receive
Instructions. *(LI-49)*

Glory to God, Who created
In pairs all things that
The earth produces, as well as
their own (human) kind
And (other) things of which
They have no knowledge. *(XXXVI- 36)*

... He has made
For you pairs
From among yourselves,
And pairs among cattle. *(XLII-11)*

The male-female relation is made firm through wedding. The purpose of sexual relation is not the timely appeasement of sexual desire. This relation is made firm so as to form a basis for the whole life. It ensures the well-wedding and survival of both the sexes. The Quran says:

Wed them with the leave
Of their owners, and give them
Their dowers, according to what
Is reasonable: they should be
Chaste, not lustful, nor taking
Paramours *(IV-25)*
They are your garments
And ye are their garments *(II-187)*

The Holy Prophet says: 'The whole world is a means of your benefit, and the best means of benefit is a virtuous wife. Another Tradition says: 'He who has the capability of wedding should wed; for wedding safeguards the eyes (against sinful glances and the private parts). Wedding promotes the spirit of love and sacrifice between the husband and the wife. It provides solace among hardships:

It is He Who created
You from a single person,
And made his mate
Of like nature, in order
That he might dwell with her
(in Love). *(VII-189)*
... He created
For you mates from among
Yourselves, that ye may
Dwell in tranquility with them,
And He has put love
And mercy between your (hearts):

Verily in that our Signs are for those
Who reflect. *(XXX - 21)*

The Holy Prophet said: 'You should not have seen two lovers like those who are joined in wedding lock' *(Mishkat,* Kitabun Nikah, Fast III). At another occasion he said:

> *Next to piety there is nothing more beneficial for a believer than a virtuous wife. If hecommands er, she obeys; if he looks at her, she becomes happy; if he swears by her, he has got to fulfil his word; if she is not there, he wishes well for himself and for her goods.* *(Ibid.)*

Scope of Women's Activities

If woman is allowed licentious freedom and if she is allowed to take part in every kind of activity (lawful or unlawful), it is going to disturb the institution of the family and the proper relations between the sexes. This is why in the scheme of cultural reconstruction the activities of woman are subject to real needs and the permission of her husband. Bertrand Russel gives two reasons for the social evils of western civilization: the emancipation of woman and the device of birth control. But the real reason is the lack of social control, which has created many subsidiary reasons also. Social control is a way of controling the minds and action of the individuals. Various efforts were made to achieve this social control, but these efforts have not met with any success.

The Best Means of Social Control is Religion : The best means of social control is religion, and this is the means used in the Islamic scheme of cultural reconstruction. Religion has the following bearings on human life:

(1) It induces the fear of God and the idea of answerability to God, which controls human actions and thoughts.

(2) Religion helps man to exercise control over his thoughts and feelings, which makes balanced in individual life on the one hand for social stability and solidarity on the other.

(3) It makes for peace of the soul and for the reform of inward and outward life.

(4) It determines the standard for sexual morality and social character and sets up a watch on human relations.

(5) The noble principles of religion make for the control of social evils and protect society against anti-social elements.

The above features of religion have been recognised in every age. All Sociologists affirm the constructive role played by religion in human history. Even Bertrand Russel admits that the fear of hell-fire and of pregnancy were the two factors that guaranteed the preservation of the modesty of woman in the past.

Now that the influence of religion has declined and anti-pregnancy devices have emerged both these restricting factors have disappeared and the situation has become what it is.

Possibility of Change in the Sphere of Woman's Activity : The sphere in which woman can play her role and the sphere in which she cannot are matters related to the permission of the husband and the real needs of the community. It is obvious that these determining factors are subject to change in accordance with the change of the circumstances.

However, two things must be considered before a particular task is delegated to woman. First, it should be seen that no disturbance is created in the status of woman and in the family institution.

Secondly, the laws related to both these subjects should be respected. With these precautionary measures it is not necessary that the woman should cover her face or hands when she comes out to work. The Quran says:

> *... that they*
>
> *Should not display their*
>
> *Beauty and ornaments except*
>
> *What (must ordinarily) appear*
>
> *Therein.* (XXIV -31)

'Except what (must ordinarily) appear therein' has been interpreted in various ways by exegetes. Here we quote a preferable interpretation. This has been reported by Aisha:

Once the daughter of Abu Bakr, Asma came before the Holy Prophet wearing a thin dress. The Holy Prophet turned away and said: 'when a woman comes of age it is not proper that any part of her body except the hands and the face becomes visible *(Abu Daud)*

Walking out is of less importance as compared to the face and the body. Perhaps for this reason it has not been mentioned separately. But if a society is corrupt and if the modesty of woman is in danger when she comes out, special precaution is needed. This is testified by the following Verse:

O Prophet! tell
Thy wives and daughters,
And the believing women,
That they should cast
Their outer garments over
Their persons (when abroad):
That is most convenient,
That they should be known
(as such) and not molested (XXXIII - 59)

'that they should be known (as such) and not molested' testifies to the consideration of the circumstances and the change in the law accordingly. Certainly Traditions indicate that before the days of the Holy Prophet and even in later times in Arab society there was the custom of covering the face. We need not go into details here.

But the reader can refer to the following works for his own benefit: (*Alminar* by Rashid Raza Misri, Vol. X, Chapter 11 and Vol. xiii., Chapters 9-10-11; *Hijabul Maratul Mussallema Fil Kitabe Wal Sunna* by Mohammad Nasiruddin Al Yani (Cairo and Beirut).

Societal Setup

Western Culture could not Provide a Firm Basis for Society : The basis of social life is the family. The condition of the family determines the social system. In western culture, the disruption of the family, the invention of new philosophies and the lust for money have precluded the formation of a firm basis for social life.

Consequently, life has become mechanical; every person feels himself or herself lonely and uprooted; and even the daughter of a millionaire has to work for her living by doing an ordinary job, for her father abandons the responsibility of supporting her.

Quality Relations among Men

The equality and amity in human relations has been emphasised by Islam. This is brought out by an incident in the life of the Holy Prophet. Once the Holy Prophet was talking to the Jews of Mecca on Islam.

On that occasion a ragged, blind man (Ibn-i-Umme Maktum) came in and expressed his desire to know something. The Holy Prophet did not like this interruption. At this the following Verse was revealed:

(The Prophet) frowned
and turned away
Because there came to him
The blind man (interrupting).
But what could tell thee
But that purchance he might
Grow (in spiritual understanding)?—
Or that he might receive
Admonition, and the teaching
Might profit him?
As to one who regards
Himself as self-sufficient,
To him dost thou attend;
Though it is no blame
To thee if he grow not
(in spiritual understanding).
But as to him who came
To thee striving earnestly,
And with fear
(In his heart),
Of him wast thou unmindful *(LXXX-1-10)*

Humanity and Equality

When there is slight corruption in society, ordinary reforms will do, but when the corruption is so deep that it seeps into the very fibres of a community strict measures are required and 'high' and 'low' have got to be inverted.Once Sohail b. Amr, Haris b. Hissham, Abu Sufiah and other dignitaries of the Quraish came to Omar. At the same time Sohaib, Bilal and other freed slaves also came. Omar gave priority to these slaves in giving an audience.

At this Abu Sufiah angrily said: 'I never saw such an outrage. These slaves get permission for audience (to the Caliph) and we keep standing at the door, and no attention is paid to us'. Sohail was more, he said: 'it is true; but we should complain, not against Umar, but against ourselves. Islam called equally to all, with one voice. Those of us who lagged behind out of their own negligence deserve to remain behind even today.(*Usudul Ghaba,* Vol. III, Tazkira Sohail b. Amr) It has been commanded that one should purge in oneself those elements that would cause disturbance in the social order.

The Arabic word for purgation or purification is *tazkiya.* Etymologically, it means cleansing something so as to make it capable of growth or development. The *tazkiya* of land means purifying it of weeds, levelling it, manuring, and irrigating it in order to make it capable of growing seeds. In the same way, the *tazkiya* of the self should mean purifying it of evil motives of thought and action in order to make man capable of moral and spiritual growth in accordance with the original, God-made, pattern of his nature.

Tazkiya of the self has its analogue in medicine. Just as medicine deals with the diseases of the body and their purgation or cure, in the same way *tazkiya* deals with the diseases of the soul and their purgation or cure. *Tazkiya* is needed in all spheres of life, and thus the main mission of the Prophet of Islam (peace be upon him) was *tazkiya.* Many Verses of Quran speak of it and words like *yuzakkikum* or *yuzakkihim* occur at many places.

But here we are concerned with the purification of those motives and tendencies which cause disorder in social relations. In the Islamic scheme, there are commandments for their purification. We give some examples below:

Prohibition against Riducule Slander etc. : Riduculing somebody, slandering him, taunting and calling him by bad nicknames, conceiving and propagating evil notions about him, picking up his faults, backbiting him or prying into his secrets—all such things are prohibited in Islam. The Quran says:

> *O ye who believe!*
>
> *Let not some men*
>
> *Among you laugh at others:*
>
> *It may be that*
>
> *The (latter) are better*
>
> *Than the (former):*
>
> *Nor let some women*
>
> *Laugh at others:*
>
> *it may be that*
>
> *The (latter) are better*

Than the (former):
Nor defame nor be
Sarcastic to each other,
Nor call each other
By (offensive) nicknames...
O ye who believe!
Avoid suspicion as much
(As possible): for suspicion
In some cases is a sin:
And spy not on each other,
Nor speak ill of each other
Behind their backs. Would any
Of you like to eat
The flesh of his dead
Brother? Nay, ye would
Abhor it... But fear God: *(XLIX 11-12)*

Prohibition Against Rejoicing at Another's Degradation etc.:

Islam prohibits rejoicing at another person's degradation and debasement. The Holy Prophet says: 'Do not rejoice at the degradation and debasement of your brother. Allah will take mercy on him and make you suffer in his place'. (Tirmidhi, Mishkat, Hifzullisan, *Fasl II)*

Making somebody ashamed at his wrong or sin is also prohibited.

The Holy Prophet says: 'The man who makes somebody ashamed of the sin he has repented, he will be involved in that sin himself before death comes to him'. *(Ibid)* Behaving as a tell-tale is prohibited.

The Quran says:

and heed not...
A slanderar, going about
With calumnies *(LXVIII-2)*

Tradition says:

'Those who behave as tell-tales create mischief among friends'. (Musnad-i-Ahmad, *p. 459)*

Breaking of Engagements, Duplicity and Violation of the Bonds of Kinship Prohibited.

Breaking of engagement is prohibited. The Quran says:

For (every) engagement

Will be enquired into

(On the Day of Reckoning). *(VII-34)*

The Holy Prophet has regarded the breaking of engagement as a sign of hypocrisy. He condemns the man who makes some engagement or promise and then breaks it and does the opposite. (Bukhari, Muslim)

Duplicity is also prohibited. A Tradition says: 'On the Day of Judgment the Double dealer will be in the worst plight—he is the man who shows one face to some person and another face to other person. (Bukhari, *Kitabul Adab). Another Tradition says: 'He who is a double dealer in this world, his tongue will be of fire on the Day of Judgment.* (Abu Daud, *Kitabul Adab)*

Violating the bond of kinship and showing inconsiderateness to kinsfolk has been prohibited.

The people who do it have been regarded as mischief-makers by the Quran:

Those who break God's covenant

After it is ratified,

And who sunder

What God has ordered to be joined,

And do mischief on earth:

These cause loss (only) to themselves. *(II-27)*

Evil Traits Disallowed

Pride was first manifested by Satan when he said:

... 'I am better

Than he' (Adam) (VII-12)

Pride hardens the heart or seals it up and insulates it

Thus doth God seal up

Every heart— of arrogant

And obstinate transgressors. (XL-35)

Pride deprives man of God's love. The Quran says:

For god loveth not

The arrogant, the vainglorious: *(IV-36)*

Pride or arrogance shuts the doors upon courtesies, which doors are actually the means to enter paradise. The Holy Prophet says: 'He who has a single atom of pride in his heart he will not enter paradise'.

(Abu Daud, *Kitabul Libas)*

Jealousy is the source of all social evils and it is something very dangerous. God has commanded the Holy Prophet and every Muslim to seek refuge with God from jealously—'I seek refuge'

From mischief

Of the envious one

As he practises envy. *(CXIII-5)*

The Holy Prophet says:

Beware of jealousy and avoid it, for jealousy eats the virtues just as fire eats wood.
(Abu Daud Kitabul Adab, Bab Fil Hasad)

False accusation, that is, imputing some evil to the other person, which is not there in him, is condemnable (even if the evil is there in him talking about it is backbiting). The Quran says:

And if anyone earns

Sin, he earns it against

His own soul; *(IV-111)*

And those who annoy

Believing men and women

Undeservedly, bear (On themsleves)

A calumny and a glaring sin. *(XXXIII-58)*

Moral Life

Working oneself into anger or getting enraged has been condemned by Islam. Those who overcome their anger are regarded as pious ones by the Quran. Those 'who restrain anger' (III. 134) are the righteous ones according to the Quran. They are those who forgive even 'when they are angry'. (XLII. 37). The Holy Prophet said: 'The heroic warrior is not one who flings down the other person, but one who controls himself in anger'. (Bukhari, *Kitabul Adab, Babul Hazr Minal Ghazab). Another Tradition says: 'Anger is from Satan, and Satan is made of fire. The fire is killed down and extinguished by water, therefore, he who gets anger must perform ablution.'* (Abu Daud, *Kitabul Adab)*

Malice and rancour are condemned because they hamper the fulfilment of one's duties towards God's creatures, just as joining partners with God hampers the fulfilment of one's duties towards God. We are commanded to pray to God for freedom from malice:

And leave not, in our hearts,

Rancour (or sense of injury)

Against those who have believed *(LIX-10)*

The Holy Prophet says: 'Do not have rancour and malice against one another; do not be jealous of one another; live like brothers and sisters'. *(Bukhari, Muslim)*

Regarding showing off and exultation it is said:

And be not like those

Who started from their homes

Insolently and to be seen of men. *(VIII-47)*

And how many populations

We destroyed, which existed

In their life (of ease and plenty); *(XXVIII - 58)*

Use of abusive and obscene language, whether charged with sexuality or rage, has been strictly prohibited.

Let there be no obscenity,

Nor wickedness,

nor wrangling

In the Hajj. *(II-197)*

The Holy Prophet said: 'It is a sacrilege to speak ill against a Muslim, and to murder him is infidelity'. *(Bukhari,* Kitabul Adab). In this regard, another Tradition says: 'A Believer never indulges in taunts and slanders, ill language and obscenity'. *(Tirmidhi Abwabul* Birri wal Sila).

In fact any behaviour, gesture, speech or action that creates disturbance in social life has been strictly prohibited.

Some Commandments Regarding Eating and Drinking, Dress etc.: In the Islamic scheme of cultural reconstruction, the social order has been given so much importance that etiquettes have been laid down in respect of eating and drinking, dress and appearance.

Obviously, the purpose is to prevent the social evils that arise from bad form.

With regard to eating and drinking the following commandments have been given:

1. You must eat with your right hand.
2. You must have an attitude of reverence towards food.
3. You must eat sitting. (If you eat standing, or if you sit on some high place and put your food on some low place, it is against the Islamic way of life.
4. Eat only as much as to cause no indigestion.
5. You must not eat unlawful things or things about which you have doubts as to their lawfulness.

Similarly, there are commandments regarding dress and appearance. For example:

1. You must not imitate or try to resemble any particular community in matters of dress and appearance.
2. It must not be the dress and appearance of those who are proud or indecent.
3. Silken dresses are forbidden for men.
4. The dress must not be such that it does not cover your shame— the parts that decency demands to be covered— or such as is likely to stimulate erotic feelings.
5. Women must be specially careful to maintain modesty in their dress and appearance.

One must take care of two things in matters of spending money and goods:

1. There must be no extravagance, both in terms of appropriateness and quantity of the expenditure.
2. The purpose of the expenditure must not be show-off or impressing the people of poor means with your wealth and position.

   This is no occasion for going into the details of the subject which has been discussed at length in various books dealing with the Islamic way of life.

Staunch Belief

The Muhammadan rule of faith is based upon what are called the four foundations of orthodoxy, namely, the Quran, or, as it is called Kalam Ullah, the Word of God; .the Hadith (pl. Ahadith), or the traditions of the saying and practice of Muhammad; Ijma, or the consent of the Mujtahidin, or learned doctors; and Qias, or the analogical reasoning of the learned.

In studying the Muhammadan religious system it must be well understood that Islam is not simply the religion of the Quran, but that all Muhammadans, whether Sunni, Shia, or Wahabi, receive the Traditions as an authority in matters of faith and practice. The Sunni Muhammadans arrogate to themselves the title of traditionists; but the Shias also receive the Hadith as binding upon them, although they do not acknowledge the same collection of traditions as those received by their opponents. The Wahabis receive the "six correct books of the Sunnis."

The example of Muhammad is just as binding upon the Muslim, as that of Him who said, "Learn of me" is upon the Christian, and very many were the injunctions which the "Prophet" gave as to the transmission of his sayings and practice, and very elaborate is the canon whereby Muslims arrive at what they believe to be the example of their Prophet. If, therefore, the grand and elaborate system of morals as expressed in the law of Islam has failed to raise the standard of morality amongst the nations of the earth which have embraced its creed, it is not unreasonable to conclude that its failure rests in the absence of a living example of truth.

The word Quran is derived from the Arabic Qara, which occurs at the commencement of Sura xcv., which is said to have been the first chapter revealed to Muhammad; and has the same meaning as the Hebrew kara, "to read," or "to recite," which is frequently used in Jeremiah xxxvi., as well as in other places in the Old Testament. It is, therefore, equivalent to the Hebrew mikra, rendered in Nehemiah viii. 18. "the reading." It is the title given to the Muhammadan Scriptures which are usually appealed to and quoted from as the "Quran Majid," or the "Glorious Quran"; the "Quran Sharif " or the "Noble Quran"; and is also called the "Furqan," or "Distinguisher," "Kalam Ullah," or the "Word of God" and "Al Kitab," or "the Book.

Muhammadans believe the Quran to be the inspired Word of God sent down to the lowest heaven complete, and then revealed from time to time to the Prophet by the Angel Jibbrail.

There is, however, only one distinct assertion in the Quran to Jibbrail having been the medium of inspiration, namely, Sura-i-Baqr (ii.), 91; and this occurs in a Medina Sura, revealed about seven years after the Prophet's rule had been established. In the Sura-i-Shura (xxvi.), 192, the Quran is said to have been given by the "Ruh ul Amin," or Faithful Spirit; and in the Sura-i-Najm. (iii.), 5, Muhammad claims to have been taught by the "Shad Eid-ul-Qua," or One terrible in power; and in the Traditions the agent of inspiration is generally spoken of as "an angel" (malak) .5 It is, therefore, not quite certain through what agency Muhammad believed himself to be inspired of God. According to Aishah, one of the Prophet's wives, the revelation was first communicated in dreams.

Aishah relates : "The first revelations which the Prophet received were in true dreams; and he never dreamt but it came to pass as regularly as the dawn of day. After this the Prophet was fond of retirement, and used to seclude himself in a cave in mount Hira and worship there day and night. He would, whenever he wished, return to his family at Mecca, and then go back again, taking with him the necessaries of life.

Thus, he continued to return to Khadijah from time to time, until one day the revelation came down to him, and the angel (malak) came to him and said, 'Read' (igaraa); but the Prophet said,' I am not a reader.' And the Prophet related, that he (i.e. the angel) took hold of me and squeezed me as much as I could bear, and he then let me go and said again, 'Read!' And I said,' I am not a reader.' Then he took hold to me a second time, and squeezed me as much as I could bear, and then let me go, and said 'Read!' And I said,' I am not a reader.' Then he took hold of me a third time and squeezed me as much as I could bear, and said:

"'Read! in the name of thy Lord who created;

Created man from a clot of blood in the womb.

"'Read! for thy Lord is the most beneficent,

He hath taught men the use of the pen;

He hath taught man that which he knoweth not."

"Then the Prophet repeated the words himself, and with his heart trembling he returned (i.e., from Hira to Mecca) to Khadijah, and said, 'Wrap me up, wrap me up.' And they wrapped him up in a garment till" his fear was dispelled, and he told Khadijah what had passed, and he said : 'Verily, I was afraid I should have died.' Then Khadijah said,' No, it will not be so. I swear by God, He will never make you melancholy or sad. For verily you are kind to your relatives" you speak the truth, you are faithful in trust, you bear the afflictions of the people, you spend in good works what you gain in trade, you are hospitable, and you assist your fellow men'. 'After this, Khadijah took the Prophet to Waraqa, who was the son of her uncle, and she said to him, 'O son of my uncle! hear what your brother's son says.' Then Waraqa said to the Prophet,' O son of my brother! what do you see?' Then the Prophet told Waraqa what he saw, and Waraqa said,' That is the Namus which God sent to Moses.' Aishah also relates that Harith-bin-Hisham asked the Prophet, How did the revelation come to you?' and the Prophet said,' Sometimes like the noise of a bell, and sometimes the angle would come and converse with me in the shape of a man.'"

According to Aishah's statement, the Sura-i-Alaq (xcvi.) was the first portion of the Quran revealed; but it is more probable that the poetical Suras, in which there is no express declaration of the prophetic office, or of a divine commission, were composed at an earlier period. Internal evidence would assign the earliest date to the Suras Zilzal (xcix.), Asar (ciii.), Adiyat (c.), and Fatiha (i.), which are rather the utterances of a searcher after truth than of an Apostle of God.

The whole book was not arranged until after Muhammad's death but it is believed that the Prophet himself divided the Suras and gave most of them their present titles, which are chosen from some word which occurs in the chapter. The following is the account of the collection and arrangement of the Quran, as it stands at present, as given in traditions recorded by Bukhari.'

> *"Zaid-ibn-Sabit, relates:- Abu-Bakr sent a person to me, and called me to him, at the time of the battle with the people of Zemamah; and I went to him, and Umar was with him; and Abu-Bakr said to me, "Umar came to me and said, Verily, a great many of the readers of the Quran were slain on the day of the battle with the people of Zemamah; and really I am afraid that if the slaughter should be great, much will be lost from the Quran, because every person remembers something of it; and, verily, I see it advisable for you to order the Quran to be collected into one book.' I said to Umar,' How can I do a thing which the 'Prophet has not done?' He said, I swear by God, this collecting of the Quran is a good thing.' And Umar used to be constantly returning to me and saying: You must collect the Quran,' till" at length God opened my breast so to do, and I saw what Umar had been ad-*

vising.' And Zaid-ibn-Sabit says that, Abu-Bakr said to me, "You are a young and sensible man, and I do not suspect you of forgetfulness, negligence, or perfidy; and, verily, you used to write for the Prophet his instructions from above; then look for the Quran in every place and collect it." I said, "I swear by God, that if people had ordered me to carry a mountain about from one place to another, it would not be heavier upon me than the order which Abu-Bakr has given for collecting the Quran." I said to Abu-Bakr, "How do you do a thing which the Prophet of God did not?" He said, "By God, this collecting of the Quran is a good act." And he used perpetually to return to me, until God put it into my heart to do the thing which the heart of Umar had been set upon. Then I sought for the Quran, and collected it from the leaves of the date, and white stones, and the breasts of people that remembered it, till" I found the last part of the chapter entitled Tauba (Repentance), with Abu-Khuzaimah Ansari, and with no other person. These leaves were in the possession of Abu-Bakr, until God caused him to die; after which Umar had them in his life-time; after that, they remained with his daughter, Hafsa; after that, Uthman compiled them into one book.'

"Anas-bin-Malik relates-Hudhaifa came to Uthman, and he had fought with the people of Syria in the conquest of Armenia; and had fought in Azurbaijan, with the people of Iraq, and he was shocked at the different ways of people reading the Quran. And Hudhaifa said to Uthman, "O Uthman, assist this people, before they differ in the Book of God, just as the Jews and Christians differ in their books." Then Uthman sent a person to Hafsa, ordering her to send those portions which she had, and saying, "I shall have a number of copies of them taken, and will then return them to you." And Hafsa sent the portions of Uthman, and Uthman ordered Zaid-ibn-Sabit, Ansari, and Abdullah-bin-Zubayr, and Saad-bin-Al Aas, and Abdullah-bin-Al-Harith-bin-Hisham; and these were all of the Quraish tribe, except Zaid-ibn-Sabit and Uthman. And he said to the three Quraishites, "When you and Zaid-ibn-Sabit differ about any part of the dialect of the Quran, then do ye write it in the Quraish dialect, because it came not down in the language of any tribe but theirs."

Then they did as Uthman had ordered; and when a number of copies had been taken, Uthman returned the leaves to Hafsa. And

Uthman sent a copy to every quarter of the countries of Islam, and ordered all other leaves to be burnt, and Ibn-Shahab said, "Khadijah, son of Zaid-ibn-Sabit, informed me, saying, 'I could not find one verse when I was writing the Quran, which, verily, I heard from the Prophet; then I looked for it, and found it with Khuzaimah Ansari, and entered it into the Sura-i-Ahzab.'"

This recension of the Quran produced by Khalifah Uthman has been handed down to us unaltered; and, as Sir William Muir remarks, "There is probably no other book in the world Which has remained twelve centuries with so pure a text."

That various readings (such as Christians understand by the term) did exist when. Uthman produced the first uniform edition is more than probable, and the Shias have always charged the Ansars with having mutilated and changed and made the Quran what they pleased;" a charge, however, which they do not attempt to prove, beyond the mere assertion that certain passages were omitted which favoured the claims of Ali to be the first Khalifah.

The various readings (Qiraat) in the Quran are not such as are usually understood by the term in English authors, but different dialects of the Arabic language. Ibn Abbas says the Prophet said, "Jibbrail taught me to read the Quran in one dialect, and when I recited it he taught me to recite it in another dialect) and so on until the number of dialects increased to seven.

Muhammad seems to have adopted this expedient to satisfy the desire of the leading tribes to have a Quran in their own dialect; for Abdul Haqq says," The Quran was first revealed in the dialect of the Quraish, which was the Prophets native tongue; but when the Prophet saw that the people of other tribes recited it with difficulty then he obtained permission from God to extend its currency by allowing it to be recited in all the chief dialects of Arabia, which were seven:- Quraish, Tay, Hawazin, Ahl-i-Yaman, Saqif, Huzail, and Bani-Tamin. Everyone of these tribes accordingly read the Quran in its own dialect, till" the time of Uthman, when these differences of reading were prohibited." These seven dialects are called Sabata-Ahruf and the science of reading the Quran in the correct dialect is called *Ilm-i-Tajwid.*

The chronological arrangement of the chapters of the Quran is most important. In the present Urdu edition, as well as in all Arabic editions, the Suras are placed as they must have been arranged by Zaid-ibn-i-Sabit, who put them together regardless of all chronological sequence. If, therefore, we arrange them according to the order which is given in Syruty's Itqan, we shall not fail to mark the gradual development of Muhammad's mind from that of a mere moral teacher and reformer, to that of a prophet and warrior chief.

The contrast between the earlier, middle, and later Suras is very striking. He who at Mecca is the admonisher and persuader, at Medina is the legislator and the warrior, who dictates obedience, and uses other weapons than the pen of the poet and the scribe. When business pressed, as at Medina, poetry makes way for prose; and although touches of the poetical element occasionally break forth, and he has to defend himself up to a very late period against the charge of being merely a poet, yet this is rarely the case in the Medina Suras, in which we so frequently meet with injunctions to obey God and the Prophet.

To fully realize the gradual growth of Muhammad's religious system in his own mind, it is absolutely necessary to read the Quran through, not in the order in which it now stands, but that in which Muslim divines admit that it was revealed. At the same time it must be remembered that all Muhammadan doctors allow that in most of the Suras there are verses which belong to a different date from that of other portions of the chapter; for example, in the Sura-i-Alaq the first five verses belong to a much earlier date than the others; and in Sura-i-Baqr, verse 234 is acknowledged by all commentators to have been revealed after verse 240, which it abrogates.

The Quran is divided into :

1. *Harf* (pl. *Huruf*), Letters; of which there are said to be 323,671.
2. *Kalima* (pl. *Kalimat*), Words; of which there arc 77,934.
3. *Ayat* (pl. *Ayat*), Verses. Ayat is a word which signifies "signs," and it was used by Muhammad for short sections or verses of his supposed revelation. There are said to be 6,616 verses inn the whole book; but the division of verses differs in different editions of the Arabic Quran. The number of verses in the Arabic Qurans are recorded after the title of the Sura, and the verses distinguished in the text by a small cypher of circle.
4. *Sura* (pl. *Suwar*), Chapters. A word which signifies a row or series, but which is now used exclusively for the chapters of the Quran, which are one hundred and fourteen in number. These chapters are called after some word which occurs in the text, and if the Traditions are to be trusted, they were so named by Muhammad himself, although the verses of their respective Suras were undoubtedly arranged after his death, and sometimes with little regard to their sequence. Musalman

doctors admit that the Khalifah Uthman arranged the chapters in the order in which they now stand in the Quran.

5. *Ruku'* (pl. *Rukuat*), Prostrations. These are of two kinds, the Ruku, of a Sura and the Ruku, of a Sipara, and are distinguished in the Arabic Quran by the letter *ain* on the margin. Muhammadans generally quote by the Ruku and not by the verse.
6. *Ruba'*, The quarter of a Sipara.
7. *Nisf*, Three-quarters of a Sipara.
8. *Suls*, Three-quarters of a Sipara.
9. *Sipara* '20 the Persian for the Arabic Juz. The Siparas or Juz, are thirty in number, and it is said that the Quran is so divided to enable the pious Muslim to recite the whole of the Quran in the thirty days of Ramadan. Muhammadans generally quote their Quran by the Sipara and Ruku', and not by the Sura and Ayat.
10. *Manzil* (pl. *manazil*), Stages. These are seven in number, and are marked by the letters F, M, Y, B, Sh, W, and Q, which words are said to spell Famibeshauq, i.e., "My mouth with desire." They have been arranged to enable the devout Muslim to recite the whole in the course of a week.

Ilm-ul-Usul, or the Exegesis of the Quran, is a science, some knowledge of which is absolutely necessary to enable the Christian controversialist to meet a Muhammadan opponent.

The words (alfaz) of the Quran are of four classes:—*Khass, Amm, Mushtarak,* and *Muawwal.*

1. *Khass*, Words used in a special sense. These are of three kinds:- Khusus-ul-jins, Special genus; Khusus-un-nau, Special species; *Khusus-ul-ain*, Special individuality.
2. *Amm*, Collective or common, which embrace many individuals or things.
3. *Mushtarak*, Complex words which have several significations; e.g. 'ain, a word which signifies an Fye, a Fountain, the Knee, or the Sun.
4. *Muawwal*, Words which require to be explained: e.g. Salat may mean either the Liturgical daily prayer (Namaz), or simple prayer (Dud).

II. The Sentences (Ibarat) of the Quran are either Zahir or Khafi', i.e., either Obvious or Hidden.

Obvious sentences are of four classes:- *Zahir, Nass, Mufassar, Muhkam.*

1. *Zahir*-Those sentences, the meaning of which is Obvious or clear, without any assistance from the context (karina).
2. *Nass*-Those sentences the meaning of which is Manifest from the text: e.g. "Take in marriage of such other women as please you, two, three, or four." Here it is manifest that the expression "such other women as please you" is restricted.
3. *Mufassar*-Sentences which are explained by some expression in the verse: e.g. "And the angles prostrated themselves all of them with one accord save Iblis". Here it is explained that Iblis did not prostrate himself.
4. *Muhkam*-Perspicuous sentences, the meaning of which is inconvertible: e.g. *Sura-i-Maida* (v.), 98, "He (God) knoweth all things."

Hidden sentences are either *Khafi, Mushkil, Mujmal,* or *Mutashabih.*

1. *Khaji*-Sentences in which other persons or things are hidden beneath the plain meaning of a word or expression contained therein: e.g. *Sura-i-Maida.* (v), 42, "As for a thief whether male or female cut ye off their hands in recompense for their doings." In this sentence the word Sariq, "thief," is understood to have hidden beneath its literal meaning, both pickpockets and highway robbers.
2. *Mushkil*-Sentences which are ambiguous: e.g., *Sura-i-Dahr* (ixxvi.), 15, "Vessels of silver and decanters which are of glass, decanters of glass with silver whose measure they shall mete."
3. *Mujmal*-Sentences which are compendious, and have many interpretations : e.g., Sura-i-Marij (Ixx.), 19, "Man truly is by creation hasty."
4. *Mutashabih*-Intricate sentences, or expressions, the exact meaning of which it is impossible for man to ascertain until the day of resurrection, but which was known to the Prophet: e.g., the letters Alif, Lam, Mim (A.L.M.); Alif, Lam, Ra (A.L.R.); Alif, Lam, Mim, Ra (A.L.M.R.), etc., at the commencement of different Suras or chapters. Also Sura-i-Mulk (xvii.) 1, "In whose hand is the Kingdom," i.e., Gods hand (Arabic, gad); and Sura-i-Ta Ha (xx.), "He is most merciful and sitteth on His throne," i.e., God sitteth (Arabic, istawa); and Sura-i-Baqr (ii.), 115, "The face of God" (Arabic, wajh-Ullah).

III. The use (istimal) of words in the Quran is divided into four classes. They are either Haqiqat, Majaz, Sarih, or Kinayah.

1. *Haqiqat*-Words which are used in their literal meaning: e.g., ruku, a prostration; zina, adultery.
2. *Majaz*-Words which are figurative.
3. *Sarih*-Words the meaning of which is clear and palpable; e.g., "Thou art free," "Thou art divorced."
4. *Kinayah*-Words which are metaphorical in their meaning: e.g., "Thou art separated"; by which may be meant "thou art divorced."

IV. The deduction of arguments, or istidlal, as expressed in the Quran, is divided into four sections: Ibarat, Isharat, Dalalat, and Iqtiza.

1. *Ibarat*-The plain sentence.
2. *Isharat*-A sign or hint: e.g., "Born of him;" meaning, of course, the father.
3. *Dalalat*-The argument arising from a word or expression: e.g., Sura-i-Bani Israil (xvii.), 23," Say not unto your parents fie" (Arabic, uff); from which it is argued that children are not either to abuse or beat their parents.
4. *Iqtiza*-Demanding certain conditions: e.g., Sura-i-Nisa (iv.), 91, "Whoso killeth a Mumin (believer) by mischance shall be bound to free a slave." Here the condition demanded is that the slave shall be the property of the person who frees him.

An acquaintance with the use of these expressions used in the exegetical commentaries of the Quran is of great assistance to the Bazaar-preacher, for it often happens that Maulavis interrupt the preacher by putting some difficult question, which the most able missionary will find it difficult to answer to the satisfaction of a mixed assemblage. For instance, an interesting discourse or discussion is often interrupted by a Maulavi putting the following question: "What did Jesus mean when He said, 'All that ever came before me were thieves or robbers?'" The best reply to such an one would be, "Maulavi Sahib, you know, sentences are Zahir or Khafi, hidden or evident.

That is Khafi. Hidden sentences you know are of four kinds, Khafi, Mushkil, Mujmal, or Mutashabih. I consider the text you have quoted to be Mujmal, and you must admit that it would take up too much time to explain a Mujmal sentence in the midst of my present discourse." Most probably the Maulavi -will be satisfied, for the preacher has applied a little flattering unction, in supposing that the Maulavi is learned in the principles of exegesis. It is often painful to observe how some of our preachers will attempt to explain the sacred mysteries of our faith in the midst of an ignorant mob. Whereas learned Muslim doctors, if placed in the same position, would decline to discuss mysterious questions under such conditions.

They would say, as the Christian Divine might also say, "Many things in God's word are hidden (Khafi), and cannot be explained to such a mixed audience as this, and besides this, in speaking of the nature (zat) of God, there is always some fear of blasphemy (kufr); I prefer speaking to you on that subject alone, after the preaching is over."

Muhammadan law consists of two divisions, Rawa and Narawa, i.e., Things lawful and Things unlawful.

I. That which is lawful is divided into five classes:

1. *Farz*-That which has been enjoined in the Quran.
2. *Wajib*-That of which there is some doubt as to its Divine institution.
3. *Sunnat*-The example of Muhammad, which consists of three kinds:

   Sunnat-i-Faili'-That which Muhammad himself did.

   Sunnat-i-Qauli'-That which Muhammad said should be practised.

   Sunnat-i-Taqriji'-That which was done in the presence of Muhammad and which he did not forbid.
4. *Mustahab*-That which Muhammad sometimes did and sometimes omitted.
5. *Mubah*-That which may be left unperformed without any fear of Divine punishment.

II. Things-unlawful are of three classes:-

1. *Haram*-That which is distinctly forbidden in the Quran and Hadith.
2. *Makruh*-That of which there is some doubt as to its unlawfulness, but which is generally held to be unclean or unlawful.
3. *Mufsid*-That which is corrupting and pernicious.

The divisions of lawful and unlawful do not merely apply to food, but also to ablutions and other customs and precepts.

Concept of Sin

The Muhammadan doctors divide sins into two classes, very much as the Roman Catholic divines do; the usual Roman designation being that of mortal and venial sin, whilst Muhammadans use the expressions Kabira and Saghira, "Great" and "Little". Kabira are those great sins, of which, if a Musalman do not repent, he will go to the purgatorial hell reserved for sinful Muslims. The divines of Islam are not agreed amongst themselves as to the exact number of Kabira sins, but they are generally considered to be seventeen (vide Fawaid-us-Shariat).

1. Kufr, or infidelity.
2. Constantly committing Saghira, or little sins.
3. Despairing of the mercy of God.
4. Considering one's self safe from the wrath of God.
5. False witness.
6. Qazaf, or falsely charging a Musalman with adultery.
7. Taking a false oath.
8. Magic.
9. Drinking wine.
10. Appropriation of the property of orphans.
11. Usury.

Chapter 4

Economic Life Under Islam

The Problem with Islamic Banking and Finance

Contemporary discourse on Islamic economics is too narrowly focused on issues related to Islamic banking and finance (IBF), whereas Islamic Economics, by definition, involves also domains of exchange other than the purely financial or commercial or market-driven.

As a matter of fact, it can be shown from Islamic economic history and the formal fiqh of mu'amala that by far the major domain of exchange in an Islamic economy is the voluntary, devotional and communal one, involving the operative mechanisms of zakat, sadaqa, waqf, hiba, qard hasan, hadiya, fara'id/mirath, wasiyya, including non-monetary lending and borrowing of tools and facilities, and reciprocal non-financial exchange of skills, services and expertise, and even goods. I think that it can be argued quite empirically that these non-market exchange mechanisms were in fact just as efficient, if not more, in the just, equitable and timely allocation of natural and cultural resources to those who needed them most.

One fundamental problem with current IBF, as has been pointed out by Meera, Larbani, Cook, El Diwany, Vadillo, and many others, is its adherence to the Fractional Reserve Banking (FRB) model also adhered to by conventional, usurious banks by which deficit-based money is created as credit as a multiple of the capital base in accordance with the capital requirements set out by the Bank of International Settlements (BIS) in the 1988 Basel Accord. So we have a situation in which an Islamic bank may be fully compliant on paper in its contractual form with the basic principle of loss and profit sharing in its business relations with customers, but the fact remains that at bottom the bank is still funding its investment through fiat money it creates out of nothing thanks to the usurious FRB principle.

According to Cook, "this reality is at best not made clear by Islamic banks and is at best deliberately obscured," and thus he concludes that "Islamic banking as currently practiced is an Islamic veneer on an un-Islamic reality." As Meera and Larbani elaborates:

Fractional reserve banking (FRB) is the basis of the present day monetary systems. In most countries, Islamic Banking and Finance too operates under this principle.... FRB has effects on the ownership structure of assets in the economy, and that this effect violates the Islamic principles of ownership money creation through FRB is creation of purchasing power out of nothing which brings about unjust ownership transfers of assets in the economy, to the bank effectively, paid for by the whole economy through inflation.

This transfer of ownership is not based on human effort by taking on legitimate risks and neither with the knowledge nor the consent of the initial owners. These violate the ownership principles in Islam and tantamount to theft. It also has the elements of riba.

On the same basis, Islamic governments should not create fiat money since this is equivalent to taking assets of the people, rich and poor alike, forcefully without compensation. It is, therefore, important that Shariah scholars come up with a fatwa on both the fiat money and the fractional reserve banking system. Such a fatwa is urgent and pertinent before Islamic banking and finance that operate under these systems, takes a course that may prove to be difficult to reverse later. The Islamic economic and finance system cannot be founded upon a money system that is fundamentally equivalent to theft and riba.

In short, fractional reserve banking allows the very few to consume the wealth of the great majority, wrongly and unjustly, in direct disregard of the divine injunction: wa la ta'kulu amwalakum baynakum bi al-batil = and do not consume your wealth amongst yourselves in vanity... (al-Baqara: 188).

As a matter of fact, quantitative studies have shown a direct correlation between FRB and compound interest, and the systemic destruction of both the cultural and natural environments in both so-called first and third world countries. It is also this system that privileges the short-term interests of the present generation over the long-term interests of future generations, who are forced to bear the debt-burden of our current lifestyle of profligate consumption and the systemic wastage of resources that goes with it.

Another problem in the current obsession with IBF is what has been called the murabaha (rent-seeking) syndrome, which is the emphasis on loan- or debt-financing (even though this may be "asset-backed") by means of elaborate mark-up instruments to ensure lucrative, risk-free profit on the part of the financing institution, regardless of the economic situation of the borrower or the financial performance of the borrowing enterprise.

This predilection for loan-/debt-financing results in the systemic marginalisation of venture capital financing (or commend, qirad/mudaraba) and financing by means of the business partnership (shirka, musharaka) in which the financing institution or investor provides (i.e., gives instead of lends) capital and participates in the conduct and outcome of the enterprise, which is thus seen and treated as a truly common enterprise.

To my limited knowledge (especially since I have taken a serious interest in economic issues only during the past two years or so), there is only one Islamic banking group in the whole world that is exclusively devoted to equity-financing and venture capital financing, while the rest are mainly devoted to conventional murabaha, rent-seeking instruments, with venture capital or commenda (qirad), business partnership (sharika), and the goodly loan (qard hasan) thrown in only as an afterthought to justify the label "Islamic."

Even when it comes to equity or venture capital financing, as in the case of that particular bank or rather venture capital investment company, the question arises as to whether the investment portfolio is spread out more or less evenly over both up-scale projects yielding high financial returns and medium- to small-scale ones yielding relatively low financial (but perhaps higher "social") returns, or concentrated on the up-scale ones. If the latter, then it is no better in essence than conventional western venture capital firms, whose motivation is mainly very high profit margins over the short and medium terms, with little or no concern for contributing to, and participating in, the larger communal well-being in which a particular enterprise is located.

In contrast, Islamic venture capital would be one whose investment portfolio is more or less evenly spread out over both market-driven and community-driven productive investment projects. In this way equitable allocation and reallocation of productive wealth is built into the general business culture in which the focus is not on financial growth per se but, much more importantly, on communal well-being and cohesion. Such a way of doing business will still make money and generate moderate profit and even moderate growth over time up to a certain size, beyond which a part of the company could break off and become a separate, autonomous entity, thus preempting over-accumulation and over-concentration of capital and wealth in the hands of a few powerful individuals or organisations.

The ideal company or corporate organisational structure would then be in the form of a management-cum-employee-owned enterprise (or common-ownership enterprise) instead of the present conventional structure in which ownership is largely vested in far-away absentee investors or shareholders (financially headquartered and coordinated for the most part at Wall Street) who don't really care a jot about the enterprise except as a disembodied, moneymaking machine.

This means we also have to realy, realy rethink the conventional notion of the corporation as a legal person. So, while the Islamic Gift Economy (IGE) willingly participates in the well-being of the community, the Wall Street Scoop Economy (WSSE) deliberately free-rides parasitically on communal wealth and sucks it dry, which explains the current system-wide financial and economic meltdown in the United States, Ireland, Greece, Spain, Iceland and Italy.

Rethinking Money, Finance and Economics

Of course, if we think along these radical (i.e., values-based-going-to-the-root-of-the-problem) lines, then we obviously have to rethink the concepts of 'bank' and 'banking', including the mutually related concepts of 'money', 'cost', 'benefit', 'revenue', and 'profit'; the concepts of the 'firm' and the 'corporation', employer-employee and management-owner relationships; the organisation of labour and commerce, and ultimately the concepts of 'economics', 'growth', 'wealth' and 'development'; including the largely unexamined concept of the GDP/GNP (Gross Domestic Product/Gross National Product) as a measure of well-being which has been so hegemonic over our economic thinking for the past five decades. It is beyond the scope of this general revisioning to go into these rethinking in any detail. I myself have started researching these issues only recently and am still in the process of critically synthesizing them within a coherent and viable counter-economic framework which engages conventional economics leading to a positive counter-economics and while systemically grounding itself in our worldview, tradition sacred law and history. But if we have more like-minded intellectuals, researchers and ulama joining hands and minds in systemically rethinking these foundational mu'amala issues, then eventually something positive will bear fruit, intellectually and operationally, in the very near future, in sha Allah.

By way of example, I believe everyone should seriously consider Chris Cook's very sound and practical ideas on "21st Century Islamic Finance," based on various forms of "debt-free asset-based finance" and "mutual interest-free deficit-finance or credit" that are "entirely consistent with the values underpinning Islam."

It is also pertinent here to say that this manner of systemic rethinking has been taking place for some time amongst the more conscientious economic and social thinkers and intellectuals of the West, such as Karl Polanyi, E. F. Schumacher, Kenneth Boulding, Bill McKibben, Herman Daly, Howard Zinn, Noam Chomsky and Hazel Henderson, including Mark Anielski (with his interesting book, Economics of Happiness), many of whose proposed solutions are in harmony, at least in spirit, with the Islamic imperatives of giving, gifting, sharing, temperance, moderation, justice, mutuality and gratitude, as these were realized in the long history of our traditional, community-centred socio-economic institutions. As a case in point, I see much of the traditional Islamic economic ethos reflected in the "green economics" of Molly Scott Cato and in Tim Watson's economics of "growth-less" prosperity.

Muslim economists, including intellectuals, policy makers, fuqaha and ulama in general, should make it an aspect of their communal obligation (fard kifaya) to take a deep, critical and proactive interest in these constructive trends toward an alternative or counter-economics, and thereby contribute a systemic and creative Islamic viewpoint to the global post-economic discourse. One important aspect of this communal intellectual obligation would be for ulama, researchers and intellectuals to work together to rearticulate traditional Islamic economic ethics in contemporary terms, and then to systemically work out the implications of this ethical framework for what is actually happening on the ground now in the modern economy.

Thus the IGE outlined here can be the basis of a comprehensive, long term Islamic Economics Research Program (IERP) leading to the eventual reclaiming and reviving of our civilizational heritage in the economic domain of life. We should view our tradition as the beacon of the present toward the future.

In tandem with the growing worldwide trend away from the Scoop toward the Gift economy, leading eventually to a future of global conviviality, Muslims today should remind themselves (through the works of Professor Murat Cizakca, for instance) that they do have a 1000 year civilizational track record in developing a successful and prosperous global gift economy, and that they should start revisiting, reviving and reliving that track record, both for their own well-being and for the well-being of humanity at large, and both for today and for the future: wa ja'alnakum shu'uban wa qaba'ila li yaiaarafu = and We have made you nations and tribes that you may become acquainted with one another (al-Hujurat: 13).

wa man yashkur
fa innama yashkuru li nafsihi
and whosoever gives thanks,
he gives thanks for the good of his own soul.

Revival of the Islamic Gift Economy

The Islamic Gift Economy (IGE; al-Iqtisad al-Infaqi) can be envisioned as an integrative economic system based on the operative principles of cooperation (ta'awun), mutual consent ('an taradin/ muradattin) and partnership (musharaka), and these are in turn founded on the principal ethics of rahma (mercy), gratitude (shukr), generosity (karam/ihsan), moderation (tawazun/ 'iffa), khilafa (trusteeship) and amana (trustworthiness/responsibility).

These operational and ethical principles are grounded in the foundational psychocosmological outlook expressed in the belief that (i) the natural and cultural resources of the world are abundant, while (ii) the material needs, wants and desires of human beings are limited and should be limited. The natural and cultural resources of the world seen as blessings and bounties (fadl) from the Merciful Creator (ni'am/ ala' al-Khaliq) are abundant and even unlimited in principle because wa-in ta'uddu ni'mataLlahi la tuhsuha: if you would count the bounty of Allah you cannot exhaust it (Ibrahim: 34).

Viewed in the light of belief (iman), these resources are gifts and favours (ala') from the realm of transcendence to which the human ethico-cognitive response is gratitude (shukr), which in turn results in contentment (qana'a). Hence man will take according to his need but not his greed, for because of abundance there is no anxiety over scarcity that feeds greed (tama') and accumulation (takathur/jam' al-mal wa ta'diduhu). Moreover, shukr itself becomes an existential and psychological state of being that is generative of abundance (ziyada) both material and spiritual, for la-in shakartum la'azidannakum = verily, if you give thanks, I will indeed give you more (Ibrahim: 7). Thus by definition, Islamic economics is an economics of abundance, and never an economics of scarcity.

In the secular darkness of disbelief and ingratitude (kufr), however, these resources are cut off from their transcendent, spiritual source, and restricted to their limited, purely quantitative level of being; hence man views these resources as limited and scarce, despite its actual abundance, and they will engage in mutual, unending competition over them out of anxiety over their perceived scarcity: al-shaytanu ya'idukum al-faqra wa ya'murukum bi alfahsha'i wa Allahu ya'idukum maghfiratan minhu wa fadlan = the devil promises you destitution and enjoins on you lewdness, but Allah promises you forgiveness from Him with bounty (al-Baqara: 268). Without belief, man will, out of anxiety, take these resources according to his greed (tama') without any sense of recognition of, and reliance on, their true, transcendent source, which in turns results in ingratitude (kufr al-ni'ma) and hence loss of contentment, leading to an existential and psychological state of perpetual anxiety and endless yearning: wa la-in kafartum inna 'azabi la shadid = but if you are thankless, then indeed my punishment is dire (Ibrahim: 7).

In this state, which can be referred to as the "pathology of consumption," what is attained is never really felt to be attained, and satisfaction is fleeting leaving in its wake disillusionment and boredom, and of course, ecological desolation of the cultural and natural landscape. The Australian economist Clive Hamilton has referred in his book to this state of perpetual anxiety and endless yearning that is never satisfied as a disease called "affluenza." Although he was not referring to the Islamic perspective on the situation, his thinking is of some significance in the interests of what my friend Faizel Katkodia of South Africa has referred to as cross-cultural "convergence on commonalities" in the quest toward finding common solutions to the common problems of humankind.

Thus, Muslims, if they are sensitive to the worldview of Islam, cannot go on agreeing explicitly or implicitly with the standard secular definition of economics that more or less asserts that it is the study of "the allocation of scarce resources to fulfill unlimited wants." This is because this and similar definitions of economics in the standard economics textbooks used throughout the world are based on two basic mistaken and largely unexamined dogmatic assumptions, one cosmological and the other psychological.

The cosmological assumption, as implicit in the phrase "scarce resources," is that nature is purely material without a transcendent source of being, renewal and regeneration, and so it must be a closed system, hence finite and limited.

The psychological assumption, as implicit in the phrase "unlimited wants," makes a claim about the nature of man, in that he is limited to his physical self and materialistic ambition without deeper spiritual substance and higher transcendent aspiration, hence he lives only to realize his immediate sensual, bodily desires and to create new desires, thus leading, from the Islamic point of view, to his seduction into "rivalry in worldly increase" as the only goal of his purely temporal life: alhakum al-takathur hatta zurtum al-maqabir = rivalry in worldly increase distracts you until you visit your graves (al-Takathur: 1-2).

In contrast, Muslims believe that (i) both nature and culture and their resources have a transcendent source of being, regeneration and renewal, and hence natural and cultural resources are not limited in respect of that transcendent source of renewal and regeneration, but rather they are abundant: wa atakum min kulli ma sa'altumuhu = and He gives you of all that you ask of him (Ibrahim: 34); and that (ii) man's self is both physical and spiritual in which the physical is embedded in and serves the spiritual. Hence man voluntarily limits his material desires through cultivating the self-discipline of zuhd (spiritual detachment and economic downshifting) in order that he might better realize his higher and truer spiritual aspirations by which he finds his true self and place in the larger order of creation and being.

He pursues his short-term material needs only in the conscious context of higher, more encompassing and long-term non-material goals and objectives and thereby attains to meaning and happiness in service of those higher imperatives. Thus man's material needs and wants are limited by virtue of his own impulse toward self-realisation of his higher, spiritual (i.e., intellectual, ethical and moral) calling, which transcends the temporal, sensual life of the world; bal tu'thiruna al-hayata al-dunya wa al-akhiratu khayrun wa abqa = Indeed, you prefer the life of the world, but the Hereafter is better and more lasting (al-A'la: 16-17). In other words, he finds his identity and destiny in the service of the transcendent and not in serving his whimsical ego.

This foundational Islamic cosmo-psychological outlook has deep and far reaching implications for how we should understand and engage both Islamic and Western economics.

Muslims need to be critically and creatively self-conscious about these two cosmo-psychological principles in order to formulate an authentic, integrative Islamic economic system that is viable in the contemporary age; namely, one that is autonomous and can stand and prosper on its own ethical and economic principles while in constructive engagement with the West, instead of one that is coopted, wittingly or unwittingly, into the mainstream, neoliberal free-market system, as is largely the case with what currently goes by the name of Islamic Banking & Finance (IBF).

This foundational consideration brings us to the notion of the Islamic Gift Economy and the manner in which we should go about defining it and outlining its general conceptual and operative parameters.

Defining the Islamic Gift Economy (IGE)

For our limited, critically reflective and programmatic purpose here, the Islamic Gift Economy (IGE) can be provisionally defined as: the provisioning and sharing, by mutual giving and receiving, of natural and cultural abundance for realisingmaterial and spiritual well-being. This definition takes into consideration that the world and humankind are not only material or physical but more fundamentally they are also spiritual and have a higher, spiritual or metaphysical significance. They serve a cognitive and moral purpose that transcends their immediate physicality or sensuality; namely, a purpose which is indicative of a higher, more encompassing Reality (al-Haqq) on which they depend, in which they are embedded, and to which they respond.

This definition of the IGE is made operative in practice by a systematic, integrative revival of the mechanisms of religious, social and commercial exchange as formally embodied in the traditional fiqh of 'ibada and mu'amala, such as zakat (obligatory charity), waqf (charitable endowment), sadaqa (voluntary charity), hiba (gift-giving), fara'id/irth (estate division), wasiyya (bequest), qard hasan (goodly personal loan), 'ariyya (lending something for use), ijara (renting and hiring), jatala (job wages), mudaraba (venture capital or financing a profit-sharing venture) and musharaka/sharika (business partnership).

Here the foundational notion of the 'gift' or rather gifting, giving and provisioning (sadaqa, hadiya, hiba and infaq) is significant, for deep reflection on the above-mentioned religious, social and commercial exchange mechanisms will show that they have less to do with taking than with giving, and hence, ultimately more about serving wider, communal/public rather than narrow, individual/private interests. As a matter of fact, even the so-called individual 'private interest' that is served in formal commercial exchange is inseparably embedded in the larger fabric of communal 'public interest', for it is a principal axiom of Islamic law that public, communal interest (maslaha 'amma) has precedence over private, individual interest (maslaha nafsiyya). Hence, the commercial is never in spite of the communal.

To illustrate this point, let us look at the institution and mechanism of fara'id/irth (the Islamic law of inheritance and estate division). Because of this law even the most greedy and accumulative of people will be compelled at the end of his life to redistribute his accumulated wealth amongst members of his extended family, such that at the end of the day he gives away, in a redistributive manner, very much more than what he has actually consumed of his hard-earned wealth. Another case in point is the august institution of zakat, which ensures that the urgent, material needs of the most vulnerable members of the community are immediately taken care of through a system of obligatory giving by its relatively more well-off members.

Even in the various formal systems of commercial exchange, such as the business partnership (musharaka/sharika) and the venture capital (madaraba/ qirad), the basic, underlying governing vision is still that of giving, i.e., mutual giving, of capital by the investor, on the one hand, and of skill, by the entrepreneur, on the other hand, to a common business enterprise, and the mutual sharing of the risks that go together with the benefits inherent in that common enterprise. Hence, what we have here is an economics of giving and receiving, not one of taking and hoarding.

We can glean from a close, intelligent and creative reading of, say, Ja'far ibn 'Ali al-Dimashqi's (circa 600 H) slim treatise the underlying message that good management of the self (ethics, akhlaq) is the basis for good management of the household (the original meaning of 'economics', or tadbir al-manzil), and this in turn is the basis for good management of society (politics, siyasa), and therefore the material economy should be embedded in the moral economy in order to realize a true economy of the common good leading to felicity in temporal and eternal life. As Essid explains:

We see here the beginnings of an ideology of the common good in which commercial exchange satisfies the common necessity, with trade raised to the rank of an eminently social link.

And so, in this mode of thinking, the market aspects and the welfare aspects are both integral, constituent aspects of the same economy, which, in this regard can be termed as the 'market-welfare' economy, or the Islamic Gift Economy (al-itqtisad al-infaqi), or an economics of "provisioning," in which profits and surpluses are to be reinvested into serving local communal well-being rather than the speculative interests and bottom-lines of far-way, indifferent absentee stockholders, or rather, free-riders.

This understanding of the underlying notion of "giving" or "gifting" finds support in Michael Bonner's careful study of early, pre-Dimashqian economic thought in Islam as exemplified in al-Shaybani's important Kitab al-Kasb. Here the corresponding notion is that of a virtuous circulative exchange between rich and poor or an economics of interdependence between rich and poor in which the surplus of the rich is "returned" (radd, ruju') to the poor in order to maintain order, peace and balance in society, especially in urban society. So the "gift" economy is the "return" economy, in which the circulation of wealth is from the rich to the poor and not from the rich to the rich, so that it does not become something which circulates among the wealthy in your midst (al-Hashr: 7).

The kind of run-away speculative, overly money-centred economics that has been systematically destroying middle-class America for the past few years or so would be something unfathomable to the Dimashqian and Shaybanian economic vision. As a matter of fact, al-Dimashqi devotes a number of pages of his treatise to warn hardworking, honest business people against the temptations of all sorts of speculative enterprises marketed by the sophisticated smooth talkers of his time, the kind of economic predators we now call "economic hit-men."

Similarly, his lucid explanation of why gold and silver have been the commonly-agreed medium of exchange and unit of value among all people doves tail perfectly well with the current call—in the face of the ongoing financial meltdown—for abandoning the overly centralized fiat, paper-money system and returning to the gold and silver system, and other forms of community-based "healthy" money and currency systems. This governing vision of mutuality, participativeness and partnership, or common interest and common good instead of self-interest, can be contrasted to the generally one-sided affair in conventional banking (including so-called 'Islamic' banking) in which capital is merely rented out by one party, say the bank, to another, the businessman/ entrepreneur, through various elaborate mark-up instruments, thus ensuring guaranteed returns to the bank without obliging it in any way to participate in the risks inherent in the enterprise, risks which are to be borne exclusively by the businessman/entrepreneur. Even informal, social giving or general voluntary charity and alms giving (sadaqa) has been institutionalized in Islam into a system called waqf (charitable endowment or trust).

Chapter 5

Concept of Justice in Islamic Law

Introduction

It is argued that Islamic extremism/fundamentalism has economic causes. Of greatest concern, however, is that a triumphant extremism/ fundamentalism has, without fail, seen justice to be synonymous with oppressive practices.

In Malaysia, for example, when the Islamic party PAS regained power in its stronghold north-eastern peninsular state of Kelantan, it attempted to enact the hudud. Only the Federal Constitution spared the people of Kelantan the horrors of severe punishments claimed to be divine in origin and, therefore, immutable. In a situation where the legal infrastructure is nominal the shariah courts were ill-equipped to bear the enormous burdens of a harsh system that involves such sentences as amputation of limbs and stoning to death. Muslims everywhere cast their everyday lives around the simple faith of a merciful and beneficent God: "In the name of Allah, the Beneficent, the Merciful". How is it possible then that Islam as practiced for well over a millennium, has been unable to allow love, mercy and kindness to surface?

Sources of Islamic Law

Is the law in Islam "divinely revealed or socially grounded? Positive or supernatural? Immutable or adaptive?" The answer to this question is fundamental towards an understanding of what divides the Muslim world today.

There are four sources of law in Islam: the Quran which is the Holy Book of revelations; the sunna or the exemplary actions of the

Prophet Mohammad as embodied in the Hadith; ijma' (the consensus of the umma as represented by the scholars); and, qiyas (conclusions by analogy). For purposes of analysis, it is convenient to categorise these sources into: the basic sources (namely, the former, i.e., Quran and the *sunna*) and the rational sources embodying both the latter.

Ijma' is arrived at through the practice of *ijtihad*, the method by which jurists recognize and make known the legal meaning of a Quranic rule or a sunna. *Ijtihad* gives rise to theories that are either accepted or rejected by *ijma'*.

These then formed what is commonly referred to as *usul al fiqh*, the sources of Islamic law. Note that here *fiqh* is used to mean law. It is not uncommon, however, for the body of Islamic law to be referred to as shariah and often these two terms are used uncritically as interchangeable. The shariah is one comprehensive system of law that is divine in origin, religious in essence and moral in scope. Although it does not exclude *fiqh* it is, in fact, not identical with it. *Fiqh* is the science of the shariah and unlike it is a human product arrived at through 'systematic' intellectual endeavour in an effort to interpret and apply the shariah accurately. It is also socially grounded. The confusion arises when there is uncritical usage of the term shariah to designate not only that portion of the law which is divinely revealed but also the human subsidiary sciences. As a consequence of such interchangeability in popular usage those who subscribe to the notion of divine origin and hence unchangeable nature of the essence of Islamic law view the whole legal system as being identical with the shariah in the pure sense. This renders the whole corpus, which evolved over some two hundred years, immutable.

As Hammudah 'Abd al 'Ati suggests:

> *"...much of this confusion can probably be avoided if the analytical distinction between the shari'ah (sic) and* fiqh *is borne in mind and if it is realized that Islamic law is held... to encompass two basic elements: the divine which is unequivocally commanded... is designated a Sharia in the strict sense of the word; and the human, which is based upon and aimed at interpretation and/or application of Sharia and is designated as fiqh or applied Sharia."*

Justice According to the Quran and Sunna

A Muslim may offend in two ways. Firstly, an offence directly against God for one may not claim rights against God. One has only duties towards Him. For instance, one cannot question God's existence or, as Islam is a monotheistic faith, believe in other than the one God [Quran: 73;9]. One may also offend against God by not performing the ritual duties enjoined – praying and fasting. Secondly, one offends God by offending one's fellow human. It is here that we confront the notion of ethical and social justice in Islam – our mutual rights and obligations in society; justice amongst and between persons.

> *"Thus it would appear there is a sense in which man as such has no rights within a theocentric perspective where God, the only reality, is in the centre: he has only duties to his Maker. But these duties in their turn gives rise to all the rights, human rights in the modern sense included."*

However, the secular concept of justice itself is an area of much contention. There is no one received definition for rendering unto everyone his or her due. D.D. Raphael in his book, "Moral Philosophy," writes:

> *"Left-wingers give priority to 'social justice' with an intention to reform society in the direction of greater equality and the removal of poverty. A right-winger's concept of justice (he is unlikely to use the phrase 'social justice') sets more store by the virtue of law and order, of stability, of reward for enterprise and merit."*

These are the two polarities of rational justice. The left-wing ideal is based on equality of well-being, where equality is synonymous with perfect justice, where discrimination towards any particular individual or group is permissible only so that they might attain 'greater equality' or achieve a higher level of well-being that is already the privilege of the better off. The right-wing meanwhile, gives priority to merit the concomitant of which is free competition. In the final analysis, therefore, justice must of necessity reflect the dominant ideology of the particular society.

The 19th century English philosopher, John Stuart Mill, sees the origins of legal justice in terms of man's desire to wreak vengeance. But this in itself has no moral value because the law, for it be acceptable, must reflect the common good of society.

"What is moral is, the exclusive subordination of it to the social sympathies... when moralised by the social feeling, it only acts in directions comfortable to the general good: just persons resenting a hurt to society, though not otherwise a hurt to themselves, and not resenting a hurt to themselves, however painful, unless it be the kind that society has a common interest with in the repression of." Views of what constitutes fairness often vary between different societies. The Quran, hence Muslim societies, endorses the concept of 'blood money' as recompense for a human life taken should the bereaved family wish it. In other societies, however, in the not too distant past, a thief could easily hang. In short, depending on where one commits a crime, a murderer may get away with his life but not a thief. Hence, Aristotle's observation that justice is relative to the constitutionally established principle of distribution of the particular polity.

In its form, then, there is a sense in which justice, be it legal, social or economic, is neither unchanging nor immutable in endeavouring to fulfil a function (its utility) in society. And, in essence, justice with its always ethical heart is a moral imperative. Possibly, in a completely harmonious society, egalitarian maybe, justice can become uncontentious.

In Islam, under conditions of freedom (not enslaved), everyone is equal before God. Before God a free man and a free woman is indistinguishable, one from the other, in their virtues and vices [Quran: 57;18, 33;35, 16;96]. Spiritually then, there is no mistaking that all free persons are equal. The Quran does, however, acknowledge the existence of social inequalities: one's neighbour's bounties shall not be coveted; the poor and the destitute must be fed and be given alms [Quran: 107;1-8, 9;60]. Now, how is this possible?

Voltaire wrote:

> *"all men would necessarily be equal if they were without needs. The poverty characteristic of our species subordinates one man to another. It is not inequality that is the real evil, but dependence."*

The key word here is 'dependence'. As there can be no such thing as spiritual dependence, before God then, as per our duties towards Him, everyone who is a free agent is equally liable. Unfortunately, society's less than egalitarian constructs do not lend themselves easily to equality. For example, much is said about us all being equal before the law, but in exercising our rights some are more equal then others because having money buys some better access to legal justice than others.

This is why in the Quran, the social milieu gives emphasis to the bonds between members of the umma and their relationship of interdependence built upon the principles of brotherhood that transcends physical boundaries. "Men, We have created you from a male and a female and divided you into nations and tribes that you might get to know one another. The noblest of you in Allah's sight is he who fears Him most." [Quran: 49;13]

For its part, the sunna is explicit. The Prophet Mohammad was once asked, "When will justice be realized on earth?" He was reported as having replied, "Not until he who sees injustice being done to another suffers from the sight of the injustice being perpetrated as much as its victims." This, therefore, is what justice must be in Islam.

Islamic justice can then be best understood in today's perceptions, dominated as it is by western philosophical concepts, as imaginative sympathy. As a result, social relations within the umma must be premised upon one among equals where everyone is viewed as an end-in-him/herself. Once this underlying principle of justice is understood the means to its application is obvious. In Surah Al-Balad the right path is defined as: "the freeing of a bondsman; the feeding, in the day of famine, of an orphaned relation or a needy man in distress; to have faith and to enjoin fortitude and mercy."

And no choice is left to the believer: "Those that do this shall stand on the right hand; but those that deny Our revelations shall stand on the left, with Hell-fire close above them". Accordingly, charity in Islam loses its voluntary nature and becomes for the recipient a legal right. That is how significant alms are in Islam, a condition made even more manifest in the Quranic prescriptions for their use.

"Those that give their wealth for the cause of Allah and do not follow their almsgiving with taunts and insults shall be rewarded by their Lord...

A kind word with forgiveness is better than giving charity followed by insult." [Quran: 2;262-263]

Indeed, it is possible from verse 9;60 to deduce that the Quran expects alms to be a sizeable enough source of public income.

"Alms shall be used only for the advancement of Allah's cause, for the ransom of captives and debtors, and for distribution among the poor, the destitute, the wayfarers, those that are employed in collecting alms, and those that are converted to the faith." [Quran: 9;60]

Thus, it is clear that alms in Islam are more akin to modern day taxation with its expenditure aimed at securing social welfare and defending social integrity. These are the moral imperatives that then "is the function of law to enforce", matters that have "a direct bearing on the regulation of life of man in relation to his fellowmen" and that the "fundamental rule of law is liberty."

In the Quran "God has set a bound to human activity in order to make legitimate liberty possible to all; without the 'bounds of God' liberty would degenerate into license, destroying the perpetrator himself along with the social fabric. This 'bound' is precisely what is called law which restrains human action within certain limits, forbidding some acts and enjoining others, and thus restraining the primitive liberty of man, so as to make it as beneficial as possible either to the individual or to society. Whatever their form, these rules tend to the same end and have the same purpose, that is the public weal *(maslahah)*. Accordingly, law [in Islam] is divine in origin, human in its subject-matter, has no other end but the welfare of man..."

But is the welfare of man served by harsh punishments of amputation of limbs? Is it served when women are regarded as "prisoners with you (men) having no control of their persons"?

The Secular Western Equivalent

According to Janet Radcliffe Richards, justice falls into two categories. Firstly, 'substantial justice', the principles of which determine "who should have what; how things should be shared out". In relation to the law this means that the law of the land would reflect the justice or otherwise expressed by this body of principles. Secondly, 'formal justice', which consists of the consistent and impartial application of the laws or actions within society that are deemed just. Or, outside the realm of law, formal justice is expressed in the rules and conventions of society. And, Radcliffe Richards argues that the one can indeed differ from the other.

And, because substantial justice is the core principles determining acts of justice, as in the constitutions of nations, it can never be right to suffer a substantial injustice. Substantial injustice can, however, occur when the principles that make up substantial justice have been overtaken by time. Take the obvious example from the West's not too distant past, of women's exclusion from ownership. If justice demands that in essence all adults are equal, why then were women excluded from ownership?

Therefore, to correct this very basic wrong an action not in conformity with the current body of laws has to be taken. In short a formal injustice (i.e. the passing of a law that contradicts the relevant principle of the extant substantial justice) is needed to correct this substantial injustice.

In Islam the Quran is the source book of law and hence that of substantial justice. It is Divine in origin and so infallible and eternal. It cannot be the cause for any injustice. Yet, it is the Quran that prescribes both gender equality and inequality; kindness and apparent cruelty. Why is this?

Even a cursory reading of the Quran leaves one with a sense that there are two elements of justice here: one dealing in broad principles and mainly to do with the notion of justice before God, implying compliance of conventions and rules and of moral decisions. Here gender equality and kindness is emphatic, with rewards and retribution being solely dependent on observance of duty. These are the Quranic principles that are equivalent to Radcliffe Richards' substantial justice.

And the other is written laws that leave little room for maneuver in the way of interpretation. Verse 4;34 appears to be a very good example: "Men have authority over women because Allah has made the one superior to the other, and because they spend of their wealth to maintain them." As a group these laws can be equated with Radcliffe Richards' formal justice. These would include the laws on inheritance, adultery, marriage, child custody and the punishment for theft, to name but a few. For the most part the punishments are harsh and where it treats of women these laws, taken on their own, are seemingly discriminatory.

The problem then for contemporary Islam is the existence of these inconsistencies in the Quran itself, between substantial justice (the tenor of the whole Text as represented by the relationship of humans to the Maker) and formal injustice (the laws). The egalitarian arrangement of humanity before God is not reflected in the social prescriptions of the relationships between human beings. The Quranic social organization appears to prefer men over women. There is then, a shift in perception from an egalitarian, equal before God perspective, to an unequal amongst humans social position.

[It is worth bearing in mind here that some fourteen hundred years ago the Quranic laws affecting women's social position were very enlightened. Fourteen hundred years ago most societies were patriarchal and women were mere chattels. To give women the right to inherit then was revolutionary; to consider women as witnesses, albeit worth only half the testimony of men, was outrageous for its time.]

Confronting the Muslim's Quandry

To go on; as practiced, in areas of the law where the Quran is not explicit, human ingenuity may take into account the needs of the prevailing circumstances. But in areas where it is explicit and at odds with modern day living only reasonable modifications can be made, reasonable in that it does not veer away from the letter of the pertinent parts of the Text.

Legal science in Islam, under these circumstances, cannot take into account the spirit of the Quran if it means altering the letter of the law. For example, to change the inheritance law to reflect gender equality is not something Muslim jurists have attempted to do as this would alter the letter of the Quranic law. The problem here is twofold: the problem of coinage, i.e., the language of communication between the Divine Author and the fallible reader, which is paramount; and, man's inability to transcend time and space thus limiting the comprehension of Divine expression. Man is limited to and by his historical context.

"...'The mind of the Divine Author' and the mind of the fallible readers are meeting, by the very hypothesis of revelation, in the same verbal territory. The one is necessarily using the categories of speech and literal symbol which are the realm of the fallibilities, and of all the right apprehensions, of the other."

In relation to this difficulty, the Quran is itself culpable:

> *"It is He who revealed to you the Quran (sic). Some of its verses are precise in meaning* [muhkamat] *– they are the foundation of the Book – and others ambiguous* [mutashabihat]. *Those whose hearts are infected with disbelief follow the ambiguous part, so as to create dissension by seeking to explain it. But no one knows its meanings except Allah..." [Quran: 3;7]*

But in verse 39;23 the Quran says: "Allah has now revealed the best of scriptures, a book uniform in style...." Which makes for Cragg's argument that "explicit", i.e., precise in meaning, and "implicit" or ambiguous should be taken to mean "literal" and "literary" respectively.

"For these are the associations of the roots from which they derive, and of the form of derivative. The *muhkam* (singular masculine) is that which is decreed or determined from authority, whether of rule or of wisdom. It denotes the legal and the authoritarian, the 'thus-it-is' quality of a sovereign will or of a competent tribunal. *Mutshabih,* however, has artistry and allusion in its nature. It relies on an image or of a figure from one realm for the illumination and expression of another."

This view, when acceptable, is permitting of a reading of the Quran as the complete and consistent whole that it is. To restrict oneself to only the obvious and then to discover apparent contradictions is to suggest that the Divine Author is in some way limited. As such, it is a Muslim's obligatory duty to limit the damage imposed by a fallibility we share with the ancestral language and appreciate the true majesty of the Message, for the fault can only lie with us and never Him. This is the essence of our faith in God. Any less would make it meaningless. To resist this possibility is to establish the arrogance that is man. For, is not contempt that allows us to blame God for what is cruel and conceit to applaud man for all that is good? This cannot be the basis of true faith.

Islamic Banking

Also known as participant banking Islamic banking refers to a system of banking or banking activity that is consistent with the principles of Islamic law (*Sharia*) and its practical application through the development of Islamic economics. Sharia prohibits the payment or acceptance of interest fees for loans of money (Riba, usury), for specific terms, as well as investing in businesses that provide goods or services considered contrary to its principles (Haraam, forbidden). While these principles were used as the basis for a flourishing economy in earlier times, it is only in the late 20th century that a number of Islamic banks were formed to apply these principles to private or semi-private commercial institutions within the Muslim community.

History of Islamic Banking

During the Islamic Golden Age, early forms of proto-capitalism and free markets were present in the Caliphate, where an early market economy and an early form of mercantilism were developed between the 8th-12th centuries, which some refer to as "Islamic capitalism". A vigorous monetary economy was created on thc basis of the expanding levels of circulation of a stable, high-value currency (the dinar) and the integration of monetary areas that were previously independent. A number of economic concepts and techniques were applied in early Islamic banking, including bills of exchange, the first forms of partnership (*mufawada*) such as limited partnerships (*mudaraba*), and the earliest forms of capital (*al-mal*), capital accumulation (*nama al-*

mal), cheques, promissory notes, trusts, transactional accounts, loaning, ledgers and assignments. Organizational enterprises independent from the state also existed in the medieval Islamic world, while the agency institution was also introduced during that time. Many of these early capitalist concepts were adopted and further advanced in medieval Europe from the 13th century onwards.

Riba

The word "Riba" means excess, increase or addition, which according to Shariah terminology, implies any excess compensation without due consideration (consideration does not include time value of money). The definition of *riba* in classical Islamic jurisprudence was "surplus value without counterpart", or "to ensure equivalency in real value", and that "numerical value was immaterial." During this period, gold and silver currencies were the benchmark metals that defined the value of all other materials being traded. Applying interest to the benchmark itself (*ex natura sua*) made no logical sense as its value remained constant relative to all other materials: these metals could be added to but not created (from nothing). Applying interest was acceptable under some circumstances. Currencies that were based on guarantees by a government to honour the stated value (i.e. fiat currency) or based on other materials such as paper or base metals were allowed to have interest applied to them. When base metal currencies were first introduced in the Islamic world, the question of "paying a debt in a higher number of units of this *fiat* money being *riba*" was not relevant as the jurists only needed to be concerned with the real value of money (determined by weight only) rather than the numerical value. For example, it was acceptable for a loan of 1000 gold dinars to be paid back as 1050 dinars of equal aggregate weight (i.e., the value in terms of weight had to be same because all makes of coins did not carry exactly similar weight)..

Modern Islamic Banking

Interest-free banking seems to be of very recent origin. The earliest references to the reorganisation of banking on the basis of profit sharing rather than interest are found in Anwar Qureshi (1946), Naiem Siddiqi (1948) and Mahmud Ahmad (1952) in the late forties, followed by a more elaborate exposition by Mawdudi in 1950. The writings of Muhammad Hamidullah 1944, 1955, 1957 and 1962 should be included in this category. They have all recognised the need for commercial banks and their perceived "necessary evil," have proposed a banking system based on the concept of Mudarabha-profit and loss sharing.

In the next two decades interest-free banking attracted more attention, partly because of the political interest it created in Pakistan and partly because of the emergence of young Muslim economists. Works specifically devoted to this subject began to appear in this period. The first such work is that of Muhammad Uzair (1955). Another set of works emerged in the late sixties and early seventies. Abdullah al-Araby (1967), Nejatullah Siddiqi (1961, 1969), al-Najjar (1971) and Baqir al-Sadr (1961, 1974) were the main contributors.

The early 1970s saw institutional involvement. The Conference of the Finance Ministers of the Islamic Countries held in Karachi in 1970, the Egyptian study in 1972, the First International Conference on Islamic Economics in Mecca in 1976, and the International Economic Conference in London in 1977 were the result of such involvement. The involvement of institutions and governments led to the application of theory to practice and resulted in the establishment of the first interest-free banks. The Islamic Development Bank, an inter-governmental bank established in 1975, was born of this process.

The first modern experiment with Islamic banking was undertaken in Egypt under cover without projecting an Islamic image—for fear of being seen as a manifestation of Islamic fundamentalism that was anathema to the political regime. The pioneering effort, led by Ahmad Elnaggar, took the form of a savings bank based on profit-sharing in the Egyptian town of Mit Ghamr in 1963. This experiment lasted until 1967 (Ready 1981), by which time there were nine such banks in country.

In 1972, the Mit Ghamr Savings project became part of Nasr Social Bank which, currently, is still in business in Egypt. In 1975, the Islamic Development Bank was set-up with the mission to provide funding to projects in the member countries. The first modern commercial Islamic bank, Dubai Islamic Bank, opened its doors in 1975. In the early years, the products offered were basic and strongly founded on conventional banking products, but in the last few years the industry is starting to see strong development in new products and services. Islamic Banking is growing at a rate of 10-15% per year and with signs of consistent future growth. Islamic banks have more than 300 institutions spread over 51 countries, including the United States through companies such as the Michigan-based University Bank, as well as an additional 250 mutual funds that comply with Islamic principles. It is estimated that over US$822 billion worldwide sharia-compliant assets are managed according to The Economist. This represents approximately 0.5% of total world estimated assets as of 2005.

According to CIMB Group Holdings, Islamic finance is the fastest-growing segment of the global financial system and sales of Islamic bonds may rise by 24 percent to $25 billion in 2010. The Vatican has put forward the idea that "the principles of Islamic finance may represent a possible cure for ailing markets."

Largest Islamic Banks

Shariah-compliant assets reached about $400 billion throughout the world in 2009, according to Standard & Poor's Ratings Services, and the potential market is $4 trillion. Iran, Saudi Arabia and Malaysia have the biggest sharia-compliant assets.

In 2009 Iranian banks accounted for about 40 percent of total assets of the world's top 100 Islamic banks. Bank Melli Iran, with assets of $45.5 billion came first, followed by Saudi Arabia's Al Rajhi Bank, Bank Mellat with $39.7 billion and Bank Saderat Iran with $39.3 billion. Iran holds the world's largest level of Islamic finance assets valued at $235.3bn which is more than double the next country in the ranking with $92bn. Six out of ten top Islamic banks in the world are Iranian. In November 2010, The Banker published its latest authoritative list of the Top 500 Islamic Finance Institutions with Iran topping the list. Seven out of ten top Islamic banks in the world are Iranian according to the list.

Principles

Islamic banking has the same purpose as conventional banking except that it operates in accordance with the rules of Shariah, known as Fiqh al-Muamalat (Islamic rules on transactions). The basic principle of Islamic banking is the sharing of profit and loss and the prohibition of riba (usury). Common terms used in Islamic banking include profit sharing (Mudharabah), safekeeping (Wadiah), joint venture (Musharakah), cost plus (Murabahah), and leasing (Ijar).

In an Islamic mortgage transaction, instead of loaning the buyer money to purchase the item, a bank might buy the item itself from the seller, and re-sell it to the buyer at a profit, while allowing the buyer to pay the bank in installments. However, the bank's profit cannot be made explicit and therefore there are no additional penalties for late payment. In order to protect itself against default, the bank asks for strict collateral. The goods or land is registered to the name of the buyer from the start of the transaction. This arrangement is called Murabaha. Another approach is EIjara wa EIqtina, which is similar to real estate leasing. Islamic banks handle loans for vehicles in a similar way (selling the vehicle at a higher-than-market price to the debtor and then retaining ownership of the vehicle until the loan is paid).

An innovative approach applied by some banks for home loans, called Musharaka al-Mutanaqisa, allows for a floating rate in the form of rental. The bank and borrower form a partnership entity, both providing capital at an agreed percentage to purchase the property. The partnership entity then rents out the property to the borrower and charges rent. The bank and the borrower will then share the proceeds from this rent based on the current equity share of the partnership. At the same time, the borrower in the partnership entity also buys the bank's share of the property at agreed installments until the full equity is transferred to the borrower and the partnership is ended. If default occurs, both the bank and the borrower receive a proportion of the proceeds from the sale of the property based on each party's current equity. This method allows for floating rates according to the current market rate such as the BLR (base lending rate), especially in a dual-banking system like in Malaysia.

There are several other approaches used in business transactions. Islamic banks lend their money to companies by issuing floating rate interest loans. The floating rate of interest is pegged to the company's individual rate of return. Thus the bank's profit on the loan is equal to a certain percentage of the company's profits. Once the principal amount of the loan is repaid, the profit-sharing arrangement is concluded. This practice is called Musharaka. Further, Mudaraba is venture capital funding of an entrepreneur who provides labour while financing is provided by the bank so that both profit and risk are shared. Such participatory arrangements between capital and labour reflect the Islamic view that the borrower must not bear all the risk/cost of a failure, resulting in a balanced distribution of income and not allowing lender to monopolize the economy.

Islamic banking is restricted to Islamically acceptable transactions, which exclude those involving alcohol, pork, gambling, etc. The aim of this is to engage in only ethical investing, and moral purchasing.

In theory, Islamic banking is an example of full-reserve banking, with banks achieving a 100% reserve ratio. However, in practice, this is not the case, and no examples of 100 per cent reserve banking are observed.

Islamic banks have grown recently in the Muslim world but are a very small share of the global banking system. Micro-lending institutions founded by Muslims, notably Grameen Bank, use conventional lending practices and are popular in some Muslim nations, especially Bangladesh, but some do not consider them true Islamic banking. However, Muhammad Yunus, the founder of Grameen Bank and microfinance banking, and other supporters of microfinance, argue that the lack of collateral and lack of excessive interest in micro-lending is consistent with the Islamic prohibition of usury (riba).

Shariah Advisory Council/Consultant

Islamic banks and banking institutions that offer Islamic banking products and services (IBS banks) are required to establish a Shariah Supervisory Board (SSB) to advise them and to ensure that the operations and activities of the banking institutions comply with Shariah principles. On the other hand, there are also those who believe that no form of banking that involves interest payments can ever comply with the Shariah.

In Malaysia, the National Shariah Advisory Council, which has been set up at Bank Negara Malaysia (BNM), advises BNM on the Shariah aspects of the operations of these institutions and on their products and services. In Indonesia the Ulama Council serves a similar purpose.

A number of Shariah advisory firms have now emerged to offer Shariah advisory services to the institutions offering Islamic financial services. Issue of independence, impartiality and conflicts of interest have also been recently voiced. The WDIBF World Database for Islamic Banking and Finance has been developed to provide information about all the websites related to this type of banking.

Fundamentals of Islamic Finance

The term "Islamic banking" refers to a system of banking or banking activity that is consistent with Islamic law (Shariah) principles and guided by Islamic economics. In particular, Islamic law prohibits usury, the collection and payment of interest, also commonly called riba in Islamic discourse. In addition, Islamic law prohibits investing in businesses that are considered unlawful, or haraam (such as businesses that sell alcohol or pork, or businesses that produce media such as gossip columns or pornography, which are contrary to Islamic values). In the late 20th century, a number of Islamic banks were created to cater to this particular banking market.

Usury in Islam

The criticism of usury in Islam was well established during the Prophet Muhammad (S.A.W) life and reinforced by several of verses in the Quran dating back to around 600 AD. The original word used for usury in this text was Riba, which literally means "excess or addition". This was accepted to refer directly to interest on loans so that, according to Islamic economists Choudhury and Malik (1992), by the time of Caliph Umar, the prohibition of interest was a well-established working principle integrated into the Islamic economic system. This interpretation of usury has not been universally accepted or applied in the Islamic world.

A school of Islamic thought which emerged in the 19th Century, led by Sir Sayyed, argues for an interpretative differentiation between usury, or consumptional lending, and interest, or lending for commercial investment (Ahmed, 1958). Nevertheless, Choudhury and Malik provide evidence for "a gradual evolution of the institutions of interest-free financial enterprises across the world" (1992: 104). They cite, for instance, the current existence of financial institutions in Iran, Pakistan and Saudi Arabia, the Dar-al-Mal-al-Islami in Geneva and Islamic trust companies in North America. This growing practice of Islamic banking will be discussed more fully in a later section as a modern application of usury prohibition.

Islamic Financial Transaction Terminology

Bai' Al 'Inah (Sale and Buy-back Agreement)

Bai' al inah is a financing facility with the underlying buy and sell transactions between the financier and the customer. The financier buys an asset from the customer on spot basis. The price paid by the financier constitutes the disbursement under the facility. Subsequently the asset is sold to the customer on a deferred-payment basis and the price is payable in installments. The second sale serves to create the obligation on the part of the customer under the facility. There are differences of opinion amongst the scholars on the permissibility of Bai' al 'inah, however this is practised in Malaysia (A set of strict conditions must be complied) and the like jurisdictions.

Bai' Bithaman Ajil (Deferred Payment Sale)

This concept refers to the sale of goods on a deferred payment basis at a price, which includes a profit margin agreed to by both parties. Like Bai' al 'inah, this concept is also used under an Islamic financing facility.

Interest payment can be avoided as the customer is paying the sale price which is not the same as interest charged on a loan. The problem here is that this includes linking two transactions in one which is forbidden in islam. The common perception is that this is simply straightforward charging of interest disguised as a sale.

Bai' Muajjal (Credit Sale)

Literally *bai' muajjal* means a credit sale. Technically, it is a financing technique adopted by Islamic banks that takes the form of *murabahah muajjal*. It is a contract in which the bank earns a profit margin on the purchase price and allows the buyer to pay the price of the commodity at a future date in a lump sum or in installments. It has to expressly mention cost of the commodity and the margin of profit is mutually agreed. The price fixed for the commodity in such a transaction can be the same as the spot price or higher or lower than the spot price. Bai' muajjal is also called a *deferred-payment sale*. However, one of the essential descriptions of riba is an unjustified delay in payment or either increasing or decreasing the price if the payment is immediate or delayed.

Musharakah

Musharakah (joint venture) is an agreement between two or more partners, whereby each partner provides funds to be used in a venture. Profits made are shared between the partners according to the invested capital. In case of loss, each partner loses capital in the same ratio. If the Bank provides capital, the same conditions apply. It is this financial risk, according to the Shariah, that justifies the bank's claim to part of the profit. Each partner may or may not participate in carrying out the business. A working partner gets a greater profit share compared to a sleeping (non-working) partner. The difference between Musharaka and Madharaba is that, in Musharaka, each partner contributes some capital, whereas in Madharaba, one partner, e.g. A financial institution, provides all the capital and the other partner, the entrepreneur, provides no capital. Note that Musharaka and Madharaba commonly overlap.

Mudarabah

"Mudarabah" is a special kind of partnership where one partner gives money to another for investing it in a commercial enterprise. The investment comes from the first partner who is called "rabb-ul-mal", while the management and work is an exclusive responsibility of the other, who is called "mudarib". The Mudarabah (Profit Sharing) is a contract, with one party providing 100 percent of the capital and the other party providing its specialist knowledge to invest the capital and manage the investment project. Profits generated are shared between the parties according to a pre-agreed ratio. Compared to Musharaka, in a Mudaraba only the lender of the money has to take losses.

Murabahah

This concept refers to the sale of goods at a price, which includes a profit margin agreed to by both parties. The purchase and selling price, other costs, and the profit margin must be clearly stated at the time of the sale agreement. The bank is compensated for the time value of its money in the form of the profit margin. This is a fixed-income loan for the purchase of a real asset (such as real estate or a vehicle), with a fixed rate of profit determined by the profit margin. The bank is not compensated for the time value of money outside of the contracted term (i.e., the bank cannot charge additional profit on late payments); however, the asset remains as a mortgage with the bank until the default is settled. This type of transaction is similar to rent-to-own arrangements for furniture or appliances that are common in North American stores.

Musawamah

Musawamah is the negotiation of a selling price between two parties without reference by the seller to either costs or asking price. While the seller may or may not have full knowledge of the cost of the item being negotiated, they are under no obligation to reveal these costs as part of the negotiation process. This difference in obligation by the seller is the key distinction between Murabaha and Musawamah with all other rules as described in Murabaha remaining the same. Musawamah is the most common type of trading negotiation seen in Islamic commerce.

Bai Salam

Bai salam means a contract in which advance payment is made for goods to be delivered later on. The seller undertakes to supply some specific goods to the buyer at a future date in exchange of an advance price fully paid at the time of contract. It is necessary that the quality of the commodity intended to be purchased is fully specified leaving no ambiguity leading to dispute. The objects of this sale are goods and cannot be gold, silver, or currencies based on these metals. Barring this, Bai Salam covers almost everything that is capable of being definitely described as to quantity, quality, and workmanship.

Basic Features and Conditions of Salam

1. The transaction is considered Salam if the buyer has paid the purchase price to the seller in full at the time of sale. This is

necessary so that the buyer can show that they are not entering into debt with a second party in order to eliminate the debt with the first party, an act prohibited under Sharia. The idea of Salam is to provide a mechanism that ensures that the seller has the liquidity they expected from entering into the transaction in the first place. If the price were not paid in full, the basic purpose of the transaction would have been defeated. Muslim jurists are unanimous in their opinion that full payment of the purchase price is key for Salam to exist. Imam Malik is also of the opinion that the seller may defer accepting the funds from the buyer for two or three days, but this delay should not form part of the agreement.

2. Salam can be effected in those commodities only the quality and quantity of which can be specified exactly. The things whose quality or quantity is not determined by specification cannot be sold through the contract of salam. For example, precious stones cannot be sold on the basis of salam, because every piece of precious stones is normally different from the other either in its quality or in its size or weight and their exact specification is not generally possible.
3. Salam cannot be effected on a particular commodity or on a product of a particular field or farm. For example, if the seller undertakes to supply the wheat of a particular field, or the fruit of a particular tree, the salam will not be valid, because there is a possibility that the crop of that particular field or the fruit of that tree is destroyed before delivery, and, given such possibility, the delivery remains uncertain. The same rule is applicable to every commodity the supply of which is not certain.
4. It is necessary that the quality of the commodity (intended to be purchased through salam) is fully specified leaving no ambiguity which may lead to a dispute. All the possible details in this respect must be expressly mentioned.
5. It is also necessary that the quantity of the commodity is agreed upon in unequivocal terms. If the commodity is quantified in weights according to the usage of its traders, its weight must be determined, and if it is quantified through measures, its exact measure should be known. What is normally weighed cannot be quantified in measures and vice versa.
6. The exact date and place of delivery must be specified in the contract.

7. Salam cannot be effected in respect of things which must be delivered at spot. For example, if gold is purchased in exchange of silver, it is necessary, according to Shari'ah, that the delivery of both be simultaneous. Here, salam cannot work. Similarly, if wheat is bartered for barley, the simultaneous delivery of both is necessary for the validity of sale. Therefore the contract of salam in this case is not allowed.

Hibah (Gift)

This is a token given voluntarily by a debtor to a debitor in return for a loan. Hibah usually arises in practice when Islamic banks voluntarily pay their customers a 'gift' on savings account balances, representing a portion of the profit made by using those savings account balances in other activities.

It is important to note that while it appears similar to interest, and may, in effect, have the same outcome, Hibah is a voluntary payment made (or not made) at the bank's discretion, and cannot be 'guaranteed.' However, the opportunity of receiving high Hibah will draw in customers' savings, providing the bank with capital necessary to create its profits; if the ventures are profitable, then some of those profits may be gifted back to its customers as Hibah.

Ijarah

Ijarah means lease, rent or wage. Generally, Ijarah concept means selling the benefit of use or service for a fixed price or wage. Under this concept, the Bank makes available to the customer the use of service of assets/equipments such as plant, office automation, motor vehicle for a fixed period and price.

Advantages of Ijarah

Ijarah provides the following advantages to the Lessee:

Ijarah conserves the Lessee' capital since it allows up to 100% financing.

Ijarah gives the Lessee the right to access the equipment on payment of the first installment. This is important as it is the access and use (and not ownership) of equipment that generates income.

Ijarah arrangements aid corporate planning and budgeting by allowing the negotiation of flexible terms

Ijarah is not considered Debt Financing so it does not appear on the Lessee' Balance Sheet as a Liability. This method of "off-balance-sheet" financing means that it is not included in the Debt Ratios used by bankers to determine financing limits. This allows the Lessee to enter into other lease financing arrangements without impacting his overall debt rating.

All payments towards Ijarah contracts are treated as operating expenses and are therefore fully tax-deductible. Leasing thus offers tax-advantages to for-profit operations.

Many types of equipment (i.e computers) become obsolete before the end of their actual economic life. Ijarah contracts allow the transfer of risk from the Lesse to the Lessor in exchange for a higher lease rate. This higher rate can be viewed as insurance against obsolescence.

If the equipment is used for a relatively short period of time, it may be more profitable to lease than to buy. If the equipment is used for a long period but has a very poor resale value, leasing avoids having to account for and depreciate the equipment under normal accounting principles.

Ijarah Thumma al Bai' (Hire Purchase)

Parties enter into contracts that come into effect serially, to form a complete lease/buyback transaction. The first contract is an *Ijarah* that outlines the terms for leasing or renting over a fixed period, and the second contract is a *Bai* that triggers a sale or purchase once the term of the Ijarah is complete. For example, in a car financing facility, a customer enters into the first contract and leases the car from the owner (bank) at an agreed amount over a specific period.

When the lease period expires, the second contract comes into effect, which enables the customer to purchase the car at an agreed to price. The bank generates a profit by determining in advance the cost of the item, its residual value at the end of the term and the time value or profit margin for the money being invested in purchasing the product to be leased for the intended term. The combining of these three figures becomes the basis for the contract between the Bank and the client for the initial lease contract. This type of transaction is similar to the contractum trinius, a legal maneuver used by European bankers and merchants during the Middle Ages to sidestep the Church's prohibition on interest bearing loans.

In a contractum, two parties would enter into three concurrent and interrelated legal contracts, the net effect being the paying of a fee for the use of money for the term of the loan. The use of concurrent interrelated contracts is also prohibited under Shariah Law.

Ijarah-wal-iqtina

A contract under which an Islamic bank provides equipment, building, or other assets to the client against an agreed rental together with a unilateral undertaking by the bank or the client that at the end of the lease period, the ownership in the asset would be transferred to the lessee. The undertaking or the promise does not become an integral part of the lease contract to make it conditional. The rentals as well as the purchase price are fixed in such manner that the bank gets back its principal sum along with profit over the period of lease.

Musharakah (Joint Venture)

Musharakah is a relationship between two parties or more, of whom contribute capital to a business, and divide the net profit and loss pro rata. This is often used in investment projects, letters of credit, and the purchase or real estate or property. In the case of real estate or property, the bank assess an imputed rent and will share it as agreed in advance. All providers of capital are entitled to participate in management, but not necessarily required to do so. The profit is distributed among the partners in pre-agreed ratios, while the loss is borne by each partner strictly in proportion to respective capital contributions. This concept is distinct from fixed-income investing (i.e. issuance of loans).

Qard Hassan/Qardul Hassan (Good Loan/Benevolent Loan)

This is a loan extended on a goodwill basis, and the debtor is only required to repay the amount borrowed. However, the debtor may, at his or her discretion, pay an extra amount beyond the principal amount of the loan (without promising it) as a token of appreciation to the creditor. In the case that the debtor does not pay an extra amount to the creditor, this transaction is a true interest-free loan. Some Muslims consider this to be the only type of loan that does not violate the prohibition on riba, since it is the one type of loan that truly does not compensate the creditor for the time value of money.

Sukuk (Islamic Bonds)

Sukuk is the Arabic name for financial certificates that are the Islamic equivalent of bonds. However, fixed-income, interest-bearing bonds are not permissible in Islam. Hence, Sukuk are securities that comply with the Islamic law (Shariah) and its investment principles, which prohibit the charging or paying of interest. Financial assets that comply with the Islamic law can be classified in accordance with their tradability and non-tradability in the secondary markets.

Takaful (Islamic Insurance)

Takaful is an alternative form of cover that a Muslim can avail himself against the risk of loss due to misfortunes. Takaful is based on the idea that what is uncertain with respect to an individual may cease to be uncertain with respect to a very large number of similar individuals. Insurance by combining the risks of many people enables each individual to enjoy the advantage provided by the law of large numbers.

Wadiah (Safekeeping)

In Wadiah, a bank is deemed as a keeper and trustee of funds. A person deposits funds in the bank and the bank guarantees refund of the entire amount of the deposit, or any part of the outstanding amount, when the depositor demands it. The depositor, at the bank's discretion, may be rewarded with *Hibah* as a form of appreciation for the use of funds by the bank.

Wakalah (Power of Attorney)

This occurs when a person appoints a representative to undertake transactions on his/her behalf, similar to a power of attorney.

Islamic Equity Funds

Islamic investment equity funds market is one of the fastest-growing sectors within the Islamic financial system. Currently, there are approximately 100 Islamic equity funds worldwide. The total assets managed through these funds currently exceed US$5 billion and is growing by 12–15% per annum. With the continuous interest in the Islamic financial system, there are positive signs that more funds will be launched. Some Western majors have just joined the fray or are thinking of launching similar Islamic equity products.

Despite these successes, this market has seen a record of poor marketing as emphasis is on products and not on addressing the needs of investors. Over the last few years, quite a number of funds have closed down. Most of the funds tend to target high net worth individuals and corporate institutions, with minimum investments ranging from US$50,000 to as high as US$1 million. Target markets for Islamic funds vary, some cater for their local markets, e.g., Malaysia and Gulf-based investment funds.

Others clearly target the Middle East and Gulf regions, neglecting local markets and have been accused of failing to serve Muslim communities. Since the launch of Islamic equity funds in the early 1990s, there has been the establishment of credible equity benchmarks by Dow Jones Islamic market index (Dow Jones Indexes pioneered Islamic investment indexing in 1999) and the FTSE Global Islamic Index Series. The Web site failaka.com monitors the performance of Islamic equity funds and provide a comprehensive list of the Islamic funds worldwide.

Islamic Derivatives

With help of Bahrain-based International Islamic Financial Market and New York-based International Swaps and Derivatives Association, global standards for Islamic derivatives were set in 2010. The "Hedging Master Agreement" provides a structure under which institutions can trade derivatives such as profit-rate and currency swaps.

Islamic Laws on Trading

The Quran prohibits gambling (games of chance involving money) and insuring ones' health or property (also considered a game of chance). The Hadith, in addition to prohibiting gambling (games of chance), also prohibits bayu al-gharar (trading in risk, where the Arabic word gharar is taken to mean "risk" or excessive uncertainty).

The Hanafi madhab (legal school) in Islam defines gharar as "that whose consequences are hidden." The Shafi legal school defined gharar as "that whose nature and consequences are hidden" or "that which admits two possibilities, with the less desirable one being more likely." The Hanbali school defined it as "that whose consequences are unknown" or "that which is undeliverable, whether it exists or not." Ibn Hazm of the Zahiri school wrote "Gharar is where the buyer does not know what he bought, or the seller does not know what he sold." The modern scholar of Islam, Professor Mustafa Al-Zarqa, wrote that "Gharar is the sale of probable items whose existence or characteristics are not certain, due to the risky nature that makes the trade similar to gambling." Other modern scholars, such as Dr. Sami al-Suwailem, have used Game Theory to try and reach a more measured definition of Gharar, defining it as "a zero-sum game with unequal payoffs".

There are a number of Hadith that forbid trading in gharar, often giving specific examples of gharhar transactions (e.g., selling the birds in the sky or the fish in the water, the catch of the diver, an unborn calf in its mother's womb etc.). Jurists have sought many complete definitions of the term. They also came up with the concept of yasir (minor risk); a financial transaction with a minor risk is deemed to be halal (permissible) while trading in non-minor risk (bayu al-ghasar) is deemed to be haram.

What gharar is, exactly, was never fully decided upon by the Muslim jurists. This was mainly due to the complication of having to decide what is and is not a minor risk. Derivatives instruments (such as stock options) have only become common relatively recently. Some Islamic banks do provide brokerage services for stock trading.

Microfinance

Microfinance is a key concern for Muslims states and recently Islamic banks also. Microfinance is ideologically compatible with Islamic finance, capable of Shariah-compliancy, and possesses a sizeable potential market. Islamic microfinance tools can enhance security of tenure and contribute to transformation of lives of the poor.

The use of interest found in conventional microfinance products and services can easily be avoided by creating microfinance hybrids delivered on the basis of the Islamic contracts of mudaraba, musharaka, and murabaha. Already, several microfinance institutions (MFIs) such as FINCA Afghanistan have introduced Islamic-compliant financial instruments that accommodate sharia criteria.

Controversy

In Islamabad, Pakistan, on June 16, 2004: Members of leading Islamist political party in Pakistan, the Muttahida Majlis-e-Amal (MMA) party, staged a protest walkout from the National Assembly of Pakistan against what they termed derogatory remarks by a minority member on interest banking: Taking part in the budget debate, M.P. Bhindara, a minority MNA [Member of the National Assembly]... referred to a decree by an Al-Azhar University's scholar that bank interest was not un-Islamic. He said without interest the country could not get foreign loans and could not achieve the desired progress.

A pandemonium broke out in the house over his remarks as a number of MMA members...rose from their seats in protest and tried to respond to Mr Bhindara's observations. However, they were not allowed to speak on a point of order that led to their walkout.... Later, the opposition members were persuaded by a team of ministers...to return to the house...the government team accepted the right of the MMA to respond to the minority member's remarks.... Sahibzada Fazal Karim said the Council of Islamic ideology had decreed that interest in all its forms was haram in an Islamic society. Hence, he said, no member had the right to negate this settled issue.

Some Islamic banks charge for the time value of money, the common economic definition of Interest (Riba). These institutions are criticized in some quarters of the Muslim community for their lack of strict adherence to Sharia.

The concept of Ijarah is used by some Islamic Banks (the Islami Bank in Bangladesh, for example) to apply to the use of money instead of the more accepted application of supplying goods or services using money as a vehicle. A fixed fee is added to the amount of the loan that must be paid to the bank regardless if the loan generates a return on investment or not.

The reasoning is that if the amount owed does not change over time, it is profit and not interest and therefore acceptable under Sharia.

Islamic banks are also criticized by some for not applying the principle of Mudarabah in an acceptable manner. Where Mudarabah stresses the sharing of risk, critics point out that these banks are eager to take part in profit-sharing but they have little tolerance for risk. To some in the Muslim community, these banks may be conforming to the strict legal interpretations of Sharia but avoid recognizing the intent that made the law necessary in the first place.

The majority of Islamic banking clients are found in the Gulf states and in developed countries. With 60% of Muslims living in poverty, Islamic banking is of little benefit to the general population. The majority of financial institutions that offer Islamic banking services are majority owned by Non-Muslims.

With Muslims working within these organizations being employed in the marketing of these services and having little input into the actual day to day management, the veracity of these institutions and their services are viewed with suspicion.

One Malaysian Bank offering Islamic based investment funds was found to have the majority of these funds invested in the gaming industry; the managers administering these funds were non Muslim. These types of stories contribute to the general impression within the Muslim populace that Islamic banking is simply another means for banks to increase profits through growth of deposits and that only the rich derive benefits from implementation of Islamic Banking principles.

Hence, the controversy that surrounds Islamic Banking continues. Is Islamic Banking really Islamic? This is a question that still is a matter of debate among the Muslim academia.

In Korea a proposal to open the country to Islamic Banking has been controversial.

The Relationship between the Waqf Institution in Islamic Law and the Rule of Law in the Middle East

Establishing a society based on the rule of law where the law is supreme and protects people against arbitrary powers is not exclusive to the West and is valued in other parts of the world including in Muslim countries. In most Muslim countries and many non-Muslim countries an effective system based on the rule of law is, as yet, unavailable. There are many reasons, including political, cultural, economic and legal realities, for the failure of the rule of law in Muslim societies.

The legal nature of the *waqf* institution and the system of land ownership in Islamic law has distinct differences to the institution of 'trust' and real property law in common law countries. These differences can be considered relevant in the failure to establish a rule of law system in Muslim countries. *Waqf*, which was established as an innovative institution from the early stages of development of Islamic law has frozen in time and arguably failed to be an effective institution in addressing wealth management in the Muslim world.

It is argued that *waqf*, which locked wealth and resources into unproductive institutions, has contributed to the weakening of civil society in the Muslim world. There is a reasonable literature available on this topic in both English and Middle Eastern languages (Arabic, Persian and Turkish). This chapter briefly reviews the historical background of trust in the common law system, and in Islamic law, and considers basic principles of *waqf* law under Islamic law. Then the paper investigates the *waqf* institution as an economic instrument in the history of the Middle East, and examines the relationship between *waqf* and the rule of law in Middle Eastern legal systems.

Historical Background of Waqf in Islam, Compared to Trust in the Common Law System

The trust, which is the major part of the Equity system, is an important area of common law legal systems. According to Frederic Maitland, "the greatest and the most distinctive achievement performed by Englishmen in the field of jurisprudence ... [is] the development from century to century of the trust idea." The origin of trust in the common law system goes back to medieval England.

After the Normans conquered England in 1066, most of the land in England became the property of the King. In order to effectively administer the land, the King granted land to noblemen, in exchange for the rendering of military services. These noblemen, in turn, granted smaller parcels of land to other noblemen. These grants of land formed the basis for the feudal system of land ownership in England. By 1086 (Domesday Book), the feudal system was well-established in England, and the land surveyed in the Domesday Book was held by the King (one fifth), the Church (one quarter), and by the King's followers (one half).

The King's followers, numbering about 1500, known as 'tenants in chief', provided services to the King. However, the King remained the paramount land-lord, and granting land on behalf of the King was the basis of all landholding in England. This doctrine of absolute land-holding by the King, and granting to tenants in chief in return for military and other services, is known as the doctrine of tenure, and became the basis of land law in English common law.

Over time, an intricate set of hierarchical relationships grew up through the tenurial system, with the King at the top, and various groups of landholders possessing rights to parcels of land. The complexity of the system resulted, by the 13th century, in the feudal system becoming both unwieldy and open to numerous claims to the same parcel of land.

By the end of the 13th century, the common law system, originated at 1066 when the Normans conquered England, became bound by a rigid formalism in which remedies could only be obtained through existing forms of writs, and further there were only a limited numbers of writs in land law. Further, alienation of land by ordinary tenants was limited by the claims of the feudal overlord and the tenant's own heirs (whether *inter vivos* or by will).

Land owners turned to a new innovative legal institution in order to avoid those obstacles in managing their land interests. The institution known as the 'use' is the basis of trust law and the Equity system in the common law systems. A trust exists in the case when the owner of a legal interest, for example, a land owner, transfers the legal title to another person, to be used for the benefit of other person or persons, or for some other purposes.

In other words, through a trust, equitable obligations will be created to deal with a property in a particular way. Indeed, by the creation of a trust, the legal title (in law), the equitable title (in Equity) and the beneficial title are separated in three elements, which are the trustee (title holder), trust property and the beneficiary or object of the trust. Initially, the courts of common law in England did not recognise the 'use' (*feoffees to uses*), but the practice was widespread and impacted on royal revenues to the extent that Henry VIII, in 1530, enacted legislation (the *Statute of Uses 1535* (27 Hen VIII c 10)) to abolish uses.

However, land owners and lawyers developed the device of a 'use upon a use' which was accepted by 1635, by which people created an extra 'use' to bypass the Statute of Uses. Following the passing of the Statute of Uses, and under pressure from the landholders, in 1540, the *Statute of Wills* (32 Hen VIII c 1) was passed, in which a statutory right was created to enable landholders to make conditional testamentary gifts of land. In addition, in 1645, the feudal tenure was abolished and the modern trust emerged.

The law of trusts, in common law countries, has been consistently amended and has acted to counter state intervention in wealth transmission and management by eliminating or reducing taxes, and limiting the government's regulation of individuals' wealth and property. According to Austin W. Scott:

It was chiefly by means of uses and trusts that the feudal system was undermined in England, that the law of conveyancing was revolutionized, that the economic position of married women was ameliorated, that family settlements have been effected, whereby daughters and younger sons of landed proprietors have been enabled modestly to participate in the family wealth, that unincorporated associations have found a measure of protection, that business enterprises of many kinds have been enabled to accomplish their purposes, that great sums of money have been devoted to charitable enterprises; and by employing the analogy of a trust, by the invention of the so-called constructive trust, the courts have been enabled to give relief against all sorts of fraudulent schemes whereby scoundrels have sought to enrich themselves at the expense of other persons.

Therefore, in contemporary common law systems, trust is acting as an important economic institution for management of properties, particularly for future purposes, as well as a legal mechanism in Equity to provide a cushion against instances of rigidness in common law principles. Indeed, the success and effectiveness of common law systems in the contemporary world can, to a great extent, be attributed to the development of a flexible equitable system within the English common law system. Furthermore, most of the principles of Equity have been developed through trust law.

Therefore, trust is both an important economic institution, which enhances flexible economic activities, and a legal mechanism which provides more effective justice.

Historical Background of Waqf in Islam

Under Islamic law, *waqf* (plural: *awqaf*) is an Islamic law institution originated in the sayings of the Prophet Muhammad (*Sunna*) which have had important impacts on the social and economic life of Muslim societies for centuries. According to Islamic jurisprudence texts, *waqf* did not exist in *jahiliya* (pre-Islamic Arabia – before 610 CE) and was inferred by the Prophet Muhammad (Pbuh). In early sayings of the Prophet (*hadiths*) what is now known as *waqf* is referred to as the '*sadaqato jariyeh* [continuous charity]'. During the time of the Prophet, properties such as mosques, water bores, land and horses were made *waqf* for charitable purposes. According to Islamic jurisprudence texts, and leading *Hadith* scholars, real property was the first incident of *waqf* in Islam, made by the second Caliph on the order of the Prophet.

Chapter 6

Psychology of Law in Islam

Islamic psychology translates the term Ilm-al Nafsiat the science of the *Nafs* ("self" or "psyche") and refers to the medical and philosophical study of the psyche as it flowered during the Islamic Golden Age (8th–13th centuries). Concepts from medieval Islamic thought have been reexamined by Muslim psychologists and scholars in the 20th and 21st centuries.

Terminology

Modern attempts at reviving the medieval Islamic study of the mind have referred to it as "Islamic psychology",. In the writings of Muslim scholars, the term Nafs (self or soul) was used to denote individual personality and the term fitrah for human nature. Nafs encompassed a broad range of faculties including the qalb (heart), the ruh (spirit), the aql (intellect) and irada (will). Muslim scholarship was strongly influenced by Greek and Indian philosophy as well as by the study of scripture. In medieval Islamic medicine in particular, the study of "mental illness was a speciality of its own", and was variously known as "diseases of the mind," al-'ilaj al-nafs (approximately "curing/ treatment of the ideas/soul/vegetative mind," also translated more simply as "psychotherapy"), al-tibb al-ruhani ("the healing of the spirit," or "spiritual health") and tibb al-qalb ("healing of the heart/self," or "mental medicine").

Ethics and Theology

Most ancient and medieval societies believed that mental illness was caused by either demonic possession or as punishment from a god, which led to a negative attitude towards mental illness in Judeo-Christian and Greco-Roman societies. On the other hand, Islamic ethics and theology held a more sympathetic attitude towards the mentally ill, as exemplified in Sura 4:5 of the Quran:

> *"Do not give your property which God assigned you to manage to the insane: but feed and cloth the insane with this property and tell splendid words to him."*

This Quranic verse summarized Islam's attitudes towards the mentally ill, who were considered unfit to manage property but must be treated humanely and be kept under care by a guardian, according to Islamic law. This positive neuroethical understanding of mental health consequently led to the establishment of the first mental hospitals in the medieval Islamic world from the 8th century, and an early scientific understanding of neuroscience and psychology by medieval Muslim physicians and psychological thinkers, who discovered that mental disorders are caused by dysfunctions in the brain.

Philosophical Approach

Intellect and Consciousness Studies

In the philosophy of mind, certain hadiths indicate that dreams consist of three parts, and early Muslim scholars also recognized three different kinds of dreams: false dreams, patho-genetic dreams, and true dreams.

One of the earliest Muslim psychological thinkers was Abu Bakr Muhammad Ibn Sirin (654–728), who was renowned for his *Tabir al-Ruya and Muntakhab al-Kalam fi Tabir al-Ahlam*, a book on dreams. The work is divided into 25 sections on dream interpretation, from the etiquette of interpreting dreams to the interpretation of reciting certain Surahs of the Quran in one's dream. He writes that it is important for a layperson to seek assistance from an Alim (Muslim scholar) who could guide in the interpretation of dreams with a proper understanding of the cultural context and other such causes and interpretations. Al-Kindi (Alkindus) (801–873) also wrote a treatise on dream interpretation entitled *On Sleep and Dreams*.

Avicenna (Ibn Sina) (980-1037), while he was imprisoned in the castle of Fardajan near Hamadhan, wrote his famous "Floating Man" thought experiment to demonstrate human self-awareness and self-consciousness and the substantiality of the soul. He referred to the living human intelligence, particularly the active intellect, which he believed to be the hypostasis by which God communicates truth to the human mind and imparts order and intelligibility to nature. His "Floating Man" thought experiment tells its readers to imagine themselves suspended in the air, isolated from all sensations, which includes no sensory contact with even their own bodies. He argues that, in this scenario, one would still have self-consciousness. He thus concludes that the idea of the self is not logically dependent on any physical thing, and that the soul should not be seen in relative terms, but as a primary given, a substance. Avicenna also wrote about the potential intellect (within man) and active intellect (outside man) and that cognition cannot be produced mechanically but involves intuition at every stage. As an analogy, he compares the ordinary human mind to a mirror upon which a succession of ideas reflects from the active intellect. He writes that a mirror can be rusty at first (i.e. before acquiring knowledge from the active intellect), but when the mirror is polished (i.e. when one thinks), the mirror can then readily reflect light from the Sun (i.e. the active intellect).

H. Chad Hillier writes the following on the contributions made by Averroes (Ibn Rushd) (1126–1198) to the field of psychology:

> *"There is evidence of some evolution in Ibn Rushd's thought on the intellect, notably in his Middle Commentary on* De Anima *where he combines the positions of Alexander and Themistius for his doctrine on the material intellect and in his Long Commentary and the* Tahafut *where Ibn Rushd rejected Alexander and endorsed Themistius' position that "material intellect is a single incorporeal eternal substance that becomes attached to the imaginative faculties of individual humans." Thus, the human soul is a separate substance ontologically identical with the active intellect; and when this active intellect is embodied in an individual human it is the material intellect. The material intellect is analogous to prime matter, in that it is pure potentiality able to receive universal forms. As such, the human mind is a composite of the material intellect and the passive intellect, which is the third element of the intellect. The passive intellect is identified with the imagination, which, as noted above, is the sense-connected finite and passive faculty that receives particular sensual forms. When the material intellect is actualized by information received, it is described as the speculative (habitual) intellect. As the speculative intellect moves towards perfection, having the active intellect as an object of thought, it becomes the acquired intellect. In that, it is*

> *aided by the active intellect, perceived in the way Aristotle had taught, to acquire intelligible thoughts. The idea of the soul's perfection occurring through having the active intellect as a greater object of thought is introduced elsewhere, and its application to religious doctrine is seen. In the Tahafut, Ibn Rushd speaks of the soul as a faculty that comes to resemble the focus of its intention, and when its attention focuses more upon eternal and universal knowledge, it become more like the eternal and universal. As such, when the soul perfects itself, it becomes like our intellect."*

"Ibn Rushd succeeded in providing an explanation of the human soul and intellect that did not involve an immediate transcendent agent. This opposed the explanations found among the Neoplatonists, allowing a further argument for rejecting of Neoplatonic emanation theories. Even so, notes Davidson, Ibn Rushd's theory of the material intellect was something foreign to Aristotle."

Ibn Khaldun's *Muqaddimah* (1377) states the following on dream interpretation:

> *"Often, we may deduce (the existence of) that high spiritual world and the essences it contains, from visions and things we had not been aware of while awake but which we find in our sleep and which are brought to our attention in it and which, if they are true (dreams), conform with actuality. We thus know that they are true and come from the world of truth. "Confused dreams," on the other hand, are pictures of the imagination that are stored inside by perception and to which the ability to think is applied, after (man) has retired from sense perception."*

Sensory Perception

Ibn al-Haytham's psychology in his *Book of Optics* (1021) may have also possibly been influenced by Buddhist philosophy, echoes of which can be in some of his views on pain and sensation. He writes that every sensation is a form of 'suffering' and that what people call pain is only an exaggerated perception; that there is no qualitative difference but only a quantitative difference between pain and ordinary sensation.

Avicenna was the first to divide human perception into five external senses (the classical senses of hearing, sight, smell, taste and touch known since antiquity) and five internal senses which he discovered himself: the *sensus communis* (seat of all senses) which integrates sense data into percepts; the imaginative faculty which conserves the perceptual images; the sense of imagination which acts upon these images by combining and separating them, serving as the seat of the practical intellect; *Wahm* (instinct) which perceives qualities (such as good and bad, love and hate, etc.) and forms the basis of a person's character whether or not influenced by reason; and intentions (*ma'ni*) which conserve all these notions in memory. Al-Ghazali (Algazel) (1058–1111) stated that the self has motor and sensory motives for fulfilling its bodily needs. He wrote that the motor motives comprise of propensities and impulses, and further divided the propensities into two types: appetite and anger. He wrote that appetite urges hunger, thirst, and sexual craving, while anger takes the form of rage, indignation and revenge. He further wrote that impulse resides in the muscles, nerves, and tissues, and moves the organs to "fulfil the propensities."

Al-Ghazali was also one of the first to divide the sensory motives (apprehension) into five external senses (the classical senses of hearing, sight, smell, taste and touch) and five internal senses, which he was able to describe more accurately than Avicenna. The five internal senses discovered by al-Ghazali were: common sense (*Hiss Mushtarik*) which synthesizes sensuous impressions carried to the brain while giving meaning to them; imagination (*Takhayyul*) which enables someone to retain mental images from experience; reflection (*Tafakkur*) which brings together relevant thoughts and associates or dissociates them as it considers fit but has no power to create anything new which is not already present in the mind; recollection (*Tadhakkur*) which remembers the outer form of objects in memory and recollects the meaning; and the memory (*Hafiza*) where impressions received through the senses are stored. He wrote that, while the external senses occur through specific organs, the internal senses are located in different regions of the brain, and discovered that the memory is located in the hinder lobe, imagination is located in the frontal lobe, and reflection is located in the middle folds of the brain. He stated that these inner senses allow people to predict future situations based on what they learn from past experiences.

In *The Revival of Religious Sciences*, al-Ghazali also writes that the five internal senses are found in both humans and animals. In *Mizan al Amal*, however, he later states that animals "do not possess a well-developed reflective power" and argues that animals mostly think in terms of "pictorial ideas in a simple way and are incapable of complex association and dissociation of abstract ideas involved in reflection." He writes that "the self carries two additional qualities, which distinguishes man from animals enabling man to attain spiritual perfection", which are 'Aql (intellect) and Irada (will). He argues that the intellect is "the fundamental rational faculty, which enables man to generalize and form concepts and gain knowledge."

He also argues that human will and animal will are both different. He writes that human will is "conditioned by the intellect" while animal will is "conditioned by anger and appetite" and that "all these powers control and regulate the body." He further writes that the Qalb (heart) "controls and rules over them" and that it has six powers: appetite, anger, impulse, apprehension, intellect, and will. He states that humans have all six of these traits, while animals only have three (appetite, anger, and impulse). This was in contrast to other ancient and medieval thinkers such as Aristotle, Avicenna, Roger Bacon and Thomas Aquinas who all believed that animals cannot become angry.

Sufi Psychology

In Sufi psychology, Nafs is considered to be the lowest principle of man. Higher than the nafs is the Qalb (heart), and the Ruh (spirit). This tripartition forms the foundation of later, more complicated systems; it is found as early as the Quranic commentary by Jafar al-Sadiq. He holds that the nafs is peculiar to the zalim (tyrant), the qalb to the muqtasid (moderate), and the ruh to the sabiq (preceding one, winner); the zalim loves God for his own sake, the muqtasid loves Him for Himself, and the sabiq annihilates his own will in God's will. Bayezid Bistami, Hakim at-Tirmidhi, and Junayd have followed this tripartition. Kharraz, however, inserts between nafs and qalb the element tab', "nature," the natural functions of man.

At almost the same time in history, Nuri saw in man four different aspects of the heart, which he derived in an ingenious way from the Quran:

> *Sadr (breast) is connected with Islam (Sura 39:23); qalb (heart) is the seat of iman (faith) (Sura 49:7; 16:106); fuad (heart) is connected with marifa (gnosis) (Sura 53:11); and lubb (innermost heart) is the seat of tauhid (Sura 3:190).*

The Sufis often add the element of sirr, the innermost part of the heart in which the divine revelation is experienced. Jafar introduced, in an interesting comparison, reason, aql, as the barrier between nafs and qalb — "the barrier which they both cannot transcend" (Sura 55:20), so that the dark lower instincts cannot jeopardize the heart's purity. Each of these spiritual centres has its own functions, and Amr al-Makki has summed up some of the early Sufi ideas in a lovely myth:

> *God created the hearts seven thousand years before the bodies and kept them in the station of proximity to Himself and He created the spirits seven thousand years before the hearts and kept them in the garden of intimate fellowship (uns) with Himself, and the consciences—the innermost part—He created seven thousand years before the spirits and kept them in the degree of union (wacl) with Himself. Then he imprisoned the conscience in the spirit and the spirit in the heart and the heart in the body. Then He tested them and sent prophets, and then each began to seek its own station. The body occupied itself with prayer, the heart attained to love, the spirit arrived at proximity to its Lord, and the innermost part found rest in union with Him.*

Other Philosophical Theories of the Mind

Al-Kindi dealt with psychology in his *First Philosophy*, and *Eradication of Sorrow*. In the latter, he described sorrow as "a spiritual (*Nafsani*) grief caused by loss of loved ones or personal belongings, or by failure in obtaining what one lusts after" and then added: "If causes of pain are discernible, the cures can be found." He recommended that "if we do not tolerate losing or dislike being deprived of what is dear to us, then we should seek after riches in the world of the intellect. In it we should treasure our precious and cherished gains where they can never be dispossessed...for that which is owned by our senses could easily be taken away from us." He also stated that "sorrow is not within us we bring it upon ourselves."

In the *Encyclopedia of the Brethren of Purity* (10th century), the Brethren of Purity discussed the soul, brain, and process of thought. They divided the soul into three parts: the vegetative, animal and rational human souls.

The vegetative soul is concerned with nutrition, growth and reproduction; the animal soul is concerned with movement, sensation, perception and emotion; and the rational human soul is concerned with thinking and talking. Contrary to the Aristotelian view of the heart being the most important organ, the Brethren of Purity considered the brain as the most important organ of the body, due to it being responsible for higher functions such as perception and thought.

The Arab Muslim physician An-Naysaburi (d. 1016) wrote the *Kitab al-Uqala al-Majanin*, in which he used the term *Mahwus* for patients with delusions and hallucinations. He attempted to explain the phenomenon of madness and insanity in philosophical terms, rather than the psychopathological methods used by his contemporaries. He considered life as a blending of opposites such as health and disease, and wrote that reason is mixed with madness so that even the sane are never free from madness.

Ibn Miskawayh (941–1030) wrote the books *Tahdhib al-Akhlaq (Cultivation of Morals)* and *Al-Fauz al-Asgar (The Lesser Victory)*, in which he gives psychological advice on certain issues, such as the fear of death, the need to develop traits to restrain oneself from faults, and the concept of morality. He also introduced the concepts of "self reinforcement" and response cost, where he advises Muslims who feel guilt to learn to punish themselves physically or psychologically through charity, fasting, etc.

Al-Ghazali (Algazel) (1058–1111) discussed the concept of the self and the causes of its misery and happiness. He described the self using four terms: Qalb (heart), Ruh (spirit), Nafs (soul) and 'Aql (intellect). He stated that "the self has an inherent yearning for an ideal, which it strives to realize and it is endowed with qualities to help realize it." He also stated that there are two types of diseases: physical and spiritual. He considered the latter to be more dangerous, resulting from "ignorance and deviation from God", and listed the spiritual diseases as: self-centeredness; addiction to wealth, fame and social status; and ignorance, cowardice, cruelty, lust, waswas (doubt), malevolence, calumny, envy, deception, and greed. To overcome these spiritual weaknesses, al-Ghazali suggested the therapy of opposites ("use of imagination in pursuing the opposite"), such as ignorance & learning, or hate & love. He described the personality as an "integration of spiritual and bodily forces" and believed that "closeness to God is equivalent to normality whereas distance from God leads to abnormality."

Ibn Bajjah (Avempace) (d. 1138) "based his psychological studies on physics." In his essay, *Recognition of the Active Intelligence*, he wrote that active intelligence is the most important ability of human beings, and he wrote many other essays on sensations and imaginations. He concluded that "knowledge cannot be acquired by senses alone but by Active Intelligence, which is the governing intelligence of nature." He begins his discussion of the soul with the definition that "bodies are composed of matter and form and intelligence is the most important part of man—sound knowledge is obtained through intelligence, which alone enables one to attain prosperity and build character." He viewed the unity of the rational soul as the principle of the individual identity, and that by its contact with the Active Intelligence, it "becomes one of those lights that gives glory to God." His definition of freedom is "that when one can think and act rationally". He also writes that "the aim of life should be to seek spiritual knowledge and make contact with Active Intelligence and thus with the Divine."

Fakhr al-Din al-Razi (1149–1209) wrote the *Kitab al Nafs Wa'l Ruh*, which deals with both human psychology and animal psychology along the same lines. In this work, he analyzed the different types of pleasures as sensuous and intellectual, and explained their comparative relations with one another. He asserted that "a careful scrutiny of pleasure would reveal that it consists essentially in the elimination of pain." He then gives the following example: "the hungrier a man is, the greater is his enjoyment of pleasure of eating." He also argues that "the gratification of pleasure is proportionate to the need or desire of the animal" and that when "these needs are satisfied or desires fulfilled, the pleasure actually turns into revulsion," as "excess of food or sex results not in more pleasure, but in pain." He argued that human needs and desires are endless, and "their satisfaction is by definition impossible." He concludes that mental pleasure is more "noble and perfect than the sensual pleasure" and suggests that "the excellence and perfection" of a human is only realized by means of science, knowledge and "excellent manners," rather than "eating, drinking, and mating."

Ibn al-Nafis (1213–1288) dealt with psychology in his *Commentary on Anatomy in Avicenna's Canon*. He developed his own theories on hylomorphic psychology and philosophy, mostly on a theological basis. In particular, he made a distinction between the soul and the spirit, and he developed his own theory on the soul. He also crtiticized the ideas of Avicenna and Aristotle on the soul originating from the heart. Ibn al-Nafis rejected this idea and instead argued that the soul "is related to the entirety and not to one or a few organs." He further criticized Aristotle's idea that every unique soul requires the existence of a unique source, in this case the heart. Ibn al-Nafis concluded that "the soul is related primarily neither to the spirit nor to any organ, but rather to the entire matter whose temperament is prepared to receive that soul" and he defined the soul as nothing other than "what a human indicates by saying 'I'."

Clinical and Medical Approach

Unlike medieval Christian physicians who relied on demonological explanations for mental illness, medieval Muslim physicians relied mostly on clinical psychiatry and clinical psychology, and clinical observations on mentally ill patients. They made significant advances to psychiatry and were the first to provide psychotherapy and moral treatment for mentally ill patients, in addition to other new forms of treatment such as baths, drug medication, music therapy and occupational therapy.

Al-tibb al-ruhani and Diseases of the Mind

The concepts of *al-tibb al-ruhani* (translated as "spiritual health" in Arabic) and "mental hygiene" were introduced in Islamic medicine by the Persian physician Abu Zayd Ahmed ibn Sahl al-Balkhi (850-934), who often related it to spiritual health.

In his *Masalih al-Abdan wa al-Anfus* (*Sustenance for Body and Soul*), he was the first to successfully discuss diseases related to both the body and the soul. He used the term *al-Tibb al-Ruhani* to describe spiritual and psychological health, and the term *Tibb al-Qalb* to describe mental medicine.

He criticized many medical doctors in his time for placing too much emphasis on physical illnesses and neglecting the mental illnesses of patients, and argued that "since man's construction is from both his soul and his body, therefore, human existence cannot be healthy without the *ishtibak* [interweaving or entangling] of soul and body."

He further argued that "if the body gets sick, the *nafs* [psyche] loses much of its cognitive and comprehensive ability and fails to enjoy the desirous aspects of life" and that "if the *nafs* gets sick, the body may also find no joy in life and may eventually develop a physical illness." Al-Balkhi traced back his ideas on mental health to verses of the Quran and hadiths attributed to Muhammad, such as:

> *"In their hearts is a disease."*
>
> — Quran 2:10

> *"Truly, in the body there is a morsel of flesh, and when it is corrupt the body is corrupt, and when it is sound the body is sound. Truly, it is the* qalb *[heart]."*
>
> — *Sahih al-Bukhari*, Kitab al-Iman

> *"Verily Allah does not consider your appearances or your wealth in (appraising you) but He considers your hearts and your deeds."* — Musnad Ahmad ibn Hanbal, *no. 8707*

Mental Hospitals

As a result of the new positive Islamic understanding of mental illness, the first mental hospitals and insane asylums were built in the Islamic world as early as the 8th century.

The first mental hospitals were built by Arab Muslims in Baghdad in 705, Fes in the early 8th century, and Cairo in 800. Other famous mental hospitals were built in Damascus and Aleppo in 1270.

'Ilaj Al-nafs and Tibb Al-qalb

Ali ibn Sahl Rabban al-Tabari's *Firdous al-Hikmah* written in the 9th century was the first work to study *'al-'ilaj al-nafs* (translated as "psychotherapy" from Arabic) in the treatment of patients. His ideas were primarily influenced by early Islamic thought and ancient Indian physicians such as Sushruta and Charaka. Unlike earlier physicians, however, al-Tabari emphasized strong ties between psychology and medicine, and the need for *al-'ilaj al-nafs* and counselling in the therapeutic treatment of patients.

He wrote that patients frequently feel sick due to delusions or imagination, and that these can be treated through "wise counselling" by smart and witty physicians who could win the rapport and confidence of their patients, leading to a positive therapeutic outcome. In his chapter on mental illness, al-Tabari first described thirteen types of mental disorders, including madness, delirium, and *Fasad Al-Khayal Wal-Aql* ("damage to the imagination, intelligence and thought"). He also clearly highlighted mental illness as a speciality of its own.

The Tunisian Arab Muslim physician, Ishaq ibn Imran (d. 908), known as "Isaac" in the West, wrote an essay entitled *Maqala fil-L-Malikhuliya*, in which he first described psychosis, and also described a type of melancholia: the "cerebral type" or "phrenitis". He described the diagnosis of this mental disorder, reporting its varied symptoms. The main clinical features he identified were sudden movement, foolish acts, fear, delusions, and hallucinations of black people. This work was later translated into Latin as *De Oblivione* (*On Forgetfulness*) by Constantine the African.

The Persian physician Muhammad ibn Zakariya Razi (Rhazes) (865-925) wrote the landmark texts *El-Mansuri* and *Al-Hawi* in the 10th century, which presented definitions, symptoms, and treatments for many illnesses related to mental health and mental illness. Razi's texts made significant advances in psychiatry. Razi also managed the mental ward of a Baghdad hospital. Such institutions could not exist in Europe at the time, because of European fears of demonic possession.

In the centuries to come, Islam would serve as a critical waystation of knowledge for Renaissance Europe, through the Latin translations of many scientific Islamic texts. Razi, al-Tabari and Ahmed ibn Sahl al-Balkhi were the first known physicians to study *al-'ilaj al-nafs*.

Ali ibn Abbas al-Majusi (d. 982) discussed mental illness in his medical text, *Kitab al-Malaki*, where he discovered and observed a type of melancholia: clinical lycanthropy, associated with certain personality disorders. He wrote the following on this particular mental illness:

> *"Its victim behaves like a rooster and cries like a dog, the patient wanders among the tombs at night, his eyes are dark, his mouth is dry, the patient hardly ever recovers and the disease is hereditary."*

Avicenna (980-1037) often used psychological methods to treat his patients. One such example involved a prince of Persia who had melancholia and suffered from the delusion that he was a cow. He would low like a cow, crying "Kill me so that a good stew may be made of my flesh," and would not eat anything. Avicenna was persuaded to undertake the case, and sent a message to the patient, asking him to be happy, as the butcher was coming to slaughter him, and the sick man rejoiced.

When Avicenna approached the prince with a knife in his hand, he asked, "Where is the cow so I may kill it." The patient then lowed like a cow to indicate where he was. By order of Avicenna in his role as the butcher, the patient was also laid on the ground for slaughter. When Avicenna approached the patient, pretending to slaughter him, he said, "The cow is too lean and not ready to be killed. He must be fed properly and I will kill it when it becomes healthy and fat." The patient was then offered food, which he ate eagerly and gradually "gained strength, got rid of his delusion, and was completely cured."

Music Therapy

Al-Kindi (801–873) wrote on the therapeutic value of music. He experimented with music therapy, and he attempted to cure a quadriplegic boy using this method.

Later in the 9th century, al-Farabi also dealt with music therapy in his treatise *Meanings of the Intellect*, where he discussed the therapeutic effects of music on the soul.

Cognitive Therapy

Al-Kindi developed cognitive methods to combat depression and discussed the intellectual operations of human beings. According to the psychologist Amber Haque, the medieval Islamic scholar Abu Zayd Ahmed ibn Sahl al-Balkhi (850-934) was "probably the first cognitive and medical psychologist to clearly differentiate between neuroses and psychoses, to classify neurotic disorders, and to show in detail how rational and spiritual cognitive therapies can be used to treat each one of his classified disorders."

Al-Balkhi classified neuroses into four emotional disorders: fear and anxiety, anger and aggression, sadness and depression, and obsession. According to Haque, al-Balkhi further classified three types of depression: normal sadness (*huzn*) which is "today known as normal depression", "endogenous depression" which "originated within the body", and "reactive depression" which "originated outside the body".

Al-Balkhi also wrote that a healthy individual should always keep healthy thoughts and feelings in his mind in the case of unexpected emotional outbursts in the same way drugs and First Aid medicine are kept nearby for unexpected physical emergencies. He stated that a balance between the mind and body is required for good health and that an imbalance between the two can cause sickness. Al-Balkhi also introduced the concept of reciprocal inhibition (*al-ilaj bi al-did*), which was re-introduced over a thousand years later by Joseph Wolpe in 1969.

Physical and Psychological Disorders

The Muslim physician Abu Zayd Ahmed ibn Sahl al-Balkhi (850-934) was a pioneer of *al-'ilaj al-nafs*, and the first to compare "physical and psychological disorders" and show "their interaction in causing psychosomatic disorders." He recognized that the body and the soul can be healthy or sick, or "balanced or imbalanced", and that mental illness can have both psychological and/or physiological causes. He wrote that imbalance of the body can result in fever, headaches and other physical illnesses, while imbalance of the soul can result in anger, anxiety, sadness and other mental symptoms. He recognized two types of depression: one caused by known reasons such as loss or failure, which can be treated psychologically through both external methods (such as persuasive talking, preaching and advising) and internal methods (such as the "development of inner thoughts and cognitions which help the person get rid of his depressive condition"); and the other caused by unknown reasons such as a "sudden affliction of sorrow and distress, which persists all the time, preventing the afflicted person from any physical activity or from showing any happiness or enjoying any of the pleasures" which may be caused by physiological reasons (such as impurity of the blood) and can be treated through physical medicine.

He also wrote comparisons between physical disorders with mental disorders, and showed how psychosomatic disorders can be caused by certain interactions between them.

In the early 10th century, Muhammad ibn Zakariya Razi reported a psychotherapeutic case study from a contemporary Muslim physician who treated a woman suffering from severe cramps in her joints which made her unable to rise. The physician cured her by lifting her skirt, putting her to shame. He wrote: "A flush of heat was produced within her which dissolved the rheumatic humour."

Ali ibn Abbas al-Majusi (d. 982) elaborated on how the physiological and psychological aspects of a patient can have an effect on one another in his *Complete Book of the Medical Art*. He found a correlation between patients who were physically and mentally healthy and those who were physically and mentally unhealthy, and concluded that "joy and contentment can bring a better living status to many who would otherwise be sick and miserable due to unnecessary sadness, fear, worry and anxiety." He also first discussed various mental disorders, including sleeping sickness, memory loss, hypochondriasis, coma, hot and cold meningitis, vertigo epilepsy, love sickness, and hemiplegia. He also placed more emphasis on preserving health through diet and natural healing than he did on medication or drugs, which he considered a last resort. Avicenna (980-1037) recognized "physiological psychology" in the treatment of "illnesses involving emotions" and develop "a system for associating changes in the pulse rate with inner feelings. Avicenna identified love sickness (*Ishq*) when he was treating a very ill patient by "feeling the patient's pulse and reciting aloud to him the names of provinces, districts, towns, streets, and people." He noticed how the patient's pulse increased when certain names were mentioned, from which Avicenna deduced that the patient was in love with a girl whose home Avicenna was "able to locate by the digital examination." Avicenna advised the patient to marry the girl he is in love with, and the patient soon recovered from his illness after his marriage.

Avicenna also gave psychological explanations for certain somatic illnesses, and he always linked the physical and psychological illnesses together. He described melancholia (depression) as a type of mood disorder in which the person may become suspicious and develop certain types of phobias. He stated that anger heralded the transition of melancholia to mania, and explained that humidity inside the head can contribute to mood disorders. He recognized that this occurs when the amount of breath changes: happiness increases the breath, which leads to increased moisture inside the brain, but if this moisture goes beyond its limits, the brain would lose control over its rationality and lead to mental disorders. He also wrote about symptoms and treatments for nightmare, epilepsy, and weak memory.

Nosology and Psychopathology

In nosology, the Arab Muslim physician and psychological thinker Najab ud-din Unhammad (870-925) described in detail nine major categories of mental disorders, which included 30 different mental illnesses in total. Some of the categories he described included obsessive-compulsive disorders (anxious and ruminative states of doubt), delusional disorders (which "manifested itself by the mind's tendency to magnify all matters of personal significance, often leading to actions that prove outrageous to society"), degenerative diseases, involutional melancholia, and states of abnormal excitement. Unhammad made many careful observations of mentally ill patients and compiled them in a book which "made up the most complete classification of mental diseases theretofore known." The mental illnesses described by Najab include agitated depression, neurosis, priapism and sexual impotence (*Nafkhae Malikholia*), psychosis (*Kutrib*), and mania (*Dual-Kulb*).

Unhammad also listed nine classes of psychopathology. This included the earliest description of *Souda a Tabee* (febrile delirium), which was in turn subdivided into *Souda* where patients showed impairment of memory, loss of contact with the environment, and childish behaviour; and *Jannon* (agitated reaction) which occurs when *Souda* reaches a chronic state and is characterized by insomnia, restlessness and sometimes "beast-like roars."

Anatomy and Physiology

Ali ibn Abbas al-Majusi (d. 982), in his *Complete Book of the Medical Art*, described the anatomy, physiology and diseases of the brain.

In the *Encyclopedia of the Brethren of Purity* (10th century), the Brethren of Purity discussed the process of thought, and wrote that the thinking process begins with the five external senses which send messages through the nerves to the brain, which processes the messages in different locations of the brain. Avicenna discovered the cerebellar vermis—which he named "vermis"—and the caudate nucleus, which he named "tailed nucleus" or "nucleus caudatus". These terms are still used in modern neuroanatomy.

He was also the earliest to note that intellectual dysfunctions were largely due to deficits in the brain's middle ventricle, and that the frontal lobe of the brain mediated common sense and reasoning.

Ibn al-Nafis (1213–1288), in his *Commentary on Anatomy in Avicenna's Canon*, corrected some of the erroneous theories of Galen and Avicenna (Ibn Sina) on the anatomy of the brain. Ibn al-Nafis quoted an error made by Galen, who believed that "blood reaches the brain itself at the section called forebrain through the duramater which divides the vault longitudinally into two equal halves at the sagittal suture." Ibn al-Nafis criticized this theory and corrected it as follows:

> *"The blood permeates first to the back ventricle (hindbrain) then to the other two ventricles. Dissection confirms this and disproves what they say. The permeation of arteries into the cranium is well known not to be from the front ventricle."*

Ibn al-Nafis corrected another theory on the nerves stated by Avicenna, who believed that the glossopharyngeal nerve, vagus nerve and accessory nerve arise from the nerve ganglion and that they are attached to the sigmoid and facial nerves through membranous fascia so that these five nerves look like one nerve emerging as three branches from the back foramen lacerum. While experimenting with this theory, Ibn al-Nafis performed the earliest known dissection on the human brain, after he made the following correction to the theory:

> *"About what he [Ibn Sina] said concerning the sixth nerve being attached to the fifth through membranous facia, I have not so far found a good reason for that attachment, and I have not even verified it. This sixth pair [a confluence of the glossopharyngeal, vagus and accessory nerves] both arises and emerges from behind the fifth, so there is no way it could be attached to it."*

Another example was Galen's incorrect theory on the optic nerve, in which he stated that the optic nerve "which comes from the right side of the brain goes to the right eye, and the nerve which comes from the left side goes to the left eye." Ibn al-Nafis also proved this theory wrong and stated:

> *"In fact it is not like that, [but] each nerve goes to the opposite side."*

Neurosurgery

In al-Andalus, Abu al-Qasim al-Zahrawi (Abulcasis), considered a father of modern surgery, developed material and technical designs which are still used in neurosurgery. In Egypt, Ibn al-Nafis performed the earliest known dissections on the human brain, while he was correcting some of the incorrect theories of Galen and Avicenna on the anatomy of the brain.

Neuropsychiatric Conditions

Avicenna described a number of neuropsychiatric conditions, including hallucination, insomnia, mania, nightmare, melancholia, dementia, epilepsy, paralysis, stroke, vertigo and tremor. He dedicated three chapters of *The Canon of Medicine* (1020s) to neuropsychiatric disorders, in which he defined madness (*Junun*) as a mental condition in which reality is replaced by fantasy, and discovered that it is a disorder of reason with its origin in the middle part of the brain.

Avicenna also discovered a condition resembling schizophrenia which he described as *Junun Mufrit* (severe madness), which he clearly distinguished from other forms of madness such as mania, rabies, and manic depressive psychosis. He observed that patients suffering from schizophrenia-like severe madness show agitation, behavioural and sleep disturbance, give inappropriate answers to questions, and in some cases are incapable of speaking at times. He wrote that such patients need to be restrained, in order to avoid any harm they may cause to themselves or to others. Avicenna also dedicated a chapter of the *Canon* to mania and rabies, where he described mania as bestial madness characterized by rapid onset and remission, with agitation and irritability, and described rabies as a type of mania.

In *The Canon of Medicine,* Avicenna extended the theory of temperaments to encompass "emotional aspects, mental capacity, moral attitudes, self-awareness, movements and dreams." Avicenna's work is thus considered by some to be a "forerunner of twentieth century psychoanalysis."

Later in the 13th century, Maimonides wrote about neuropsychiatric disorders and described rabies and belladonna intoxication.

Neurology and Neuropharmacology

Avicenna's contributions in neurology include his diagnosis of facial nerve paralysis, his distinction between brain paralysis and hyperaemia, and most importantly his discovery of meningitis. He diagnosed meningitis as a disease induced by the brain itself and differentiated it from infectious brain disease, and was also able to diagnose and describe the type of meningitis induced by an infection in other parts of the body.

Ibn Zuhr (Avenzoar) gave the earliest accurate descriptions on certain neurological disorders, including meningitis, intracranial thrombophlebitis, and mediastinal tumours, and made contributions to modern neuropharmacology. Averroes suggested the existence of Parkinson's disease and attributed photoreceptor properties to the retina.

Sociological Approach

Al-Farabi's Social Psychology and Model City were the earliest treatises to deal with social psychology. He stated that "an isolated individual could not achieve all the perfections by himself, without the aid of other individuals." He wrote that it is the "innate disposition of every man to join another human being or other men in the labour he ought to perform." He concluded that in order to "achieve what he can of that perfection, every man needs to stay in the neighbourhood of others and associate with them."

Ibn Khaldun (1332–1406), considered a father of sociology and the social sciences, was another Muslim scholar who significant contributions to the area of social psychology. His book Muqaddimah (known as Prolegomena in the West) was a classic on the social psychology of the peoples of the Arabian Peninsula, particularly the Bedouins.

Animal Psychology and Musicology

The earliest works on "the social organization of ants" and "animal communication and psychology" were written by al-Jahiz (766–868), an Afro-Arab scholar who wrote many works on these subjects.

In animal psychology and musicology, Ibn al-Haytham's *Treatise on the Influence of Melodies on the Souls of Animals* was an early treatise dealing with the effects of music on animals. In the treatise, he demonstrates how a camel's pace could be hastened or retarded with the use of music, and shows other examples of how music can affect animal behaviour, experimenting with horses, birds and reptiles. Through to the 19th century, a majority of scholars in the Western world continued to believe that music was a distinctly human phenomenon, but experiments since then have vindicated Ibn al-Haytham's view that music does indeed have an effect on animals.

Islamic Military Jurisprudence

Islamic military jurisprudence refers to what has been accepted in Sharia (Islamic law) and Fiqh (Islamic jurisprudence) by *Ulama* (Islamic scholars) as the correct Islamic manner which is expected to be obeyed by Muslims in time of war.

Development of Rulings

The first military rulings were formulated during the first century after Muhammad established an Islamic state in Medina. These rulings evolved in accordance with the interpretations of the Quran (the Muslim Holy scriptures) and Hadith (the recorded traditions of Muhammad). The key themes in these rulings were the justness of war, and the injunction to Jihad. The rulings do not cover feuds and armed conflicts in general.

Jihad (Arabic for "struggle") was given a military dimension after the oppressive practices of the Meccan Quraish against Muslims. It was interpreted as the struggle in God's cause to be conducted by the Muslim community. Injunctions relating to Jihad have been characterized as individual as well as collective duties of the Muslim community. Hence, the nature of attack is important in the interpretation—if the Muslim community as a whole is attacked Jihad becomes incumbent on all Muslims. Jihad is differentiated further in respect to the requirements within Muslim-governed lands (Dar al-Islam) and non-Muslim lands (Dar al-Harb).

According to Shaheen Sardar Ali and Javaid Rehman, both professors of law, the Islamic military jurisprudence are in line with rules of modern international law. They point to the dual commitment of Organisation of the Islamic Conference (OIC) member states (representing most of the Muslim world) to Islamic law and the United Nations Charter, as evidence of compatibility of both legal systems.

Ethics of Warfare

The basic principle in fighting in the Quran is that other communities should be treated as one's own. Fighting is justified for legitimate self-defense, to aid other Muslims and after a violation in the terms of a treaty, but should be stopped if these circumstances cease to exist.

The principle of forgiveness is reiterated in between the assertions of the right to self-defence. During his life, Muhammad gave various injunctions to his forces and adopted practices toward the conduct of war. The most important of these were summarized by Muhammad's companion and first Caliph, Abu Bakr, in the form of ten rules for the Muslim army:

> *"O people! I charge you with ten rules; learn them well!*
>
> *Do no betray or misappropriate any part of the booty; do*

not practice treachery or mutilation. Do not kill a young child, an old man, or a woman. Do not uproot or burn palms or cut down fruitful trees. Do not slaughter a sheep or a cow or a camel, except for food. You will meet people who have set themselves apart in hermitages; leave them to accomplish the purpose for which they have done this. You will come upon people who will bring you dishes with various kinds of foods. If you partake of them, pronounce God's name over what you eat. You will meet people who have shaved the crown of their heads, leaving a band of hair around it. Go in Gods name, and may God protect you from sword and pestilence."

These injunctions were honoured by the second Caliph, Umar, during whose reign (634–644) important Muslim conquests took place. During the Battle of Siffin, the Caliph Ali stated that Islam does not permit Muslims to stop the supply of water to their enemy. In addition to the Rashidun Caliphs, hadiths attributed to Muhammad himself suggest that he stated the following regarding the Muslim conquest of Egypt that eventually took place after his death:

"You are going to enter Egypt a land where qirat *(money unit) is used. Be extremely good to them as they have with us close ties and marriage relationships. When you enter Egypt after my death, recruit many soldiers from among the Egyptians because they are the best soldiers on earth, as they and their wives are permanently on duty until the Day of Resurrection. Be good to the Copts of Egypt; you shall take them over, but they shall be your instrument and help. Be Righteous to God about the Copts."*

These principles were upheld by 'Amr ibn al-'As during his conquest of Egypt. A Christian contemporary in the 7th century, John of Nikiu, stated the following regarding the conquest of Alexandria by 'Amr:

"On the twentieth of Maskaram, Theodore and all his troops and officers set out and proceeded to the island of Cyprus, and abandoned the city of Alexandria. And thereupon 'Amr the chief of the Moslem made his entry without effort into the city of Alexandria. And the inhabitants received him with respect; for they were in great tribulation and affliction. And Abba Benjamin, the patriarch of the Egyptians, returned to the city of

> *Alexandria in the thirteenth year after his flight from the Romans, and he went to the Churches, and inspected all of them. And every one said: 'This expulsion (of the Romans) and victory of the Moslem is due to the wickedness of the emperor Heraclius and his persecution of the Orthodox through the patriarch Cyrus. This was the cause of the ruin of the Romans and the subjugation of Egypt by the Moslem. And 'Amr became stronger every day in every field of his activity. And he exacted the taxes which had been determined upon, but he took none of the property of the Churches, and he committed no act of spoliation or plunder, and he preserved them throughout all his days."*

The principles established by the early Caliphs were also honoured during the Crusades, as exemplified by Sultans such as Saladin and Al-Kamil. For example, after Al-Kamil defeated the Franks during the Crusades, Oliverus Scholasticus praised the Islamic laws of war, commenting on how Al-Kamil supplied the defeated Frankish army with food:

> *"Who could doubt that such goodness, friendship and charity come from God? Men whose parents, sons and daughters, brothers and sisters, had died in agony at our hands, whose lands we took, whom we drove naked from their homes, revived us with their own food when we were dying of hunger and showered us with kindness even when we were in their power."*

The early Islamic treatises on international law from the 9th century onwards covered the application of Islamic ethics, Islamic economic jurisprudence and Islamic military jurisprudence to international law, and were concerned with a number of modern international law topics, including the law of treaties; the treatment of diplomats, hostages, refugees and prisoners of war; the right of asylum; conduct on the battlefield; protection of women, children and non-combatant civilians; contracts across the lines of battle; the use of poisonous weapons; and devastation of enemy territory.

Criteria for Soldiering

Muslim jurists agree that Muslim armed forces must consist of debt-free adults who possess a sound mind and body. In addition, the combatants must not be conscripted, but rather enlist of their free will, and with the permission of their family.

Traditionally, "adults" have been defined as post-pubescent individuals above the age of 15.

Legitimacy of War

Muslims have struggled to differentiate between legitimate and illegitimate wars. Fighting in self-defense is not only legitimate but considered obligatory upon Muslims, according to the Quran. The Quran, however, says that should enemy hostile behaviour cease, then the reason for engaging such enemy also lapses. Some scholars argue that war may only be legitimate if Muslims have at least half the power of the enemy (and thus capable of winning it). Other Islamic scholars consider this command only for a particular time.

Defensive Conflict

The Hanafi school of thought holds that war can only be launched against a state that had resorted to armed conflict against the Muslims. War, according to the Hanafis, can't simply be made on the account of nation's religion. Sheikh Abdullah Azzam considers the defense by Muslims of their territory as one of the foremost obligations after faith. Abdulaziz Sachedina argues that the original Jihad according to his version of Shi'ism was permission to fight back against those who broke their pledges. Thus the Quran justified defensive Jihad by allowing Muslims to fight back against hostile and dangerous forces.

Offensive Conflict

Muhammad ibn Idris ash-Shafii (d. 820), founder of the Shafii school of thought, was the first to permit offensive Jihad. He limited this warfare against pagan Arabs only, not permitting it against non-Arab non-Muslims. Javed Ahmad Ghamidi believes that after Muhammad and his companions, there is no concept in Islam obliging Muslims to wage war for propagation or implementation of Islam. The only valid basis for military Jihad is to end oppression when all other measures have failed. Islam only allows Jihad to be conducted by a government.

According to Abdulaziz Sachedina, offensive Jihad raises questions about whether Jihad is justifiable on moral grounds. He states that the Quran requires Muslims to establish just public order, increasing the influence of Islam, allowing public Islamic worship, through offensive measures. To this end, the Quranic verses revealed in the latter part of Muhammad's career require Muslims to wage Jihad against unbelievers. This has been complicated by the early Muslim wars of expansion, which he argues were although considered Jihad by Sunni scholars, but under close scrutiny can be determined to be political. Moreover, the offensive Jihad points more to the complex relationship with the "People of the book".

International Conflict

International conflicts are armed strifes conducted by one state against another, and are distinguished from civil wars or armed strife within a state. Some classical Islamic scholars, like Shafii classified territories into broad categories: dar al-islam ("abode of Islam"), dar al-harb ("abode of war), dar al-ahd ("abode of treaty"), and dar al-sulh ("abode of reconciliation"). Such categorizations of states, according to Asma Afsaruddin, are not mentioned in the Quran and Islamic tradition.

Declaration of War

The Quran commands Muslims to make a proper declaration of war prior to the commencement of military operations. Thus, surprise attacks are illegal under the Islamic jurisprudence. The Quran had similarly commanded Muhammad to give his enemies, who had violated the Treaty of Hudaybiyyah, a time period of four months to reconsider their position and negotiate. This rule, however, is not binding if the adversary has already started the war. Forcible prevention of religious practice is considered an act of war.

Conduct of Armed Forces

During battle the Quran commands Muslims to fight against the enemy. However, there are exceptions to such combat. Torturing the enemy, and burning the combatants alive is strictly prohibited. The mutilation of dead bodies is also prohibited. The Quran also discourages Muslim combatants from displaying pomp and unnecessary boasting when setting out for battle.

According to professor Sayyid Damad, no explicit injunctions against use of chemical or biological warfare were developed by medieval Islamic jurists as these threats were not recognized. However, *Khalil al-Maliki's Book on Jihad* states that combatants are forbidden to employ weapons that cause unnecessary injury to the enemy, except under dire circumstances. The book, as an example, forbids the use of poisonous spears, since it inflicts unnecessary pain.

Civilian Areas

Islam expressly prohibits the killing of non-combatants. Harming civilian areas and pillaging residential areas is also forbidden, as is the destruction of trees, crops, livestock and farmlands. The Muslim forces may not loot travellers, as doing so is contrary to the spirit of Jihad. Nor do they have the right to use the local facilities of the native people without their consent. If such a consent is obtained, the Muslim army is still under the obligation to compensate the people financially for the use of such facilities. However, Islamic law allows the confiscation of military equipment and supplies captured from the camps and military headquarters of the combatant armies.

Negotiations

Commentators of the Quran agree that Muslims should always be willing and ready to negotiate peace with the other party without any hesitation. According to Maududi, Islam does not permit Muslims to reject peace and continue bloodshed.

Islamic jurisprudence calls for third party interventions as another means of ending conflicts. Such interventions are to establish mediation between the two parties to achieve a just resolution of the dispute.

Ceasefire

In the context of seventh century Arabia, the Quran ordained Muslims must restrain themselves from fighting in the months when fighting was prohibited by Arab pagans. The Quran also required the respect of this cease-fire, prohibiting its violation.

If, however, non-Muslims commit acts of aggression, Muslims are free to retaliate, though in a manner that is equal to the original transgression. The "sword verse", which has attracted attention, is directed against a particular group who violate the terms of peace and commit aggression (but excepts those who observe the treaty). Crone states that this verse seems to be based on the same above-mentioned rules. Here also it is stressed that one must stop when they do. Ibn Kathir states that the verse implies a hasty mission of besieging and gathering intelligence about the enemy, resulting in either death or repentance by the enemy. It is read as a continuation of previous verses, it would be concerned with the same oath-breaking of "polytheists".

Prisoners of War

Men, women, and children may all be taken as prisoners of war under traditional interpretations of Islamic law. Generally, a prisoner of war could be, at the discretion of the military leader, freed, ransomed, exchanged for Muslim prisoners, In earlier times, the ransom sometimes took an educational dimension, where a literate prisoner of war could secure his or her freedom by teaching ten Muslims to read and write. Some Muslim scholars hold that a prisoner may not be ransomed for gold or silver, but may be exchanged for Muslim prisoners. Women and children prisoners of war cannot be killed under any circumstances, regardless of their religious convictions, but they may be freed or ransomed. Women who are neither freed nor ransomed by their people were to be kept in bondage and referred to as *ma malakat aymanukum*, dispute however exist among scholars on its interpretation. Islamic law does not put an exact limit on the number that can be kept in bondage. It strictly forbids keeping female slaves as a means of sexual enjoyment and luxury according to the Islamic scholar Maududi.

Internal Conflict

Internal conflicts include "civil wars", launched against rebels, and "wars for welfare" launched against bandits. During their first civil war, Muslims fought at the Battle of Bassorah. In this engagement, Ali (the caliph), set the precedent for war against other Muslims, which most later Muslims have accepted. According to Ali's rules, wounded or captured enemies should not be killed, those throwing away their arms should not be fought, and those fleeing from the battleground should not be pursued. Only captured weapons and animals (horses and camels which have been used in the war) are to be considered war booty. No war prisoners, women or children are to be enslaved and the property of the slain enemies are to go their legal Muslim heirs. Different views regarding armed rebellion have prevailed in the Muslim world at different times. During the first three centuries of Muslim history, jurists held that a political rebel may not be executed nor his/her property confiscated. Classical jurists, however, laid down severe penalties for rebels who use "stealth attacks" and "spread terror". In this category, Muslim jurists included abductions, poisoning of water wells, arson, attacks against wayfarers and travellers, assaults under the cover of night and rape. The punishment for such crimes were severe, including death, regardless of the political convictions and religion of the perpetrator. Further, rebels who committed acts of terrorism were granted no quarter.

Prisoners of War in Islam

The rules and regulations concerning prisoners of war in Islam are covered in manuals of Islamic jurisprudence, based upon Islamic teachings, in both the Quran and Hadith. The historical legal principles governing the treatment of prisoners of war, in Sharia, Islamic law, (in the traditional madhabs schools of Islamic jurisprudence), was then a significant improvement over the pre-existing norms of society during

Muhammad's time. Men, women, and children may all be taken as prisoners of war under traditional interpretations of Islamic law. Generally, a prisoner of war could be, at the discretion of the military leader, freed, ransomed, exchanged for Muslim prisoners, or kept in bondage. In earlier times, the ransom sometimes took an educational dimension, where a literate prisoner of war could secure his or her freedom by teaching ten Muslims to read and write. Some Muslim scholars hold that a prisoner may not be ransomed for gold or silver, but may be exchanged for Muslim prisoners.

History

In pre-Islamic Arabia, upon capture, those captives not executed, were made to beg for their subsistence. During his life, Muhammad changed this custom and made it the responsibility of the Islamic government to provide food and clothing, on a reasonable basis, to captives, regardless of their religion. If the prisoners were in the custody of a person, then the responsibility was on the individual.

Historically, Muslims routinely captured large number of prisoners. Aside from those who converted, most were ransomed or enslaved. Pasquier writes:

It was the custom to enslave prisoners of war and the Islamic state would have put itself at a grave disadvantage vis-a-vis its enemies had it not reciprocated to some extent. By guaranteeing them [male POWs] humane treatment, and various possibilities of subsequently releasing themselves, it ensured that a good number of combatants in the opposing armies preferred captivity at the hands of Muslims to death on the field of battle.

However, when Muslims defeated the Jewish tribe of the Banu Qurayza "The Banu Qurayza eventually surrendered and all the men, apart from a few who converted to Islam, were beheaded, while the women and children were enslaved."

According to accounts written by Muhammad's followers, after the Battle of Badr, some prisoners were executed for their earlier crimes in Mecca, but the rest were given options: They could convert to Islam and thus win their freedom; they could pay ransom and win their freedom; they could teach 10 Muslims to read and write and thus win their freedom. William Muir wrote of this period:

> *"In pursuance of Mahomet's commands the citizens of Medina and such of the refugees as possessed houses received the prisoners and treated them with much*

> *consideration. 'Blessings be on the men of Medina', said one of these prisoners in later days, 'they made us ride while they themselves walked; they gave us wheaten bread to eat when there was little of it, contenting themselves with dates."*

During his rule, Caliph Umar made it illegal to separate related prisoners of war from each other, after a captive complained to him for being separated from her daughter.

These principles were also honoured during the Crusades, as exemplified by sultans such as Saladin and al-Kamil. For example, after al-Kamil defeated the Franks during the Crusades, Oliverus Scholasticus praised the Islamic laws of war, commenting on how al-Kamil supplied the defeated Frankish army with food:

> *"Who could doubt that such goodness, friendship and charity come from God? Men whose parents, sons and daughters, brothers and sisters, had died in agony at our hands, whose lands we took, whom we drove naked from their homes, revived us with their own food when we were dying of hunger and showered us with kindness even when we were in their power."*

Treatment of Prisoners

Upon capture, the prisoners must be guarded and not ill-treated. Islamic law holds that the prisoners must be fed and clothed, either by the Islamic government or by the individual who has custody of the prisoner. This position is supported by the verse of the Quran. The prisoners must be fed in a dignified manner, and must not be forced to beg for their subsistence. Muhammad's early followers also considered it a principle to not separate prisoners from their relatives.

After the fighting is over, prisoners are to be released, with some prospect of survival, or ransomed. The freeing or ransoming of prisoners by Muslims themselves is highly recommended as a charitable act. The Quran also urges kindness to captives and recommends, their liberation by purchase or manumission. The freeing of captives is recommended both for the expiation of sins and as an act of simple benevolence.

Women and Children

Muslim scholars hold that women and children prisoners of war cannot be killed under any circumstances, regardless of their faith, but that they may be enslaved, freed or ransomed. Women who are neither freed nor ransomed by their people were to be kept in bondage and referred to as *ma malakat aymanukum* (slaves).

Men

There has been disagreement whether adult male prisoners of war may be executed. One traditional opinion holds that executing prisoners of war is strictly forbidden; this is the most-widely accepted view, and one upheld by the Hanafi madhab.

However, the opinion of the Maliki, Shafii, Hanbali and Jafari madhabs is that adult male prisoners of war may be executed. Conventionally, execution was conditional on the reasonable belief that male prisoners would pose a genuine and immediate threat to the Muslim community if allowed to live. The decision for an execution is to be made by the Muslim leader. This opinion was also upheld by the Muslim judge, Sa'id bin Jubair (665-714 AD) and 'Abu Yusuf Yaqub a classical jurist from the Hanafi school of jurispudence. El Fadl argues the reason Muslim jurists adopted this position was largely because it was consistent with the war practices of the Middle Ages.

Most contemporary Muslim scholars prohibit altogether the killing of prisoners and hold that this was the policy practiced by Prophet Muhammad (Pbuh). The 20th century Muslim scholar, Sayyid Abul Ala Maududi states that no prisoner should be "put to the sword" in accordance with a saying of Muhammad.

Yusuf Ali, another 20th century Muslim scholar, while commenting on verse , writes. Even those the enemies of Islam, actively fighting against Islam, there may be individuals who may be in a position to require protection.

Full asylum is to be given to them, and opportunities provided for hearing the Word of Allah...If they do not see their way to accept Islam, they will require double protection: (1) from the Islamic forces openly fighting against their people, and (2) from their own people, as they detached themselves from them. Both kinds of protection should be ensured for them, and they should be safely escorted to a place where they can be safe.

But "The Banu Qurayza eventually surrendered and all the men, apart from a few who converted to Islam, were beheaded, while the women and children were enslaved." Maududi further states that Islam forbids torturing, especially by fire, and quotes Muhammad as saying, "Punishment by fire does not behoove anyone except the Master of the Fire [God]."

Peace in Islamic Philosophy

As in other religions, peace is a basic concept in Islamic thought. The Arabic term "Islam" itself is usually translated as "submission"; submission of desires to the will of God. It comes from the term *aslama,* which means "to surrender" or "resign oneself". The Arabic word *salaam* ("peace") has the same root as the word *Islam.* One Islamic interpretation is that individual personal peace is attained by utterly submitting to Allah. The greeting "As-Salaamu alaykum", favoured by Muslims, has the literal meaning "Peace be upon you".

Muhammad is reported to have said once, "Mankind are the dependents of God and the most beloved of them to God are those who are the most excellent to His dependents." "Not one of you believes until he loves for his brother what he loves for himself." Great Muslim scholars of prophetic tradition such as Ibn Hajar al-Asqalani and Sharafuddin al Nawawi have said that the words 'his brother' mean any person irrespective of faith.

Concept of Islamic Peace

Islam is a monotheistic religion and according to the Quran all people are children of Adam. Satan is considered the enemy of humanity, causing enmity among all people. The series of prophets and messengers coming from God throughout the ages is to call the people again towards their innate identity of love and friendship. The good life according to Islam is in submitting to God and in worshipping Him as The Creator and The Master and to recognize the innate nature of man. The individual who will recognize his true nature on which every person is created will be able to live together in society with peace and affection to each other. In his Last Sermon, the Prophet Muhammad (Pbuh) admonished believers:

- "Hurt no one so that no one may hurt you."

  Jeffrey Wattles holds that the compassion appears in the following statements, some of which are attributed to Muhammad and some of which come from the Quran:

- The Quran: "Woe to those... who, when they have to receive by measure from men, exact full measure, but when they have to give by measure or weight to men, give less than due"
- The Quran commends "those who show their affection to such as came to them for refuge and entertain no desire in their hearts for things given to the (latter), but give them preference over themselves"

- "None of you [truly] believes until he wishes for his brother what he wishes for himself."
- "Seek for mankind that of which you are desirous for yourself, that you may be a believer; treat well as a neighbour the one who lives near you, that you may be a Muslim [one who submits to God]."
- "That which you want for yourself, seek for mankind."
- "The most righteous of men is the one who is glad that men should have what is pleasing to himself, and who dislikes for them what is for him disagreeable."

Rules for Peace

Islamic tradition dictates that prophets were sent by God to every nation. In Islam, only Muhammad was sent finally to convey God's message to the whole world, whereas other prophets were sent to convey their messages to a specific group of people or nation. So the ideal nationhood in Islam is beyond all boundaries and differences. Prophet Muhammad (Pbuh) is the final messenger according to Islam and all mankind of our era Ummah is called *Ummat e Muhammad* (nation of Muhammad).

The establishment of Khilafa (the Islamic community) on earth based on the rules of shariah is the ultimate goal of Islam according to the jurisprudential approach. The Ummah is not confined to any particular geography, or limited to any specific race; rather it consists of all believers throughout the world from whatever background, language, creed, history or geography. Unlike race, language, history and other such involuntary criteria in nationhood, where the individual has no choice and nationalism and patriotism ask for allegiance to a particular nation and state not chosen by him/her, Ummah arms the individual by allowing a choice to be made by him/her in joining or rejecting it. It is therefore a conscious and informed choice that establishes Ummah and allegiance to it rather than non-voluntary factors as in nationhood.

Importance of Peace

One of the terms meaning peace and peacemaking in Arabic, *sulh*, which is used in the Quran, is also the root of the word islah denoting development and improvement. This term is used to refer to peacemaking. Peacemakers are agents of good and those who breach it are elements of corruption and sin. It is therefore observed that peace and peacemaking are seen in Islamic tradition as part and parcel of human development.

In other words peace and making peace are seen as *Godly acts worthy of praise and reward.* Enmity takes root within and is the cause of conflict amongst humans without; *'wars start in the minds of men'* reads the UNESCO Charter.

Therefore, the main ingredient and instigator of much of armed conflict in history, enmity and hatred, befell mankind as a result of having succumbed to Satanic temptation and deception. The commonality with Kantian as well as Hobbesian perspective in considering enmity and war as 'state of nature' (outside of the original dwelling) is all too clear. However, there is a striking difference in man's approach to the 'state of nature'. Whilst both Hobbes and Kant believe that peace is a better way of life and prescribe an artificial state of peace to promote human security, progress and stability (they, however, disagree widely on how to achieve that state) as a rational discourse, in Islam peace is advocated as a divine quality to be pursued in order to achieve the state of felicity that we were in paradise, man's former dwelling.

Peace and Justice

Justice, as outlined in *the Quran,* refers to *balance and is the foundation upon* which creation stands.

Ali Ibn Abi Talib, the fourth Caliph after the Prophet, has an incisive definition of justice. He considers justice to be *the placement of everything in their proper order.* The issue of proportionality and relativeness is thus an indispensable part of justice.

Quran states in chapter Al Maidah :O ye who believe! stand out firmly for Allah, as witnesses to fair dealing, and let not the hatred of others to you make you swerve to wrong and depart from justice. Be just: that is next to piety: and fear Allah. For Allah is well-acquainted with all that ye do.

Peace based on justice, therefore, would mean *a balanced, fair and tranquil state of affairs,* where all concerned would enjoy their due rights and protection. Muhammad is reported to have said once;

> *"Mankind are the family of God, and the most beloved of them to God are those who are the most excellent to His family." "Not one of you believes until he loves for his brother what he loves for himself."*

Great Muslim scholars of prophetic tradition such as Ibn Hajar al-Asqalani and Sharafuddin al Nawawi have said that the words 'his brother' mean any person irrespective of faith.

House of Peace

The ideal society, according to the Quran is Dar as-Salam, literally, "the house of peace" of which it intones: And Allah invites to the 'abode of peace' and guides whom He pleases into the right path. The establishment of abode of peace on earth means the establish peace in everyday lives, at all levels. This includes personal, social, state and international levels. According to Islam there will be an era in which justice, plenty, abundance, well-being, security, peace, and brotherhood will prevail among humanity, and one in which people will experience love, self-sacrifice, tolerance, compassion, mercy, and loyalty. In his sayings, our Prophet, may God bless him and grant him peace, says that this blessed period will be experienced through the mediation of the Mahdi, who will come in the end times to save the world form chaos, injustice, and moral collapse. He will eradicate godless ideologies and bring an end to the prevailing injustice. Moreover, he will make religion like it was in the days of our Prophet, cause the Quran's moral teachings to prevail among humanity, and establish peace and well-being throughout the world.

Eschatology

Muslims believe that Jesus invited the Children of Israel to follow the true path and showed them many miracles. He is the Messiah and, as the Quran says, he is the "prophet of God". Together with his return to earth in his second coming he will be the best judge among all people on earth. The lack of understanding between Christians and Muslims, who believe in the same God, share the same moral values and, as the Quran says, are closer to one another in love than all other people, will be repaired and these two greatest of the world's religious communities will be united. The members of the world's third monotheistic religion, the Jews, will also accept Jesus as their true Messiah and find their way to the true religion. So by the return of Jesus, religion will defeat the atheistic philosophies and pagan beliefs with intellectual means; the world will be saved from wars, conflicts, racial and ethnic hostility, cruelty and injustice. Humanity will enter a "Golden Age" of peace, happiness and well-being.

Bayt Al-mal

Bayt al-mal is an Arabic term that is translated as "House of money" or "House of Wealth." Historically, it was a financial institution responsible for the administration of taxes in Islamic states, particularly in the early Islamic Caliphate. It served as a royal treasury for the caliphs and sultans, managing personal finances and government expenditures. Further, it administered distributions of zakah revenues for public works. Modern Islamic economists deem the institutional framework appropriate for contemporary Islamic societies.

History

Bayt al-mal was the department that dealt with the revenues and all other economical matters of the state. In the time of Muhammad there was no permanent Bait-ul-Mal or public treasury. Whatever revenues or other amounts were received were distributed immediately. There were no salaries to be paid, and there was no state expenditure. Hence the need for the treasury at public level was not felt. In the time of Abu Bakr as well there was not treasury. Abu Bakr earmarked a house where all money was kept on receipt. As all money was distributed immediately the treasury generally remained locked up. At the time of the death of Abu Bakr there was only one dirham in the public treasury.

Establishment of Bait-ul-Maal

In the time of Umar things changed. With the extension in conquests money came in larger quantities, Umar also allowed salaries to men fighting in the army. Abu Huraira who was the Governor of Bahrain sent a revenue of five hundred thousand dirhams. Umar summoned a meeting of his Consultative Assembly and sought the opinion of the Companions about the disposal of the money. Uthman ibn Affan advised that the amount should be kept for future needs. Walid bin Hisham suggested that like the Byzantines separate departments of Treasury and Accounts should be set up.

After consulting the Companions Umar decided to establish the Central Treasury at Madinah. Abdullah bin Arqam was appointed as the Treasury Officer. He was assisted by Abdur Rahman bin Awf and Muiqib. A separate Accounts Department was also set up and it was required to maintain record of all that was spent. Later provincial treasuries were set up in the provinces. After meeting the local expenditure the provincial treasuries were required to remit the surplus amount to the central treasury at Madinah. According to Yaqubi the salaries and stipends charged to the central treasury amounted to over 30 million dirhams.

A separate building was constructed for the royal treasury by the name *bait ul maal*, which in large cities was guarded by as many as 400 guards. In most of the historical accounts, it states that among the Rashidun caliphs, Uthman ibn Affan was first to struck the coins, some accounts however states that Umar was first to do so. When Persia was conquered three types of coins were current in the conquered territories, namely Baghli of 8 dang; Tabari of 4 dang; and Maghribi of 3 dang. Umar (according to some accounts Uthman) made an innovation and struck an Islamic dirham of 6 dang.

Welfare State

The concepts of welfare and pension were introduced in early Islamic law as forms of *Zakat* (charity), one of the Five Pillars of Islam, under the Rashidun Caliphate in the 7th century. This practice continued well into the Abbasid era of the Caliphate. The taxes (including *Zakat* and *Jizya*) collected in the treasury of an Islamic government were used to provide income for the needy, including the poor, elderly, orphans, widows, and the disabled. According to the Islamic jurist Al-Ghazali (Algazel, 1058–1111), the government was also expected to stockpile food supplies in every region in case a disaster or famine occurred. The Caliphate can thus be considered the world's first major welfare state.

During the Rashidun Caliphate, various welfare programs were introduced by Caliph Umar. In his time, equality was extended to all citizens, even to the caliph himself, as Umar believed that "no one, no matter how important, should live in a way that would distinguish him from the rest of the people." Umar himself lived "a simple life and detached himself from any of the worldly luxuries," like how he often wore "worn-out shoes and was usually clad in patched-up garments," or how he would sleep "on the bare floor of the mosque." Limitations on wealth were also set for governors and officials, who would often be "dismissed if they showed any outward signs of pride or wealth which might distinguish them from the people." This was an early attempt at erasing "class distinctions which might inevitably lead to conflict." Umar also made sure that the public treasury was not wasted on "unnecessary luxuries" as he believed that "the money would be better spent if it went towards the welfare of the people rather than towards lifeless bricks." Umar's innovative welfare reforms during the Rashidun Caliphate included the introduction of social security.

This included unemployment insurance, which did not appear in the Western world until the 19th century. In the Rashidun Caliphate, whenever citizens were injured or lost their ability to work, it became the state's responsibility to make sure that their minimum needs were met, with the unemployed and their families receiving an allowance from the public treasury. Retirement pensions were provided to elderly people, who had retired and could "count on receiving a stipend from the public treasury." Babies who were abandoned were also taken care of, with one hundred dirhams spent annually on each orphan's development. Umar also introduced the concept of public trusteeship and public ownership when he implemented the *Waqf*, or charitable trust, system, which transferred "wealth from the individual or the few to a social collective ownership," in order to provide "services to the community at large." For example, Umar brought land from the Banu Harithah and converted it into a charitable trust, which meant that "profit and produce from the land went towards benefiting the poor, slaves, and travellers."

During the great famine of 18 AH (638 CE), Umar introduced further reforms, such as the introduction of food rationing using coupons, which were given to those in need and could be exchanged for wheat and flour. Another innovative concept that was introduced was that of a poverty threshold, with efforts made to ensure a minimum standard of living, making sure that no citizen across the empire would suffer from hunger. In order to determine the poverty line, Umar ordered an experiment to test how many seers of flour would be required to feed a person for a month. He found that 25 seers of flour could feed 30 people, and so he concluded that 50 seers of flour would be sufficient to feed a person for a month.

As a result, he ordered that the poor each receive a food ration of fifty seers of flour per month. In addition, the poor and disabled were guaranteed cash stipends. However, in order to avoid some citizens taking advantage of government services, "begging and laziness were not tolerated" and "those who received government benefits were expected to be contributing members in the community."

Further reforms later took place under the Umayyad Caliphate. Registered soldiers who were disabled in service received an invalidity pension, while similar provisions were made for the disabled and poor in general. Caliph Al-Walid I assigned payments and services to the needy, which included money for the poor, guides for the blind, and servants for the crippled, and pensions for all disabled people so that they would never need to beg.

The caliphs Al-Walid II and Umar ibn Abdul-Aziz supplied money and clothes to the blind and crippled, as well as servants for the latter. This continued with the Abbasid caliph Al-Mahdi. Tahir ibn Husayn, governor of the Khurasan province of the Abbasid Caliphate, states in a letter to his son that pensions from the treasury should be provided to the blind, to look after the poor and destitute in general, to make sure not to overlook victims of oppression who are unable to complain and are ignorant of how to claim their rights, and that pensions should be assigned to victims of calamities and the widows and orphans they leave behind.

The "ideal city" described by the Islamic philosophers, Al-Farabi and Avicenna, also assigns funds to the disabled. When communities were striken by famine, rulers would often support them though measures such as the remission of taxes, importation of food, and charitable payments, ensuring that everyone had enough to eat. However, private charity through the *Waqf* trust institution often played a greater role in the alleviation of famines than government measures did. From the 9th century, funds from the treasury were also used towards the *Waqf* (charitable trusts) for the purpose of building and supporting public institutions, often Madrassah educational institutions and Bimaristan hospitals.

Treatment of Conquered Peoples

Caliph Umar was the first Caliph to provide Allowance to non-Muslims, or Dhimmi, after they reached old age. The very first Non-Muslim to receive pension from the Rashidun Administration was a Jew from the following documented record:

Once Caliph Omar was in the streets of Madina when he saw a man begging. He went to him and asked him; "why are you begging? Are you not receiving maintenance (allowance) from Bait al-mal". The man replied; "I am a Jew and I am doing this so that I can pay the Jizya". Hearing this the Caliph Omar took him by his hand to the Bait al-mal and decreed "In the name of Allah you pay Jizya all your life and then you get betrayed when you reach old age." He ordered to provide that man Pension and from that day it was so ordered for all Jews and Christians and others. This is how non-Muslims were being given relief from Jizya, though Jizya was not abolished.

Blasphemy Law in Iran

Iran is a constitutional, Islamic theocracy. Its official religion is the doctrine of the Twelver Jaafari School. Iran's law against blasphemy derives from Sharia. Blasphemers are usually charged with "spreading corruption on earth", or mofsed-e-filarz, which can also be applied to criminal or political crimes. The law against blasphemy complements laws against criticizing the Islamic regime, insulting Islam, and publishing materials that deviate from Islamic standards. The regime uses these laws to persecute religious minorities such as the Sunni,

Bahai, Sufi, and Christians and to persecute dissidents and journalists. Persecuted individuals are subject to surveillance by the "religious police," harassment, prolonged detention, mistreatment, torture, and execution. The courts have acquitted vigilantes who killed in the belief that their victims were engaged in un-Islamic activities.

Selected Cases

On 9 June 2009, the singer Mohsen Namjoo was sentenced in absentia to a five-year jail term for ridiculing the Quran in a song. In 2008, Namjoo had apologized for the song, which he claimed was never meant for public release.

In March 2009, Iranian blogger Omid Mirsayafi died in prison while serving a 30-month sentence for propaganda against the state and criticism of religious leaders. The authorities said Mirsayafi committed suicide. In February 2009, the Iranian government launched a campaign against Mohammad Mojtehed Shabestari, a Shia Muslim cleric, for blasphemy. Shabestari's blasphemy was to say in a speech: "If in a society the three concepts of God, power, and authority are mixed up, a political-religious despotism will find strong roots.... and the people will suffer greatly."

In May 2007, authorities arrested eight students at Tehran's Amir Kabir University. The students were associated with a newspaper which had published articles suggesting that no humans were infallible, including Prophet Muhammad (Pbuh).

In October 2006, Ayatollah Hossein Kazemeyni Boroujerdi, a senior Shia cleric who advocates the separation of religion and state, and a number of his followers were arrested and imprisoned after clashes with riot police. He and seventeen of his followers were initially sentenced to death, but the death sentences were later withdrawn. In August 2007, he was sentenced to one year in prison in Tehran followed by another ten years in prison in another part of the country. In 2002, Hashem Aghajari, a member of the Shia majority, a history professor, and a veteran who lost a leg in 1980-88 war against Iraq, gave a speech in which he called for political reforms.

The authorities arrested Aghajari, charged him with blasphemy, and jailed him. A court convicted Aghajari, and made death the penalty. In June 2004, the Supreme Court substituted a charge of "insulting religious values" for the blasphemy charge, and imposed a jail term of three years among other penalties. Aghajari was released on bail on 31 July 2004.

In 1999, Iran put on trial for "insulting the Prophet, his descendants, and the Ayatollah Khomeini," and for other charges, Abdollah Nouri, the former Minister of the Interior in the Rafsanjani and Khatami cabinets.

In 1999, Nouri was the publisher of a daily newspaper that discussed the limits on the Supreme Leader's powers, the rights of unorthodox clerics and groups to air their views, the right of women to divorce, and whether laughing and clapping were un-Islamic. On 27 November 1999, the Special Court for the Clergy found Nouri guilty, and sentenced him to five years' imprisonment and a fine. Nouri was released on 5 November 2002.

In 1988, in the United Kingdom, Salman Rushdie published The Satanic Verses, a novel. Muslims in the United Kingdom accused Rushdie of blasphemy. Some Muslims called upon the Crown to prosecute Rushdie but it did not. On 14 February 1989, the Ayatollah Khomeini of Iran issued a fatwa which called for Muslims to kill Rushdie and all publishers of The Satanic Verses. In 1991, the novel's Japanese translator was stabbed to death. Shortly afterward, the Italian translator was stabbed but survived. In 1993, the Norwegian publisher of the book was injured in a gun attack.

Blasphemy Law in Pakistan

The Islamic Republic of Pakistan uses its Penal Code to prohibit and punish blasphemy against any recognized religion. While the law in theory protects blasphemy against all religions it is only applied to Islam. The Criminal Code provides penalties for blasphemy ranging from a fine to death. An accusation of blasphemy commonly subjects the accused, police, lawyers, and judges to harassment, threats, and attacks. An accusation is sometimes the prelude to vigilantism and rioting.

The Constitution

By its constitution, the official name of Pakistan is the "Islamic Republic of Pakistan." More than 96% of Pakistan's 167 million citizens (2008) are Muslims. Among countries with a Muslim majority, Pakistan has the strictest anti-blasphemy laws. The first purpose of those laws is to protect Islamic authority. By the constitution (Article 2), Islam is the state religion. By the constitution's Article 31, it is the country's duty to foster the Islamic way of life. By Article 33, it is the country's duty to discourage parochial, racial, tribal, sectarian, and provincial prejudices among the citizens.

The Blasphemy Laws

Several sections of Pakistan's Criminal Code comprise its blasphemy laws. 295 forbids damaging or defiling a place of worship or a sacred object. 295-A forbids outraging religious feelings. 295-B forbids defiling the Quran. 295-C forbids defaming the Prophet Muhammad (Pbuh). Except for 295-C, the provisions of 295 require that an offence be a consequence of the accused's intent.

Defiling the Quran merits imprisonment for life. Defaming Muhammad merits death with or without a fine. If a charge is laid under 295-C, the trial must take place in a Court of Session with a Muslim judge presiding.

298 states: Whoever, with the deliberate intention of wounding the religious feelings of any person, utters any word or makes any sound in the hearing of that person or makes any gesture in the sight of that person or places any object in the sight of that person, shall be punished with imprisonment of either description for a term which may extend to one year, or with fine, or with both. 298-A prohibits the use of any derogatory remark or representation in respect of Muslim holy personages. 298-B and 298-C prohibit the Ahmadiyya from behaving as Muslims behave, calling themselves Muslims, proselytizing, or "in any manner whatsoever" outraging the religious feelings of Muslims. Violation of any part of 298 makes the violator liable to imprisonment for up to three years and liable also to a fine.

No judicial execution of a person charged with blasphemy has occurred in Pakistan. Article 45 of the Constitution says, "The President shall have power to grant pardon, reprieve and respite, and to remit, suspend or commute any sentence passed by any court, tribunal or other authority."

The only law that may be useful in countering misuse of the Blasphemy law is PPC 153 A (a), whoever "by words, either spoken or written, or by signs, or by visible representations or otherwise, promotes or incites, or attempts to promote or incite, on grounds of religion, race, place of birth, residence, language, caste or community or any other ground whatsoever, disharmony or feelings of enmity, hatred or ill-will between different religious, racial, language or regional groups or castes or communities" shall be fined and punished with imprisonment for a term that may extend to five years.

On Jan. 12, 2011, Prime Minister of Pakistan Yousuf Raza Gilani once again said that there would be no amendments to the blasphemy law.

Shariah

The Federal Shariat Court (FSC) is a religious body which rules on whether any particular law is repugnant to the injunctions of Islam. If a law is repugnant to Islam, "the President in the case of a law with respect to a matter in the Federal Legislative List or the Concurrent Legislative List, or the Governor in the case of a law with respect to a matter not enumerated in either of those Lists, shall take steps to amend the law so as to bring such law or provision into conformity with the Injunctions of Islam" (Constitution, Article 203D). In October 1990, the FSC ruled that 295-C was repugnant to Islam by permitting life imprisonment as an alternative to a death sentence. The Court said "the penalty for contempt of the Holy Prophet... is death." The FSC ruled that, if the President did not take action to amend the law before 30 April 1991, then 295-C would stand amended by its ruling.

Promptly after the FSC's ruling in 1990, Bishop Dani L. Tasleem filed an appeal in the Supreme Court of Pakistan, which has the power to overrule the FSC. In April 2009, the Shariat Appellate Bench of the Supreme Court considered the appeal. Deputy Attorney-General Agha Tariq Mehmood, who represented the federal government, said that the Shariat Appellate Bench dismissed the appeal because the appellant did not pursue it. The appellant did not present any argument on the appeal because the appellant, according to reports, was no longer alive. Consequently, it appears to be the law in Pakistan that persons convicted under 295-C must be sentenced to death with or without a fine.

Vigilantism

Those who are accused of blasphemy may be subject to harassment, threats, and attacks. Police, lawyers, and judges may also be subject to harassment, threats, and attacks when blasphemy is an issue. Those accused of blasphemy are subject to immediate incarceration, and most accused are denied bail to forestall mob violence. It is common for those accused of blasphemy to be put in solitary confinement for their protection from other inmates and guards. Like those who have served a sentence for blasphemy, those who are acquitted of blasphemy usually go into hiding or leave Pakistan.

United Nations

Pakistan's opposition to blasphemy has caused Pakistan to be active in the international arena in promoting global limitations on freedom of religion or belief and limitations on freedom of expression. In March 2009, Pakistan presented a resolution to the United Nations

Human Rights Council in Geneva which calls upon the world to formulate laws against the defamation of religion.

Internet Censorship

In May 2010, Pakistan blocked access to Facebook because the website hosted a page called Everybody Draw Muhammad Day. Pakistan lifted the block after Facebook prevented access to the page. In June 2010, Pakistan blocked seventeen websites for hosting content that the authorities considered offensive to Muslims. At the same time, Pakistan began to monitor the content of Google, Yahoo, YouTube, Amazon, MSN, Hotmail, and Bing.

Selected Cases

On March 4, 2011, thousands of Christians and Muslims gathered in Khushpur, a Christian village in the Punjab province of Pakistan, at the funeral of late Shahbaz Bahtti, Federal Minister for Minorities Affairs. He was assassinated on March 2 in Islamabad. Bhatti was killed because he had been struggling to bring changes in the blasphemy laws. Pakistani authorities charged 647 people with offences under the blasphemy laws between 1986 and 2007.

Fifty percent of the people charged were non-Muslim (3% of the national population). 20 of those charged were murdered. On March 2nd, 2011 Shahbaz Bhatti, a Roman Catholic member of the National Assembly, was killed by gunmen in Islamabad as he was travelling to work, a few weeks after he had vowed to defy death threats over his efforts to reform Pakistan's blasphemy laws.

In November 2010, Asia Bibi was sentenced to death by hanging on a charge of blasphemy; the case that has yet to be upheld by the Lahore High Court has sparked international reactions. Punjab Governor Salman Taseer was shot dead by his security guard for supporting Asia Bibi. Salman Taseer visited Asia Bibi in Jail and held a press conference with her. He told media that Asia Bibi will be released soon and the President of Pakistan will soon demolish her death sentence. Mass protests in Pakistan were held in Pakistan against his support to Asia Bibi. Many local Mosque's Imams across Pakistan said that Salman Taseer has defied Mohammed and he should also be sentenced to death.

On December 12, 2010, during a press conference major Islamic parties in Pakistan launched a campaign for upholding the sanctity of Muhammad against the proposed amendment in the blasphemy laws.

In July 2010, the Lahore High Court ordered the release of Zaibun Nisa, a woman who was jailed in 1996 on a charge of blasphemy when police were investigating a complaint that a Quran had been defiled. Nisa's lawyer reported, "There was no evidence linking her to the crime."

In July 2010, a trader in Faisalabad complained that one of his employees had been handed a pamphlet which contained disrespectful remarks about Muhammad. According to the police, the pamphlet appeared to have the signatures and addresses of Pastor Rashid Emmanuel and his brother Sajid, who were Christians. While the police were escorting the brothers from a district court, gunmen shot and killed both. Allama Ahmed Mian Hammadi, a Pakistani Muslim cleric, has claimed that Shahbaz Bhatti, Pakistan's Federal Minister for Minorities has himself committed blasphemy by branding the recently murdered Christian brothers as victims of Pakistan blasphemy laws.

Bhatti had spoken out about the murder last week of Rashid Emmanuel, 30, and his brother Sajid, 27, by unidentified masked gunmen inside a courthouse in Faisalabad. The brothers had been accused of blaspheming Muhammad earlier this month, a charge that they had both denied.

According to Mr Hammadi's statement, published in Daily Jasarat, a Pakistani Urdu daily newspaper, the Muslim cleric said that Muslims cannot tolerate blasphemy against Muhammad. "It is not a cruelty to kill blasphemers, rather blasphemy itself is such an enormous brutality that the one who commits it neither has got a right to live in this world nor is there any pardon for the blasphemer," Daily Jasarat quoted Mr Hammadi as saying.

"Muslims won't tolerate even a slightest blasphemy against Prophet Muhammad (Pbuh). If Shahbaz Bhatti committed blasphemy he would be beheaded."

On 4 August 2009, a Muslim mob attacked a factory-owner by the name of Najeebullah and others at Sheikhupura in the Punjab. The mob killed Najeebullah and two others, and set fire to the factory. The mob complained that Najeebullah had placed an outdated calendar, which contained verses from the Quran, on a table. For that offence, a worker accused Najeebullah of blasphemy. The workers may have been in a dispute with Najeebullah over wages.

On 30 July 2009, hundreds of members of Sipah-e-Sahaba, a banned Muslim organization, torched Christian homes and killed Christians in the Punjabi city of Gojra and in the nearby village of

Korian. The professed reason for the violence was that a Christian had defiled a Quran. Christian mobs retaliated. Fighting between Muslim and Christian groups went on through 1 August 2009.

On 28 January 2009, the police in Punjab arrested a labourer and four students for blasphemy. All those arrested were Ahmadi. The accusation against them was that they wrote "Prophet Muhammad (Pbuh)" on the wall of a toilet in a Sunni mosque. The senior superintendent of police investigated and reported to the Ministry of the Interior at the end of March 2009 that the accusation was baseless.

On 22 January 2009, Hector Aleem a Christian Human Rights Activist in Pakistan was arrested due to a blasphemy charge. According to the FIR someone sent a blasphemous text message to the leader of Sunni Tehreek. After the investigation, that sender had once contacted Hector Aleem. So he is guiltiy by association. Since they could not find that person so they arrested him. Police raided Hector's house situated in sector G-11/2 of Islamabad on January 22, 2009 at 1:30 am.

Hector Aleem the Chairman of Peace Worldwide was working for a church destroyed by CDA (capital development authority) in Islamabad Pakistan. The church was destroyed because according to CDA it was built illegally. When Hector Aleem objected to the destruction of the church he faced with several lawsuits ranging from fraud to criminal charges. He fought all of them in the courts and proved his innocence. His opponents tried to assassinate him several times. The Maulvies threatened him that if he continues to work for the Church they would kill him and his sons, and would force his daughters to convert to Islam. During this time Hector Aleem received a Peace award by Mr. Yousaf Raza Gillani the Prime minister of Pakistan. When Hector Aleem was arrested, the Police severely beat him and tortured him mentally and physically. After 24 hours of not knowing what were the charges, we was told that his offence is blasphemy, a charge that caries death penalty in Pakistan. His name is not even mentioned in the FIR (First Information Report) but still he is tried in the Rawalpindi Judicial Court. In May 2008, Punjabi police jailed Robin Sardar, a Christian physician, upon an accusation of blasphemy from a Muslim street-vendor who wanted to install himself in front of Sardar's clinic.

In February 2008, Special Rapporteurs of the United Nations Human Rights Council reminded Pakistan's representative of the matter regarding Raja Fiaz, Muhammad Bilal, Nazar Zakir Hussain, Qazi Farooq, Muhammad Rafique, Muhammad Saddique and Ghulam Hussain. According to the allegations received, the men were members of the Mehdi Foundation International (MFI), a multi-faith institution utilizing the name of Riaz Ahmed Gohar Shahi. They were arrested on 23 December 2005 in Wapda Town.

The police confiscated posters on which Gohar Shahi was shown as "Imam Mehdi." On 13 July 2006, the Anti-Terrorism Court No. 1 in Lahore sentenced each accused to five years of imprisonment, inter alia, under § 295-A for having outraged others' religious feelings. Since 27 August 2006, the seven men have been detained in Sahiwal Jail, Punjab, where they were forced to parade naked, and were suspended from the ceiling and beaten. The prisoners' records were posted outside the cell and falsely indicated that they had been sentenced under 295-C.

For this reason, they were constantly threatened and intimidated by prison staff as well as by other detainees. One MFI member was targeted by several other inmates and sexually assaulted. Subsequently, other staff members sexually abused him and pushed burning cigarette butts into his anus.

On 28 October 2007, the police arrested Muhammad Imran of Faisalabad under § 295-B for allegedly setting fire to a Quran. For three days, the police kept Imran in a torture-cell where they tortured him. Then the police sent him to a jail where other inmates attacked him. His jailers put Imran into solitary confinement without attending to his injuries. On 14 April 2009, an Additional Sessions judge released Imran. On 9 May 2007, Raja Riaz, a servant, accused his master, Walter Fazal Khan Khan, 84, a Christian, of burning a Quran at his house. The police arrested Khan under § 295-B. Kahn's family and others said Riaz's accusation was part of a plot to take Khan's valuable house and land from him.

In April 2007, upon a charge of blasphemy, the police in Toba Tek Singh jailed five Christians: Salamat Masih, his son Rashid, and their relatives Ishfaq, Saba, and Dao Masih. The allegation against the Christians was that they desecrated pieces of paper that bore Muhammad's name. On 25 January 2009, the authorities released the Christians, and Muslim clerics agreed to issue a fatwa which declared that the accusation of blasphemy was unsound.

Christians and Muslims in Pakistan condemned Dan Brown's novel The Da Vinci Code as blasphemous. On 3 June 2006, Pakistan banned the film. Culture Minister Ghulam Jamal said: "Islam teaches us to respect all the prophets of God Almighty and degradation of any prophet is tantamount to defamation of the rest."

Two Christians, both elderly men from Faisalabad, Punjab, were acquitted by the Lahore High Court in April 2009. In November 2006, the two had been sentenced to 10 years in prison for allegedly burning pages from the Quran. The allegation arose apparently out of a dispute over land.

In March 2006, the police arrested Shafeeq Lateef for making derogatory remarks about Muhammad and for desecrating a Quran. On 18 June 2008, a District and Sessions court sentenced Lateef to death for his alleged remarks and demanded that he pay a fine of 500,000 rupees for desecrating a Quran. Arshed Masih, 38, is still fighting for his life in Holy Family Hospital in Rawalpindi, a city not far from Pakistan's capital. With the help of police, Muslim extremists last Friday set him on fire for refusing to convert to Islam and raped his wife, local sources told AsiaNews.it. The incident occurred in front of a local police station.

In 2005, Masih and his wife began working for a wealthy Muslim businessman, he as driver and she as his wife's maid. Recently, the two fell out of favour with their employer and his family because they insisted on remaining Christian.

During the incident, Masih's wife, Martha, "was raped by police agents," local sources said. The couple's three children, ranging in age from 7 and 12, were forced to watch their parents being brutalised. No action taken by the Government. On 11 August 2005, Judge Arshad Noor Khan of the Anti-Terrorist Court found Younus Shaikh guilty of defiling a copy of the Quran, outraging religious feelings, and propagating religious hatred among society. Shaikh's conviction occurred because he wrote a book: Shaitan Maulvi (Satanic Cleric).

The book said stoning to death (Rajam) as a punishment for adultery was not mentioned in the Quran. The book said also that four historical imams (religious leaders) were Jews. The judge imposed upon Shaikh a fine of 100,000 rupees, and sentenced him to spend his life in jail.

On 20 November 2003, the police arrested Anwar Masih, a day labourer, a Christian, a married father of four (at that time), a resident of Shahdara, a town next to Lahore. The police charged Masih under § 295-B. The charge arose out of an encounter that Masih had with a neighbour who had grown a beard. The neighbour disclosed that he had converted from Christianity to Islam. Masih and the neighbour exchanged harsh words. The neighbour reported to the police that Masih had insulted Muhammad. The Lahore High Court acquitted Masih on 24 December 2004.

In August 2005, Masih took a job in a factory. In November 2007, he lost the job when his employer was threatened for employing a "blasphemer." Masih went into hiding.

In August 2003, the police arrested a Christian, Samuel Masih, for allegedly defiling a mosque by spitting on its wall. While in prison, Masih contracted tuberculosis. The authorities transported him to a hospital. There, on 24 May 2004, a police constable used a hammer to kill Masih. The constable said it was his duty as a Muslim to kill Masih.

In October 2000, Pakistani authorities charged Dr. M. Younus Shaikh M.D., a physician, with blasphemy on account of remarks that students claimed he made during a lecture. The students alleged that, inter alia, Shaikh had said Muhammad's parents were non-Muslims because they died before Islam existed. A judge ordered that Shaikh pay a fine of 100,000 rupees, and that he be hanged. On 20 November 2003, a court retried the matter and acquitted Shaikh, who fled Pakistan for Europe soon thereafter.

In 2000, a court sentenced Naseem Ghani and Mohammed Shafiq to seven years imprisonment upon allegations that they had burned a Quran.

The police arrested Ayub Masih, a Pakistani Christian bricklayer for blasphemy on 14 October 1996 and jailed him for violation of 295-C. Muhammad Akram, a Muslim neighbour to Masih, complained to the police that Masih had said Christianity was right, and Masih had recommended that Akram read Salman Rushdie's Satanic Verses. The same day that Masih was arrested, Muslim villagers forced the entire Christian population of Masih's village (fourteen families) to leave the village. Masih's family had applied under a government program that gave housing plots to landless people. Local landlords resented Masih's application because the landlords had been able to oblige landless Christians to work in the fields in exchange for a place to live. Masih's application gave him a way out of his subservience to the landlords. Upon Masih's arrest, the authorities gave Masih's plot to Akram.

Akram shot and injured Masih in the halls of the Session Court at Sahiwal on 6 November 1997. Four assailants attacked Masih in jail. The authorities took no action against Akram or against the other assailants.

On 20 April 1998, Judge Abdul Khan sentenced Masih to death and levied a fine of 100,000 rupees. Two judges of the Lahore High Court heard Masih's appeal on 24 July 2001. Shortly thereafter, the judges affirmed the judgment of the trial court. On 16 August 2002, the Supreme Court of Pakistan set aside the judgment of the lower courts.

The Supreme Court noted Akram's acquisition of Masih's property and concluded the case had been fabricated for personal gain. The court also noted other breaches in the law of due process.

Judge Arif Iqbal Hussain Bhatti was assassinated on 19 October 1997 in his Lahore office after acquitting two people who were accused of blasphemy.

Riaz Ahmad, his son, and two nephews (Basharat Ahmad, Qamar Ahmad and Mushtaq Ahmad), all Ahmadis, were arrested and jailed on 21 November 1993. They were detained for having "said something derogatory." Local people in Piplan, Mianwali District, said that rivalry over Ahmad's position as village headman was the real motivation for the complaint against him. The Sessions Court rejected the bail applications of the accused. The Supreme Court granted bail in December 1997.

In February 1993, Anwar Masih, a Christian from Samundri in Punjab, went to jail upon a Muslim shopkeeper's allegation that, during an argument over money, Masih had insulted Muhammad.

In November 1992, Gul Masih, a Christian, was sentenced to death after having remarked to his neighbour Mohammad Sajjad, a Muslim, he had read "that Mohammed had 11 wives, including a minor."

LGBT Topics and Islam

LGBT topics and Islam are influenced by both the cultural-legal history of the nations with a large Muslim population, along with how specific passages in the Quran and statements attributed to the Prophet Muhammad (Pbuh) are interpreted. The mainstream interpretation of Quranic verses and Hadith condemn homosexuality and cross-dressing. In this, Islam resembles mainstream interpretations of other Abrahamic religions such as Judaism and Christianity.

The Quran cites the story of the "people of Lot" (also known as the people of Sodom and Gomorrah), destroyed by the wrath of Allah because they engaged in "lustful" carnal acts between men.

Eminent scholars of Islam, such as Sheikh ul-Islam Imam Malik, and Imam Shafi amongst others, ruled that Islam disallowed homosexuality and ordained capital punishment for a person guilty of it. Homosexual activity is a crime and forbidden in most Muslim-majority countries. In the Islamic regimes of Iran, Mauritania, Saudi Arabia, Sudan and Yemen, homosexual activity is punished with the death penalty. In Nigeria and Somalia the death penalty is issued in some regions. The legal punishment for sodomy has varied among juristic schools: some prescribe capital punishment; while other prescribe a milder discretionary punishment such as imprisonment. In some relatively secular Muslim-majority countries such as Indonesia, Jordan and Turkey this is not the case. By contrast, homoerotic themes were present in poetry and other literature written by some Muslims from the medieval period onwards and which celebrated love between men.

Islamic Law—The Quran

Sharia, or traditional Islamic law, is based on the Quran, Allah's revelation to humankind, and on the Hadith, sayings attributed to Muhammad according to tradition. Both the Quran and the Hadith have been generally interpreted as condemning sexual relations between persons of the same sex.

The Quran is the central text of Islam, believed by Muslims to be the revelation of God. It contains seven references to "the people of Lut," the biblical Lot, but meaning the residents of Sodom and Gomorrah (references 7:80-84, 11:77-83, 21:74, 22:43, 26:165-175, 27:56-59, and 29:27-33), and their destruction by Allah is associated explicitly with their sexual practices:

"And (We sent) Lut when he said to his people: What! do you commit an indecency which any one in the world has not done before you? Most surely you come to males in lust besides females; nay you are an extravagant people. And the answer of his people was no other than that they said: Turn them out of your town, surely they are a people who seek to purify (themselves). So We delivered him and his followers, except his wife; she was of those who remained behind. And We rained upon them a rain; consider then what was the end of the guilty."

The sins of the people of Lut became proverbial, and the Arabic words for homosexual behaviour (*liwat*) and for a person who performs such acts (*luti*) both derive from his name. There is, however, only one passage in the Quran which can be interpreted as prescribing a legal position towards homosexual behaviour:

> *"And as for those who are guilty of an indecency from among your women, call to witnesses against them four (witnesses) from among you; then if they bear witness confine them to the houses until death takes them away or Allah opens some way for them. And as for the two who are guilty of indecency from among you, give them*

both a punishment; then if they repent and amend, turn aside from them; surely Allah is oft-returning (to mercy), the Merciful."

The Hadith and Akhbar

Given the vagueness of the Quran regarding the punishment of *liwat*, Islamic jurists have turned to the collections of the Hadith (sayings of Muhammad) and akhbar (accounts of his life). These, on the other hand, are perfectly clear and particularly harsh.

Ibn al-Jawzi records Muhammad as cursing sodomites in several Hadith, and recommending the death penalty for both the active and passive partners in same-sex acts. Sunan al-Tirmidhi, again reports Muhammad as having prescribed the death penalty for both the active and the passive partner: "Whoever you find committing the sin of the people of Lut, kill them, both the one who does it and the one to whom it is done." The overall moral or theological principle is that a person who performs such actions (*luti*) challenges the harmony of God's creation, and is therefore a revolt against God.

Al-Nuwayri in his *Nihaya* reports that the Prophet is alleged to have said what he feared most for his community were the practices of the people of Lot (although he seems to have expressed the same idea in regard to wine and female seduction). Such Hadith nevertheless show that, while probably not very common in Bedouin society, homosexuality was not totally unknown in Arabia of the pre-Islamic period.

Jurisprudence

The various traditional schools of Sharia (Islamic law) disagree on what punishment is appropriate for *liwat*. The Hanafi school holds that it does not merit any physical punishment, on the basis of a Hadith that "Muslim blood can only be spilled for adultery, apostasy and homicide"; against this the Hanbali school, identifying sodomy with adultery, holds that it must incur the death penalty.

Abu Bakr, condemned a homosexual to be buried beneath the debris of a wall, and prescribed burning alive as the penalty for all those guilty of such practices. In this respect he was followed by Abd Allah bin al-Zubayr and Hisham bin Abd al-Malik. For his part, Ali bin Abi Talib ordered the stoning of a *luti* and had another thrown head-first from the top of a minaret; according to Ibn Abbas, this last punishment must be followed by stoning. Abd Allah bin Umar went a step beyond the condemnation by the Prophet, reckoning that these people would be resurrected in the form of monkeys and pigs.

Rulings by Modern Scholars of Islam

Based on the principles of the Quran and the Hadith, several eminent scholars of Islam, such as Imam Malik, Imam Shafi, Ahmad and Ishaaq have ruled that the person guilty of homosexuality should be stoned regardless of his married or unmarried nature. Ibn Kathir's commentary on the words of Quran with respect to homosexuality are;

> *"The words of Allah 'And the two persons (man and woman) among you who commit illegal sexual intercourse, hurt them both' mean, those who commit immoral actions, punish them both. Ibn 'Abbaas (may Allah be pleased with him), Sa'eed ibn Jubayr and others said: By condemning them, shaming them and hitting them with shoes. This was the ruling until Allah abrogated it and replaced it with whipping and stoning. 'Ikrimah, 'Ata, al-Hasan and 'Abd-Allah ibn Katheer said: This was revealed concerning a man and woman who commit fornication. Al-Saddi said, it was revealed concerning young people before they get married. Mujaahid said: it was revealed concerning two men if they admit it bluntly; a hint is not sufficient-as if he was referring to homosexuality. And Allah knows best."*

Ibn al-Qayyim is reported to have said;

> *"Both of them – fornication and homosexuality – involve immorality that goes against the wisdom of Allah's creation and commandment. For homosexuality involves innumerable evil and harms, and the one to whom it is done would be better off being killed than having this done to him, because after that he will become so evil and so corrupt that there can be no hope of his being reformed, and all good is lost for him, and he will no longer feel any shame before Allah or before His creation. The semen of the one who did that to him will act as a poison on his body and soul. The scholars differed as to whether the one to whom it is done will ever enter Paradise."*

Ahmad Kutty, senior lecturer and Islamic scholar at the Islamic Institute of Toronto, Ontario, Canada, in his lectures on the subject has expressed the view a Muslim practicing homosexuality needs to give it up since it is considered "one of the most abominable sins in Islam". Muslims like Dr. Nadia El-Awady, the Health & Science Editor at IslamOnline, have attempted to discuss and understand homosexuality in an Islamic as well as a scientific light, citing its apparent ill-effects for the Islamic as well as the moral society. The Islamic UK-based group, the Shari'ah Court of the UK has issued a fatwa calling for a death sentence for playwright Terrence McNally for depicting Jesus and his followers as a group of homosexuals.

Many scholars of Sharia, or Islamic law, interpret homosexuality as a punishable offence as well as a sin. There is no specific punishment prescribed, however, and this is usually left to the discretion of the local authorities on Islam.

However, there do exist some dissenting opinions amongst Ulema. Mohamed El-Moctar El-Shinqiti, a contemporary Mauritanian scholar, has argued that "[even though] homosexuality is a grievous sin...[a] no legal punishment is stated in the Quran for homosexuality...[b] it is not reported that Prophet Muhammad (Pbuh) has punished somebody for committing homosexuality...[c] there is no authentic Hadith reported from the Prophet prescribing a punishment for the homosexuals..." He argues that both hadiths on stoning and killing homosexuals are weak: Hadith scholars such as Al-Bukhari, Yahya ibn Ma`in, An-Nasa'i, Ibn Hazm, Al-Tirmidhi, and others impugned the two hadiths.

Abu Bakr Al-Jassas (d. 981 AD/370 AH) argued that the hadiths on killing homosexuals "are not reliable by any means, and no legal punishment can be prescribed based on them."

History of Homosexuality in Islamic Society

Medieval Era

Increasing prosperity resulting from Muslim conquests in the centuries following Muhammad's death, was accompanied by what some Muslims bemoaned as a general "corruption" of morals in the two holy cities of Mecca and Medina. The accumulation of wealth and power in the hands of a privileged few, combined with the continuance of and regularization of polygamy and concubinage, severely restricted the sexual opportunities available to young men. Such opportunities were only opened via Jihad or through some form of illicit sex.

Therefore, in spite of its condemnation by religious authorities, homosexuality persisted in a subterranean manner. And it seems to have become less of a rarity as the process of acculturation sped up. Information relating to the development of music and song reveals the presence of *mukhannathun*, who were apparently for the most part of foreign origin. The arrival of the Abbasid army to Arabia in the 8th century seems to have meant that tolerance for homosexual practice subsequently spread more widely under the new dynasty. The ruler Al-Amin, for example, was said to have required slave women to be dressed in masculine clothing in the hope of inducing him to adopt more conventional morals.

There are other examples from the following centuries. The Aghlabid Emir, Ibrahim II of Ifriqiya (ruled 875-902), was said to have been surrounded by some sixty catamites, yet whom he was said to have treated in a most horrific manner. Caliph al-Mutasim in the 9th century and some of his successors were accused of homosexuality. The popular stories says that Cordoba, Abd al-Rahman III had executed a young man from Leon who was held as a hostage, because he had refused his advances at 10th century. Mehmed the Conqueror, the Ottoman sultan living in the 15th century, European sources say "who was known to have ambivalent sexual tastes, sent a eunuch to the house of Notaras, demanding that he supply his good looking fourteen year old son for the Sultan's pleasure. When he refused, the Sultan instantly ordered the decapitation of Notaras, together with that of his son and his son-in-law; and their three heads ... were placed on the banqueting table before him". Another youth Mehmed found attractive, and who was presumably more accommodating, was the brother of the famous Vlad the Impaler, "Radu, a hostage in Istanbul whose good looks had caught the Sultan's fancy, and who was thus singled out to serve as one of his most favoured pages." After the defeat of Vlad, Mehmed placed Radu on the throne of Wallachia as a vassal ruler. However, Turkish sources deny these stories.

Literature

Whatever the legal strictures on sexual activity, the positive expression of male homeoerotic sentiment in literature was accepted, and assiduously cultivated, from the late eighth century until modern times. First in Arabic, but later also in Persian, Turkish and Urdu, love poetry by men about boys more than competed with that about women, it overwhelmed it. Anecdotal literature reinforces this impression of general societal acceptance of the public celebration of male-male love (which hostile Western caricatures of Islamic societies in medieval and early modern times simply exaggerate)....

In a tradition from the *Arabian Nights (A* set of myths and folk tales), The author wrote the story, in the story Muhammad was said to have warned his followers against staring at youth because of their beauty: "Be careful, Do not gaze at beardless youth, for they have eyes more tempting than the houris." Beyond that, despite the ban on homosexuality by mainstream Islam, homosexual practise was generally tolerated, though thinly veiled, in many parts of the Arab/ Muslim world, until early modern times, when the emergence of a Westernized elite caused it to be frowned upon. Some observers have compared the status of homosexuality in the premodern Muslim world to its status in Ancient Greece, though the parallel is shaky.

Modern Day

As the fact that *liwat* is regarded as a temptation indicates, anal intercourse is not seen as repulsively unnatural so much as dangerously attractive: "one has to avoid getting buggered precisely in order not to acquire a taste for it and thus become addicted." In practise, the segregation of women and the strong emphasis on virility can lead to adolescents and unmarried young men seeking sexual outlets with males younger than themselves-in one study in Morocco, with boys in the age-range 7 to 13. But deep shame attaches to the passive partner. Similar sexual sociologies are reported for other Muslim societies from North Africa to Pakistan and the Far East. In Afghanistan in 2009, the British Army was forced to commission a report into the sexuality of the local men after British soldiers reported the discomfort at witnessing adult males involved in sexual relations with boys. The report stated that though illegal, there was a tradition of such relationships in the country, known as "bache bazi" or *boy play*, and that it was especially strong around Kandahar.

Raphael Patai in *The Arab Mind*, has argued that among some Arabs and Turks homosexuality can be justified as an expression of power. The "active homosexual act is considered as an assertion of one's aggressive masculine superiority, while the acceptance of the role of the passive homosexual is considered extremely degrading and shameful because it casts the man or youth into a submissive, feminine role".

Legal Status in Modern Islamic Nations

Homosexual relations are a crime and face punishment in some Islamic countries such as Saudi Arabia, or Islamic Republics such as Iran. The death penalty is currently in place in Saudi Arabia, Iran, Mauritania, northern Nigeria, Sudan, and Yemen. It formerly carried the death penalty in Afghanistan under the Taliban, but subsequently has changed from a capital crime to one that is punished with fines and a prison sentence. The legal situation in the United Arab Emirates is unclear. In many Muslim nations, such as Bahrain, Qatar, Algeria and the Maldives, homosexuality is punished with jail time, fines, or corporal punishment. This has led to controversy regarding Qatar, which is due to stage the 2022 World Cup. Human rights groups have questioned the awarding in 2010 of the right to host the competition, due to the possibility that gay football fans may be jailed. In response, Sepp Blatter, head of FIFA, joked that they would have to "refrain from sexual activity" while in Qatar. He later withdrew the remarks after condemnation from rights groups.

In Saudi Arabia, while the maximum punishment for homosexual acts is public execution, the government will generally use lesser punishments—e.g., fines, jail time, and whipping—as alternatives, unless it feels that individuals are challenging state authority by engaging in LGBT social movements. Iran is perhaps the nation to execute the largest number of its citizens for homosexual acts. Since the 1979 Islamic revolution, the Iranian government has executed more than 4,000 such people.

In Egypt, openly gay men have been prosecuted under general public morality laws. On the other hand, homosexuality, while not legal, is tolerated to some extent in Lebanon.

In some Muslim-majority nations, such as Albania, Turkey, Jordan, Indonesia or Mali, same-sex intercourse is not forbidden by law.

Most international human rights organizations, such as Human Rights Watch and Amnesty International, condemn laws that make homosexual relations between consenting adults a crime. Since 1994, the United Nations Human Rights Committee has also ruled that such laws violate the right to privacy guaranteed in the Universal Declaration of Human Rights and the International Covenant on Civil and Political Rights. However, most Muslim nations (except for Turkey), insist that such laws are necessary to preserve Islamic morality and virtue. Of the nations with a majority of Muslim inhabitants, Lebanon has an internal effort to legalize homosexuality.

Cultural Acceptance or Hostility

Most Muslim-majority countries are not liberal in terms of tolerance for homosexual rights. Some like Iran, Saudi Arabia, Pakistan, Sudan, Yemen, Afghanistan, Iraq, and Malaysia have high levels of hostility due to the influence of religion and politics. Among these countries, Iran is seen by some as being considerably more intolerant. In one case that caused international controversy, Iran executed Mahmoud Asgari and Ayaz Marhoni on July 19, 2005, after they were convicted for the rape of a 13-year-old boy. Soon after, a

British group alleged that the teenagers were executed for consensual homosexual acts and not rape. While Iran has outlawed homosexuality, Iranian Shia thinkers such as Ayatollah Khomeini have allowed for transsexuals to change their gender so that they can enter heterosexual relationships. This position has been confirmed by the Supreme Leader of Iran, Ayatollah Ali Khamenei, and is also supported by many other Iranian clerics. The state will pay a portion of the cost for a sex-change operation. Despite support for transsexuals from Iranian religious leaders, Iranian society itself is less accepting of them.

In India, where Muslims form a large minority, the largest Islamic seminary (Darul Uloom Deoband) has vehemently opposed recent government moves to abrogate and liberalize archaic laws from the British Raj era that banned homosexuality.

Some secular Muslim countries like Albania, Indonesia, Turkey, Kazakhstan, Lebanon, etc. have more liberal attitudes. In the UK, a Gallup poll showed that almost zero Muslims believed homosexuality to be "morally acceptable", compared with 35% of French Muslims.

Gender Variant and Transgender People

In Islam, the term mukhannathun is used to describe gender-variant people, usually male-to-female transsexuals. Neither this term nor the equivalent for "eunuch" occurs in the Quran, but the term does appear in the Hadith, the sayings of Muhammad, which have a secondary status to the central text. Moreover, within Islam, there is a tradition on the elaboration and refinement of extended religious doctrines through scholarship. This doctrine contains a transpositive passage by the scholar and Hadith collector An-Nawawi: A mukhannath is the one ("male") who carries in his movements, in his appearance and in his language the characteristics of a woman.

There are two types; the first is the one in whom these characteristics are innate, he did not put them on by himself, and therein is no guilt, no blame and no shame, as long as he does not perform any (illicit) act or exploit it for money (prostitution etc.). The second type acts like a woman out of immoral purposes and he is the sinner and blameworthy.

Iran carries out more sex change operations than any other nation in the world except for Thailand. It is sanctioned as a supposed "cure" for homosexuality, which is punishable by death under Iranian law. The government even provides up to half the cost for those needing financial assistance and a sex change is recognised on the birth certificate.

LGBT Movements within Islam

The Al-Fatiha Foundation is an organization which advances the cause of gay, lesbian, and transgender Muslims. It was founded in 1998 by Faisal Alam, a Pakistani American, and is registered as a nonprofit organization in the United States. The organization was an out shoot of an internet listserve that brought together many gay, lesbian and questioning Muslims from various countries. The Foundation accepts and considers homosexuality as natural, either regarding Quranic verses as obsolete in the context of modern society, or pointing out that the Quran speaks out against homosexual lust, and is silent on homosexual love. In 2001, Al-Muhajiroun, a banned and now defunct international organization who sought the establishment of a global Islamic caliphate, issued a fatwa declaring that all members of Al-Fatiha were murtadd, or apostates, and condemning them to death. Because of the threat and coming from conservative societies, many members of the foundation's site still prefer to be anonymous so as to protect their identity while continuing a tradition of secrecy. Al-Fatiha has fourteen chapters in the United States, as well as offices in England, Canada, Spain, Turkey and South Africa. In addition, Imaan, a social support group for Muslim LGBT people and their families, exists in the UK. Both of these groups were founded by gay Pakistani activists. The UK also has the Safra Project for women.

Although it is a minority viewpoint, some Muslims such as the lesbian writer Irshad Manji and academic author Scott Kugle argue that Islam does not condemn homosexuality. Author Scott Kugle, South Asian scholar and author Ruth Vanita, and Muslim scholar and writer Saleem Kidwai even contend that ancient Islam has a rich history of homoerotic literature. There are also a number of Islamic ex-gay (i.e. people claiming to have experienced a basic change in sexual orientation from exclusive homosexuality to exclusive heterosexuality) groups aimed at attempting to guide homosexuals towards heterosexuality. The StraightWay Foundation is a UK based ex-gay organization which works with homosexual Muslims who seek to eliminate their same-sex attractions. Al-Tawbah is an internet based ex-gay group.

Islam and Slavery

Historically, the major juristic schools of Islam traditionally accepted the institution of slavery. The Islamic Prophet Muhammad (Pbuh) and many of his companions bought, sold, freed, and captured slaves. In Islamic law the topic of slavery is covered at great length. The Quran (the holy book) and the *Hadith* (the sayings of Muhammad) see slavery as an exceptional condition that can be entered into under certain limited circumstances. Only children of slaves or non-Muslim prisoners of war could become slaves, never a freeborn Muslim. They also consider manumission of a slave to be one of many meritorious deeds available for the expiation of sins. According to Sharia, slaves are considered human beings and possessed of some rights on the basis of their humanity. In addition, a Muslim slave is equal to a Muslim freeman in religious issues and superior to the free non-Muslim. In practice, slaves played various social and economic roles from Emir to worker. Slaves were widely employed in irrigation, mining, pastoralism and the army. Even some rulers relied on military and administrative slaves to such a degree that they seized power.

However, people do not always treat with slaves in accordance with Islamic law. In some cases, the situation has been so harsh as to have led to uprisings such as Zanj Rebellion. However, this was usually the exception rather than the norm, as the vast majority of labour in the medieval Islamic world consisted of free, paid labour. For a variety of reasons, internal growth of the slave population was not enough to fulfil the demand in Muslim society. This resulted in massive importation, which involved enormous suffering and loss of life from the capture and transportation of slaves from non-Muslim lands. In theory, slavery in Islamic law does not have a racial or colour component, although this has not always been the case in practice. The Arab slave trade was most active in West Asia, North Africa and East Africa. By the end of the 19th century, such activity had reached a low ebb. In the early 20th century (post World War I) slavery was gradually outlawed and suppressed in Muslim lands, largely due to pressure exerted by Western nations such as Britain and France. However, slavery claiming the sanction of Islam is documented presently in the African republics of Chad, Mauritania, Niger, Mali and Sudan.

Slavery in Pre-Islamic Arabia

Slavery was widely practiced in pre-Islamic Arabia, as well as in the rest of the ancient and early medieval world. The majority of slaves within Arabia were of Ethiopian origin, through whose sale merchants grew rich. The minority were white slaves of foreign extraction, likely brought in by Arab caravaners (or the product of Bedouin captures) stretching back to biblical times. Native Arab slaves had also existed, a prime example being Zayd ibn Harithah, later to become Muhammad's adopted son. Arab slaves, however, usually obtained as captives, were generally ransomed off amongst nomad tribes. The slave population was added to by the custom of child abandonment, the kidnapping, or, occasionally, the sale of small children. There is no conclusive evidence of the existence of enslavement for debt or the sale of children by their families; the late and rare accounts of such occurrences show them to be abnormal, Bruschvig states (According to Brockopp, debt slavery was persistent.) Free persons were also able to sell their offspring, or even themselves, into slavery. Enslavement was also possible as a consequence of committing certain offences against the law, as in the Roman Empire. Two classes of slave were apparent: a purchased slave, and a slave born in the master's home. Over the latter the master had complete rights of ownership, though these slaves were unlikely to be sold or disposed of by the master.

Female slaves were at times forced into prostitution for the benefit of their masters in accordance with Near Eastern customs. The historical accounts of the early years of Islam report that "slaves of non-Muslim masters... suffered brutal punishments. Sumayya bint Khubbat is famous as the first martyr of Islam, having been killed with a spear by Abu Jahl when she refused to give up her faith. Likewise, Bilal was freed by Abu Bakr when his master, Umayya ibn Khalaf, placed a heavy rock on his chest in an attempt to force his conversion."

Slavery in the Quran

The Quran includes multiple references to slaves, slave women, slave concubinage, and the freeing of slaves. It accepts the institution of slavery. It may be noted that the word 'abd' (slave) is rarely used, being more commonly replaced by some periphrasis such as ma malakat aymanukum ("that which your right hands own"). The Quran recognizes the basic inequality between master and slave and the rights of the former over the latter. The historian Bruschvig states that from a spiritual perspective, "the slave has the same value as the free man, and the same eternity is in store for his soul; in this earthly life, failing emancipation, there remains the fact of his inferior status, to which he must piously resign himself."

Whereas a master may marry a female slave, concubinage is strictly prohibited in Islam. However, the practice of concubinage among the elite (most notably with Harems) is well-known but outside the allowed practices of Islam (adultery). The Quran urges, without commanding, kindness to the slave and recommends, their liberation by purchase or manumission. The freeing of slaves is recommended both for the expiation of sins and as an act of simple benevolence. It exhorts masters to allow slaves to earn or purchase their own freedom (manumission contracts)." Slaves are mentioned in at least twenty-nine verses of the Quran, most of these are Medinan and refer to the legal status of slaves. The legal material on slavery in the Quran is largely restricted to manumission and sexual relations. According to Sikainga, the Quranic references to slavery as mainly contain "broad and general propositions of an ethical nature rather than specific legal formulations."

The Quran accepts the distinction between slave and free as part of the natural order and uses this distinction as an example of God's grace, regarding this discrimination between human beings as in accordance with the divinely established order of things. "The Quran, however, does not consider slaves to be mere chattel; their humanity is directly addressed in references to their beliefs, their desire for manumission and their feelings about being forced into prostitution. In one case, the Quran refers to master and slave with the same word, rajul.

Later interpreters presume slaves to be spiritual equals of free Muslims. For example, urges believers to marry 'believing maids that your right hands own' and then states: "The one of you is as the other," which the Jalaalayn interpret as "You and they are equal in faith, so do not refrain from marrying them." The human aspect of slaves is further reinforced by reference to them as members of the private household, sometimes along with wives or children. Pious exhortations from jurists to free men to address their slaves by such euphemistic terms as "my boy" and "my girl" stemmed from the belief that God, not their masters, was responsible for the slave's status.

There are many common features between the institution of slavery in the Quran and that of neighbouring cultures. However, the Quranic institution had some unique new features. Bernard Lewis states that the Quranic legislation brought two major changes to ancient slavery which were to have far-reaching effects: presumption of freedom, and the ban on the enslavement of free persons except in strictly defined circumstances.

According to Brockopp, the idea of using alms for the manumission of slaves appears to be unique to the Quran, assuming the traditional interpretation of verses and. Similarly, the practice of freeing slaves in atonment for certain sins appears to be introduced by the Quran (but compare Exod 21:26-7). The forced prostitution of female slaves, a Near Eastern custom of great antiquity, is condemned in the Quran. Murray Gordon notes that this ban is "of no small significance." Brockopp writes: "Other cultures limit a master's right to harm a slave but few exhort masters to treat their slaves kindly, and the placement of slaves in the same category as other weak members of society who deserve protection is unknown outside the Quran. The unique contribution of the Quran, then, is to be found in its emphasis on the place of slaves in society and society's responsibility toward the slave, perhaps the most progressive legislation on slavery in its time."

Muhammad's Traditions

The Islamic Prophet Muhammad (Pbuh) encouraged manumission of slaves, even if one had to purchase them first. On many occasions, Muhammad's companions, at his direction, freed slaves in abundance. Muhammad personally freed 63 slaves, and his wife Aisha freed 67. In total his household and friends freed 39,237 slaves. The most notable of Muhammad's slaves were: Safiyya bint Huyayy, whom he freed and married; Maria al-Qibtiyya, given to Muhammad by a Sassanid official, whom he freed and who may have become his wife; Sirin, Maria's sister, whom he freed and married to the poet Hassan ibn Thabit and Zayd ibn Harithah, whom Muhammad freed and adopted as a son.

Chapter 7

Understanding Women's Rights in Islam

Last year, P. K. K. Ahmed Kutty Moulavi, the head Imam of the Palayam Jumma Masjid in Thiruvananthapuram, created a stir by issuing a *fatwa* (ruling) permitting women to enter the mosque and offer prayers, including the late evening prayers during the month of Ramzan. Soon, a section of the Imam's Council in the city issued a counter *fatwa* denying women such entry: It speaks for the conservatism of the community and the moral bankruptcy of its so-called leaders that the example of the progressive Imam was ignored. He reacted to the Council's *fatwa* by pointing out that gender parity was central to the virtues of Islam. Prophet Muhammad (Pbuh), his foster son, Anas, and the Hadith (traditions and sayings of the Prophet) had all said in various contexts that women eager to pray in mosques should be allowed to do so. He said the *Sahih al-Bukhari* and *Sahih al-Muslim* texts too had emphasised that women could pray in places of worship. These two are regarded as leading works of Hadith.

Dr. Zeenat Shaukat Ali, Professor of Islamic Studies at St. Xavier's College, Mumbai, cites that very collection of the Prophet's tradition (Hadith), Sahih al-Bukhari, on this point. "Some examples of women's participation in various activities, as the early history of Islam and the traditions of Prophet Muhammad (Pbuh) point out, are the following: Women took part in national activities, acted as advisors and while they were efficient managers of the household, nonetheless joined in congregational prayers in the mosque There is ferment among Muslim women, especially the intellectuals, which has not been much noticed. Faezeh Hashemi is a member of Iran's Parliament, chairperson of the

Islamic Women's Olympics Committee and, incidentally, daughter of former President Ali Akbar Hashemi. She had some sharp comments to make on the subject in a little noticed interview to a Western news agency (DPA). It will come as a surprise to many. She said that Islam had always been interpreted by men in a way that secured their own interests. "Men have always been the main Islamic scholars, those who interpreted the Islamic laws and implemented these interpretations." She added: "Men manipulated Islamic laws during the course of history and implemented them to secure their own interests. What we are doing in the Majlis (Parliament) right now is to separate this and get some advantages for women."

Terming Islam as a very progressive religion, she observed that traditions had become enmeshed with the Muslim religion. "That was the reason why the West considers our religion not as today's Islam but that of 1,400 years ago. We must make use of the positive things (in the West) and make them compatible with our own Islamic values."

All these three books are written by women, the first two by particularly devout Muslims. All are scholars of impeccable credentials. Fatima Mernissi is Professor of Sociology at the University of Rabat, Morocco. Barbara Freyer Stowasser is Director of the Centre for Contemporary Arab Studies at Georgetown University and Professor of Arabic. The authors' concern is with Islam and the woman's place in it. They have studied the Quran, the Prophet's sayings and tradition (Hadith, the second source of law in Islam) and are familiar with modern literature on gender equality. Stowasser, unlike the other two, is not concerned in her book with advocacy of women's rights as much as with a deep analysis of women's issues in the Quran and the Hadith and the strands in modern Muslim thinking.

Fatima Mernissi may well shock many Muslims in India. An Arab intellectual, she has carefully but critically read through volumes of commentaries on the Quran and of the Hadith. She has not hesitated to challenge the most respected compiler of Hadith, Al-Bukhari himself. "This Hadith is the sledgehammer argument used by those who want to exclude women from politics." Zeenat Shaukat Ali is no less ardent in her advocacy of reform. But nothing in her work will offend the *feelings* of the devout. She draws on her erudition to compel them to reflect on cherished but wholly groundless and harmful beliefs about women's rights in Islam.

A powerful appeal to Indian Muslims was also made by Turan Jamshidian Ghaleh Sefidi, editor of the Iranian magazine *Muhjubah.*

Seventy-eight per cent of Iranian women are literate, she noted. The national literacy rate was 80 per cent. She appealed to Muslim men to motivate their women to learn and to Muslim women to take more interest in education. Addressing a press conference in Kozhikode in Kerala on January 30, 1997, Sefidi said: " We attend all mosques in Iran and women form almost half of the congregations there". There is little interest in India about the reform of Muslim law even in avowedly Islamic countries like Iran.

In 1986, the Muslim leadership collaborated with Rajiv Gandhi to nullify the Supreme Court's ruling in the Shah Bano case (on divorced Muslim women's right to maintenance). It was a sordid alliance. Having agreed with the Vishwa Hindu Parishad in 1985 to unlock the gates of the Babri Mosque, he sought to mollify Muslims. They sought to legitimise their leadership. In 1996 the Bangaladesh High Court ruled on the same lines as did the Supreme Court of India. It has ruled also that Islam does not approve of polygamy.

In a Friday sermon by Ayatollah Mohammad Yazdi, head of the judiciary at Teheran University, on November 18, 1994, he declared: "If a man wished to divorce his wife, the court can, or must, investigate the amount of wealth which they have accumulated during the period from the start of their joint life to the time of divorce, and at the discretion of the court, up to half of that wealth should be given unconditionally by the man to that woman, before being able to use his right to divorce her, the same court which deals with divorce and which issues the certificate of divorce should also deal with the issue of defining the amount of income and the amount that should be paid to the wife. The court should issue the verdict and should enforce it."

Islamic law is based on scripture. Arabic, the language of the Quran, is rich in nuances. Riffat Hassan, Professor of the Religious Studies programme at the University of Louisville in the U.S. and author of *Woman and the Quran* said: "A single word in Arabic can have many meanings. But as the translators have always been men, the Quranic translations have always made a male bias. Take Chapter 4, Verse 34, which is always quoted when the issue of equality crops up. In this verse, the Quran uses the word *qawwamun* to describe the man. This word has always been translated as ruler or master. But I believe that it means breadwinner - which immediately changes the meaning of the verse. There are scores of such examples."

For historical reasons, conservatism has held sway, in recent decades, among the Muslims of the subcontinent. Muhammad Heikal, one of the Arab world's most distinguished journalists, notes with dismay that far from learning from other Muslims, they "exported" their conservatism to Arab lands. "Islam was always a political as well as religious movement, and it also had its cultural and social side.

By 1980 it was beginning to feel the influence of Muslims from Pakistan and India, where Islam had acquired a different flavour. *Asian Muslims tended to take the Quran literally, while Arabs were more inclined to interpret it. Reading the texts in their own language enabled Arabs to set it in historical context, keeping in mind observations by Arab religious authorities*, but Asians were less able to look beyond it - partly because other works had not been translated into their languages, but more importantly because the Arabic language was the tongue of Islam. *Deprived of linguistic context* the Quran inevitably takes on a slightly different character, forcing non-Arab readers to rely more on the texts than on the way the ideas are expressed."

Mernissi proceeds systematically to take each verse from the Quran which has been misinterpreted to deny the rights of Muslim women and describes its context, the situation it was concerned with. She deals not only with "occasions of revelation" but also "occasions for revelation." She, likewise, takes up major pronouncements on women's status in Hadith and shows how little credence some of them deserve.

Zeenat Shaukat Ali does not go so far. But in her own meticulous manner she also links Quranic verses to the context. The one on the hijab (veil), for instance: " O Prophet, tell thy wives and daughters that they should cast their outer garments over their persons when abroad, that is most convenient that they should be known as such and not molested.' Two points seem to be made in the above verses: One, if the women did not go out where lay the necessity for prescribing a distinctive dress or occasion for their harassment? Second, it seems that this particular injunction *was required by special circumstances which then prevailed in Medina*, where the hypocrites would molest a woman and feign innocence by suggesting that they thought that the woman was a person of ill-repute. This is plainly hinted in the following verse: 'Truly if the hypocrites and those who stir up sedition in the city desist not, We shall make thee stand up against them' Such a dress was therefore a kind of protection and not meant for suppression."

Zeenat Shaukat Ali blends history, theology and the law in one erudite whole in a work of enormous labour. She proves to the hilt that:

(a) the Quran does not sanction polygamy,

(b) the triple pronouncement of divorce in one sitting is un-Islamic. An English Judge of the Bombay High Court aptly described it as "good in law, though *bad in theology*" and

(c) the wife is equally entitled to divorce the husband. This is known as *khula*.

It is not Islamic law, the Shariat, that is practised in India but Anglo-Muhammedan law as it evolved during British rule. The Privy Council ruled early in the day against reference to the Quran or original texts of Hadith. It preferred, instead, certain commentaries of dubious worth. Muslim personal law in Pakistan grew in a progressive direction because its Supreme Court abandoned that rule of interpretation and consulted the texts themselves.

Zeenat Shaukat Ali's work is of enormous *practical* value. She has appended texts of modern marriage contracts which fully protect the wife's rights in respect of divorce by her as well as by her husband, rule out his second marriage and guarantee her other rights. All these, the book establishes, are rooted in Islamic law.

In the lectures he delivered in Chennai nearly 70 years ago, the poet-philosopher Iqbal posed a pertinent question: "Did the founders of our schools ever claim finality for their reasonings and interpretations? Never." He upheld the claim of "the present generation of Muslim liberals to reinterpret the foundational legal principles in the light of their own experience." Iqbal's remarks, made 70 years ago, are relevant now: "In view of the intense conservatism of the Muslims of India, Indian judges cannot but stick to what are called standard works. The result is that while the peoples are moving, the law remains stationery."

Muslims alone are responsible for the disgraceful and un-Islamic state of personal law in respect of marriage and divorce. As the Quran says: "Verily God does not change the state of a people until they change the state of their own lives."

Islam – Democracy's Dilemma

While the recent Arab Spring uprisings toppled both the Tunisian President Ben Ali and the Egyptian President Hosni Mubarak, other authoritarian leaders are clinging to power in Libya, Syria and Yemen. Although these developments created a considerable democratic momentum in the region not much has yet been achieved, as full, stable, and secure democracies are still nowhere in sight. Of all the challenges facing democracy in the world. Perhaps, the greatest yet lies in the Islamic world, where only a handful of states "have made significant strides towards establishing democratic systems." Therefore, now, more than ever, is the time to focus on the ultimate compatibility between the Islamic political theory and the liberal democratic discourse.

Recent agreement between Hamas and Fatah in the occupied Palestinian territories, the official registration of the first Muslim Brotherhood political party in Egypt, the success of the Kuwaiti Islamist parties in establishing a nationwide boycott of French products following the country's introduction of the ban on wearing *niqab* in public, the continuous successes of the Justice and Development Party (AKP) in Turkey, and finally the ever-more prominent presence of Hizbullah in Lebanon, all indicate sustained gains of political power by the Islamist movements in the region. Since both most of the Islamist movements and a significant percentage of Muslims in the region express widespread support for *shariah* as the ultimate source of legislation in their countries (as much as around 79 per cent of respondents of the recent Gallup poll argue for its incorporation in state's legislation), it is imperative that one questions the roles Islam may play in establishing democracy in the region.

Many among the Westerners appalled by the lack of freedoms in the Islamic word, as well as Muslims that fail to see democracy as anything more than another project of imperialism, would agree with Amir Taheri that Islam as a religion and a source of civilizational tradition is inherently incompatible with democracy. This paper, however, argues that such recognition strays from a long-standing theoretical tradition of moral and political values of plurality, communal consensus seeking, and non-autocratic, consultative mode of governance that find themselves well within the scope of a democratic paradigm.

The scope of this paper requires initially a quick introduction to three different models of democracy: electoral, participatory and liberal, that will be then assessed in terms of their presence in and compatibility with the Islamic political theory of governance. Moreover, the question posed here introduces the initially self-evident logical distinction between Islam as a moral and axiological faith system, and democracy as a political and morally neutral system of governance. The intricacy of this distinction lies at the core of the fundamental dispute over the question of sovereignty in Islamic societies, which will be then discussed as one of the challenges democracy faces in a predominantly Muslim environment. Despite considerable popular variance in understanding the origins of power in a Muslim society, there appears to be a set of social and political values, and legalistic institutions, such as *shura*, *bay'a*, *ijtihad*, *tasamuh*, *qist*, *maslaha* and *ikhtilaf* that may constitute a strong future basis for establishing democracy in an Islamic setting. Finally, the focus of this paper will turn to the recent Arab Spring, its potential for the future of democracy in the region, as well as some other potential repercussions it may cause.

Democracy... but which?

Democracy, one of the most misused and misinterpreted modern political concepts, connotes a number of various, often-conflicting understandings. Adequate appreciation for the complexities of various theoretical paradigms associated with democratic theory, although of secondary importance to this paper, allows a more adequate reading of contemporary experiments with democracy in the Middle East and other parts of the Islamic world.

For the purpose of this research it is relevant to briefly introduce three, arguably, most important theoretical frameworks of electoral, liberal and participatory democracy. Joseph Schumpeter's model essentially focuses on the notion of democracy as "an institutional arrangement for reaching political decisions in which individuals acquire the power to decide by means of competitive struggle for people's votes." Although this model indubitably separates itself from authoritarianism and instead confers the legislative powers on the wider public, it does not require the elimination of separate domains of power reserved for the military, the clergy and others, as in the *valyi al-faqih* system in Iran, notes Esposito.

Liberal democracy, on the other hand, is "a political system marked not only by free and fair elections, but also by the rule of law, a separation of powers, and the protection of basic liberties of speech, assembly, religion, and property." Not only does it emphasise the essentially fair and open electoral process but also stresses on the most basic liberal requirement of protecting the individual and all the minority groups within a given society. However, despite being the most popular and widespread model of democracy, the liberal constitutional theory found itself a number of significant critics both in the Western world and elsewhere.

Barber's participatory democracy represents one such criticism of liberal democracy. As a truly Rousseauian counter argument to Schumpeterian elective oligarchy it aims to develop a model comfortably comparable to both Habermas' 'discoursive democracy', and Cohen and

Sabel's 'directly-deliberative polyarchy', in which they attempt to offset the dangers of the tyrant of the majority while retaining the basic individual rights. Moreover, democracy in its participatory mode offers a response to, what some believed was, a transparent democratic deficit of liberal democracy, as "incompatible with freedom," and "producing distrustful, passive citizens."

Islam – religion or Politic?

In spite of a huge diversity of opinion on the nature of democracy among the scholars, there appears to be a clear consensus on the common denominators of any democratic system of governance. Democracy is believed to be a system of popular sovereignty that respects the freedom of speech and assembly, as well as grants the universal right to protest against, object to and oppose the government that both stems from a periodic, open and fair electoral process, and recognises the separation of its executive, legislative and the essentially independent judicial branches. It is therefore, imperative that we question the compatibility of those concepts with Islam.

However, is it not slightly erroneous to examine the affinity of a modern political system of democracy and a religious faith system of Islam? Similar question was also often posed at the onset of democracy in the West, then arguing for the incompatibility of Christianity and democracy. It appears that the indispensable here is to establish whether Islam represents an independent political system. Here again, the opinion is widely split between two major groups, the Islamic political rejectionists and their opposition – the accomodationists.

The rejectionists, such as 'Ali 'Abd al-Raziq & Muhammad Sa'id al-'Ashmawy, commonly 'depoliticise' Islam and argue for a fundamental distinction between Islam as a religion, and democracy as a political construct that is alien to any given religion for it originates in a secular theory of governance, widely independent of any religious ethical bases. In his book, *Islamisme contre l'Islame*, al-'Ashmawy not only argues that Islamists misuse such ideas as the "application of the *shariah*" (*taqnin al shariah*), arguably in order to get popular support for their political programme, but they also totally disregard the fact that "political rule had not been part of the prophetic mission of Muhammad and that religion and government should be separate in Islam," as noted by Shepard. Furthermore, 'liberal' modernists, like al-Ashmawy, insist that the *shariah* is predominantly "the way or method of Islam," and that "in the Quran it does not mean either law (*qanun*) or legislation (*tashri'*)."

The accomodationists, on the other hand, are adamant in their claim that one can clearly discern a specific Islamic political system based on the message of the Quran and the Sunnah, thus rendering democracy in the Islamic context as only additional to or enhancing the overall political Islamic legacy. Sayyid and Muhammad Qutb go even further to denounce any other political systems, including democracy as "un-Islamic." In spite of this clearly negative message, many of their contemporary followers accept some aspects of democracy. The Islamist liberals, a clear minority in the wider Islamist movement, call for incorporation of the basic liberal concepts into the Islamic political system. However, the majority of Islamist subscribe themselves to, what could be called, an electoral accomodationist wing and while emphasising majoritarianism they accept the Schumpeterian definition of democracy. Islamist organisations and parties, like Hamas, Hizbullah, AKP and the Muslim Brotherhood, would certainly fit this description, as they strive to enhance their popular following in an open electoral process. There has been, however, a considerable fear among the policy makers that those movements are inclined to misuse the system and allow for the so-called "one man, one vote – once." predicament

However, are the Islamist right to claim there is a clear-cut political system of Islam? I believe they are not. As governance and the use of political power in any given country stems from a particular understanding of the underlying legal system, the Islamic system should be then based on the *Shariahh*. This is precisely, where the whole problem starts, for; although theoretically disputed by radicals, such as Khomeini and others; shariah and the Quran provide us with a set of fundamental values rather than any fixed juristic rulings or a particular system of governance applicable to all times. Some have even argued that democracy is unlikely to spread in the Middle East, due to the persistent presence of Islam-based authoritarianism. As popular and as convincing this line of argumentation may sound, the actual truth is slightly different. Wright correctly points out the most antidemocratic and authoritarian regimes in the region – such as Brunei, Indonesia, Iraq, Oman, Bahrain, Qatar, Syria, and Turkmenistan, "are secular autocrats who refuse to share power with their brethren." Wickham advances that "as we [Muslims] have a human understanding of Islam, it is a mistake for us to say that there is a certain system that represents the Islamic system"

It would be, however, equally incorrect to overlook some of the clear political dimensions one can distinguish within Islamic philosophy.

Although Krämer is right to note that *shariah* should be primarily defined by its 'empty spaces', the overall message of Islam undoubtedly provides a set of fundamental values of a distinctly political nature. A selection of these principles and tools advanced in the Quran and the Sunnah will now facilitate the examination of both the potential bases for and the most serious challenges to democracy in the Islamic context.

Democracy – non-Islamic in Origin but yet Compatible with Islamic Society?

Historical development of the Islamic political thought spans across all the centuries of Islam and numerous schools of jurisprudence, philosophy and *kalam*. Scholarly, juristic and religious thought produced a wide-ranging set of often conflicting political concepts. Therefore, Ashour argues that "theoretical interpretations of Islam can be used to support various types of political regimes, ranging from repressive authoritarianism and 'religio-fascism' to tolerant pluralism and liberal democracy."

Even at the very beginning of the Muslim *ummah* Prophet Mohammed was not blind to various political and societal problems challenging the Arabs at that time, i.e. legal standing of women within the society, principles of just rule, tribal unrest and rivalries, criminal justice or the tradition of slavery in Arabia. Some of the rules introduced by Mohammed were truly revolutionary and could clearly now serve as a 'blueprint' for the construction of democracy. "Islam is not lacking in tenets and practices that are compatible with pluralism. Among these are the traditions of *ijtihad* (interpretation), *ijma* (consensus), and *shura* (consultation)," as noted by Wright. Nevertheless, the more orientalist scholars, such as Huntington, state "thatthe Quran may serve as a hindrance to the development of democratic ideals and believe that Islamic scripture is at least partially responsible for the lack of democratic political systems in the Muslim world."

Although Islam may, indeed, lack in certain well-established and fundamental democratic concepts and tools, and remains largely ambiguous to the extent to which democracy can be implemented in an Islamic setting, two fundamental juristic tools of the *Shariahh*: the independent interpretation of law (*ijtihad*) and the scholarly disagreement (*ikhtilaf*) provide most hope for the future of democracy in Islam. The vast historical diversity of the juristic scholarship is often used to indicate the dynamism of the *Shariahh*. This dynamism not only lies at the bottom of our deliberations and allows for a democratic re-interpretation of the Islamic political thought, but also exemplifies the essential embedment of *ijtihad* in the very structure of Islamic law. As Johnston argues, "*shariah* is divine, but in everyday life we experience it as *ijtihad*." Similarly, 'Adb Al-Rahman 'Azzam, a prominent Egyptian Arab nationalist, argues that:

> *"Islam is definite and conclusive on all general principles ... [but] when it comes to implementing these principles, one can see clearly the flexibility of the Islamic Shariah and the authority it gives to our reason and our effort (*ijtihad*)."*

In contrast, Sheikh Al-Qaradawi, the scriptualists of Qutb, some radical Salafis or the historical Zahiris, either consider *ijtihad* a matter of the enlightened Islamic past or even outright *haram* (sinful and unacceptable), and would rather prefer to follow the well-established, yet infamous longstanding tradition of imitation of the previously established rulings (*taqlid*) that arguably led to a major suspense of the Islamic sciences. One must remember that *ijtihad* was once considered to be "the ultimate act of worship (*'ibadah*)". The institution of *ijtihad*is, indeed, fundamentally and essentially inherent to the essence of both the *Shariahh*, and the Quran itself. 'Ali Ibn Abi Talib, Mohammed's cousin and the fourth rightly guided caliph, is understood to claim that the Quran is but ink and paper, it does not speak for itself. Since humans understand Quran and the sunna only as they subjectively perceive it, it is the human agency, the *ijtihad*, and our personal judgement that is central to our deliberation and can provide for the basis of democracy in the Middle East.

Human factor in political and security matters appears to be deeply grounded in the early Hadith describing the moral conditions of peace negotiations and defence engagement. Mohammed is believed to say:

> *"[...] if you [army commanders] met the enemy and then they asked for [peace] talks [based] on God's judgment [terms or conditions], then do not agree. Ask them for [peace] talks on your and your companion's judgment [terms or conditions], because you never know if you will be able to meet God's judgment regarding them or not."]*

In this particular Hadith the meaning of "talks [based] on God's judgment" refers to an understanding that peace talks must not be based on the subjective understanding of "God's judgment" by certain commanders, for what they believe to be the true meaning of the Quran and sunna may, despite all the knowledge and expertise they possess, be in fact be dissimilar to the actual meaning, which the humans are not capable of ascertaining indubitably during their worldly life. The emphasis on human agency and the role of *ijtihad* in this Hadith is certainly extraordinary. Indeed, in line with this Hadith one could argue that contemporary policy makers should feel greatly encouraged to re-examine the role of Islamic political principles in the current geographic, historical and societal setting.

Shura – the Islamic Parliament?

Authoritarianism is certainly ripe in the Islamic world. The history of Islam abounds with totalitarian, despotic, non-democratic and essentially unfair rule. But the early ages of Islamic society provide some hope to those, who wish to establish democracy in the Middle East and the wider Islamic world. Although the Prophet did not specify any particular form of governance, he continuously advanced certain guidelines for the Islamic mode of conduct based on justice, freedom, *shura* in public affairs, and enjoining the good and forbidding the evil.

The principle of *shura* is comfortably grounded in the Quran and sunna of the Prophet. In chapter *Ash-shura* one reads:

> *„...who obey their Lord, attend to their prayers, and conduct their affairs by mutual consent: who bestow in alms part of what We have given them and, when oppressed, seek to redress their wrongs."*

Whereas, sura Aal-e-Imran demands the Prophet to "take counsel with them in the conduct of affairs." Both these *ayat*clearly advocate for the popular governance to be based in communal consultation.

Although historically the Muslim scholars were divided as to the status of these *ayat*, even those of the classical scholars, who did not perceive *shura* to be *fard* (Islamic obligation), they all commonly agreed to consider it *mandub*(recommended) for all Muslim communities. Moussalli reiterates that while the Islamic scholars of the past did not use the term 'democracy' to explain the consultative form of governance of the early *ummah*, the extent of power that was vested in the people comes close to our current understanding of democracy. Al-Ghazali interestingly emphasises the role of *shura* and claims that "despotic, non- consultative, decision-making, even if from a wise and learned person is objectionable and unacceptable."

Unfortunately, establishing democracy within an Islamic setting requires more than only utilising the juristic *ijtihad* and the institution of *shura*, Some of the fundamental democratic precepts of governance, such as periodic alternation of political power through popular election, are clearly inexistent in the Islamic political thought. Nonetheless, the principle of *bay'a* (an oath of allegiance to the leader) is the closest Islamic equivalent.

The Prophet did not leave any straightforward guidelines as to the electoral process within the *ummah*. However, over the years it became clear among the Muslim community that establishing a legitimate leader of an Islamic state requires a universal oath of allegiance – *bay'a* to that individual. As in any other community or religion, so in Islam there were three different forms of gaining power within a society.

An Islamic ruler was mostly chosen either through *shura*, or through *istikhlaf* (nomination by ailing ruler), or though *ghalaba* (victory, triumph, nomination by force). All these, however, still require the communal acceptance through *bay'a*, which is also rendered potentially revocable. Additionally, the legal contractual status of *bay'a*, coupled with the notion of juristic *ijtihad* allows for a modern re-interpretation of *bay'a* and possibly implementation of periodic elections.

The Islamic concept of *shura* clearly represents a great democratic potential. However, as El Fadl indicates it is susceptible to majoritarianism. He notes, "even if the ethic of *shura* is expanded into a broader concept of a participatory government, concerns about majority tyranny underscore that the moral commitments informing the lawmaking process are as important as the process itself." Barber used similar argument in his critique of liberal democracy and his advancement of the participatory mode of governance. Barber's strong democracy "as politics in the participatory mode" will is meant to be initially introduced as a panacea for persistent democratic deficits of liberal democracy, and a truly Rousseauian counter argument to Schumpeterian elective oligarchy.

Democracy and Repression?

One of Barber's major arguments against liberal democracy regarded the inability of that system to protect the individual rights of citizens and minorities. It is often argued in the West, and quite rightly so, that the Islamic world has a very poor record of tolerance, protection of minority and individual rights, as well as human rights. The region is also notorious for political oppression and total suppression of any expression of dissent. Clearly this was one of the focal points of the Arab Spring. Political repression and discrimination, as well as lack of human rights provisions lie at the bottom of the unrest in Bahrain, Syria and Egypt. It is certainly inaccurate to attribute the regional unrest to political reasons only, for the economy played a significant role too, but one must not forget the significant role, with which these issues continue to shape the situation in the region.

However, it remains totally imperative to remember that this situation does not really stem from any underlying religious factors. In fact, one can argue that the principle of *tasamuh* (tolerance) is central to the message of Islam. Majority of scholars interpret Islam as fundamentally opposed to discrimination on the basis of race, ethnicity, class and, to a lesser extent, tribe. The Quran abounds with textual examples of this principle. Surah Hud, explicitly introduces diversity among people as God's conscious choice and will.

Moreover, according to Al-Buti, Mohammed is believed to argue that "the Arabs are not better than non-Arabs and non-Arabs are not better than Arabs, whites are not better than blacks and blacks are not better than whites, unless one is more righteous than the other." Even the contemporary empirical evidence indicates that majority of the Middle Easterners will to incorporate freedom of expression and opinion on political, social, and economic issues into their constitutions. However, there is still a difficult issue of religious, sexual and gender discrimination. Islamic societies are unfortunately quite restrictive when it comes to gay, bisexual and transgender people.

Moreover, the problem of apostasy remains to be one of the most disputed issues among the scholars. Apostates continue to be rendered state enemies in many of the Islamic countries and often face death penalty. Religious discrimination lies at the bottom of the current unrest in Bahrain, where the Sunni led regime openly discriminates against their Shia majority. Similar situation exists in Saudi Arabia, Iran, Iraq, Lebanon, Syria and others, where religious minority groups are constantly discriminated against both on personal and structural level. This is clear obstacle in the process of establishing any liberal democracy in the region.

Democratic Islam vs. God's Sovereignty

The most fundamental challenge yet, however, comes from the understanding of sovereignty within Islam. Democracy is often argued to be a product of Western civilisation, as it emphasises the rights over duties, the individual over the divine. Hence, for people like Abdul R. Moten, democracy becomes antithetical to the Islamic way of life. It is precisely the understanding of the superiority of the human over the divine that makes many Muslims most uncomfortable about democracy. Historically, laws made by a sovereign monarch were deemed illegitimate, as they appeared to substitute God's sovereignty with human authority.

As indicated by El Fadl, "it is in the *Khawarij's* rallying cry of "dominion belongs to God" or "the Quran is the judge" (*la hukma illa li'llah* or *al-hukmu li'l-Quran*)" that this situation is most explicitly apparent. These statements are, on the other hand, nearly identical to those of the contemporary Islamist, who ironically universally detest the *Khawarij*. For many of those "Quran is the only constitution," as noted by Ayubi. For organisations, such as Al Qaeda or the Islamic Jihad "the *Shariah* is the blueprint to which the structure of society and state must conform," notes Coulson. "In Islam it is not the government 'of the people'; it is the 'government of Allah'", reminds Sayyid S. A. Rizvi.

Bibliography

Ali, Abdullah Yusuf: *The Holy Qur'an: Text, Translation and Commentary.* Washington, DC : Amanah, 1989.

As-Sadr, Muhammad Baqir : *Lessons in Islamic Jurisprudence.* Translated by Roy Parviz Mottahedeh. Oxford: Oneworld Press, 2003.

Beckett, Katharine Scarfe : *Perception of the Islamic Word,* Cambridge University Press, New Delhi, 1992.

Bernard G. Weiss : *The Law Applied: Contextualizing the Islamic Shariah.* New York: I. B. Tauris, 2008.

Chaudhri, Sajedul Bar : *The Profile of an Islamic State,* Dhaka, Islamic Foundation Bangladesh, 1984.

Crone, Patricia : *Roman, Provincial, and Islamic Law: The Origin of the Islamic Patronate.* Cambridge, U.K.: Cambridge University Press, 1987.

Doi, Abdur Rahman I. : *Shariah: the Islamic Law.* Kuala Lumpur: A. S. Noordeen, 2002.

El-Awa, Mohammad : *Punishment in Islamic Law,* Indianapolis: American Trust Publications, 1982.

Enayatullah Mashriqi : *Quranic System of Law,* Akhuwat Publications, Rawalpindi, Pakistan.

Ferrari, Silvio and Anthony Bradney: *Islam and European Legal Systems.* Aldershot: Ashgate, 2000.

Frank Griffel : *Shariah: Islamic Law in the Contemporary Context.* Palo Alto, CA: Stanford University Press, 2007.

Gerber, Haim. *State, Society, and Law in Islam: Ottoman Law in Comparative Perspective.* Albany, NY: State University of New York Press, 1994.

Goldziher, Ignaz : *Introduction to Islamic Theology and Law.* Princeton, NJ: Princeton University Press, 1981.

Haeri, Shahla. *Law of Desire: Temporary Marriage in Shi'i Iran.* Syracuse, NY: Syracuse University Press, 1989.

Haleem, M. Abdel: *Criminal Justice in Islam: Judicial Procedure in the Sharî'ah.* London: I.B. Tauris, 2003.

Ilyas Ahmad : *The Social Contract and the Islamic State*, Kitab Bhavan, New Delhi, 1981.

Johansen, B.: *Contingency in a Sacred Law: Legal and Ethical Norms in the Islamic Fiqh*, Leiden 1999

Kamali, Mohammad H.: *Principles of Islamic Jurisprudence.* Cambridge, U.K.: Islamic Texts Society, 1991.

Kelsay, John. *War and the Imperatives of Justice in Islamic Law.* Cambridge, UK: Cambridge University Press, forthcoming.

Liebesny, H.J.: *The Law of the Near & Middle East: Readings, Cases & Materials* Albany 1975

Makdisi, George. *Religion, Law and Learning in Classical Islam.* Aldershot: Ashgate/Variorum, 1991.

Makdisi, George: *The Rise of Colleges: Institutions of Learning in Islam and the West.* Edinburgh: Edinburgh University Press, 1981.

Naquib, Seyd Muhammed : *Prelegomena to the Metaphysics of Islam: An Exposition of the Fundamental Elements of the Worldview of Islam.* Kuala Lumpur, Malaysia, 1995.

Peters, Rudolph : *Jihad in Classical and Modern Islam,* Princeton, NJ: Markus Wiener Publishers, 1996.

Reinhart, A Kevin: *Before Revelation: The Boundaries of Muslim Moral Thought.* Albany: State University of New York Press, 1995.

Rosen, Lawrence. *The Anthropology of Justice: Law as Culture in Islamic Society.* Cambridge, UK: Cambridge University Press, 1989.

Serjeant, R.B. *Customary and Shari'ah Law in Arabian Society.* Aldershot: Ashgate/Variorum, 1991.

Sheik, Mufti Allie Haroun : *Islamic Principles on Family Planning,* Adam Publishers, New Delhi, 2001.

Sonbol, Amira El Azhary: *Women, The Family, and Divorce Laws in Islamic History.* Syracuse, NY: Syracuse University Press, 1996.

Toshihiko Izutsu : *God and Man in the Koran,* Weltansckauung. Tokyo, 1964

Vogel, F.E.: *Islamic Law and Legal System: Studies of Saudi Arabia,* Leiden 2000

Vogel, Frank E. *Islamic Law and Legal Systems: Studies of Saudi Arabia.* Leiden: E.J. Brill, 2000.

Walker, Benjamin : *Foundation of Islam : the Making of World Faith,* Rupa & Co., New Delhi, 2001.

Weiss, Bernard G. *The Spirit of Islamic Law.* Athens, GA: University of Georgia Press, 1998.

Welchman, Lynn. *Beyond the Code: Muslim Family Law and the Shari'a Judiciary in the Palestinian West Bank.* The Hague: Kluwer Law Int'l., 2000.

Index

M

N

O

P

R

S

T

V

W

❑❑❑